Daddy
x x x x
Merry christmes
2010,
All my love
mingle + Dylan.
Bur
xxxxxxxxxx
xxxxxxx

UNROMAN
BRITAIN

UNROMAN BRITAIN

BRITAIN

EXPOSING
THE GREAT MYTH
OF BRITANNIA

MILES RUSSELL AND STUART LAYCOCK

The History Press

First published 2010

The History Press
The Mill, Brimscombe Port
Stroud, Gloucestershire, GL5 2QG
www.thehistorypress.co.uk

British Library Cataloguing in Publication Data.
A catalogue record for this book is available from the British Library.

ISBN 978 0 7524 5566 2

Typesetting and origination by The History Press
Printed in Great Britain

CONTENTS

INTRODUCTION

CIVILISATION is a matter of perspective. Nowhere is this more clear than when comparing the literary or artistic output of particular cultures, for such works represent a discrete point of view; the defining statements of distinct ethnic groups; perspectives written about a particular society by members of that society in order to educate, satirise, entertain or inform. When examined at a very basic level, most literary works appear to be driven by three basic imperatives: 'where shall I live?', 'who will I marry?' and 'what are we having for lunch?' If you take two particular, and perhaps rather exaggerated, literary masterpieces detailing the eating habits of Mediterranean Rome and Celtic north-western Europe, then the differences cannot seem more extreme.

The *Story of Mac Dathó's Pig*, one of the most famous Irish sagas, belongs to the so-called cycle of Ulster, an epic first set down in the eleventh or twelfth century AD, but it ultimately describes (and derives from) a much earlier pre-Christian world. The story of the pig covers, as its main theme, the events surrounding a feast set within the great hall of Mac Dathó, king of Leinster.

'There were seven doors in that hall, and seven passages through it, and seven hearths in it, and seven cauldrons, and an ox and a salted pig in each cauldron', the anonymous author tells us. 'Every man who came along the passage used to thrust the flesh-fork into a cauldron, and whatever he brought out at the first catch was his portion. If he did not obtain anything at the first attempt he did not have another'.[1] Having set the scene, the narrator then describes the carving of a great, spit-roasted pig and the challenges over who was entitled to the hind leg, or 'Champion's Portion'.

'It shall not be', said a tall fair hero who had risen from his place, 'that Cet should divide the pig before our faces'. 'Whom have we here?' asked Cet. 'He is a better hero than you are', said everyone; 'for he is Angus mac Lam Gábuid of Ulster'. 'Why is your father called Lam Gábuid?' asked Cet. 'We do not know indeed' said all. 'I know', said Cet. 'I once went eastward. The alarm was raised against me. Everyone came on and Lam came too. He threw a cast of his great spear at me. I sent the same spear back to him, and it struck off his hand, so that it lay on the ground. What could bring his son to give me combat?' Angus sat down. 'Keep up the contest further' said Cet, 'or else let me divide the pig'. 'It is intolerable that you should take precedence in dividing the pig' said a tall fair hero of Ulster. 'Whom have we here?' asked Cet. 'That is Eogan mac Durthacht' said everyone. 'I have seen him before', said Cet. 'Where have you seen me?' asked Eogan. 'At the door of your house, when I deprived you

of a drove of cattle. The alarm was raised around me in the country-side. You came at that cry. You cast a spear at me so that it stuck out of my shield. I cast the spear back at you so that it pierced your head and put out your eye. It is patent to the men of Ireland that you are one-eyed. It was I who struck out the other eye from your head'. Thereupon the other sat down.[2]

In contrast to *Mac Dathó's Pig*, is the *Satyricon*, an incomplete Latin work of fiction detailing the (mis)adventures of one Encolpius. This is about as far away from the smoking hearths and roasted pigs of Ireland as one could imagine. It was written in the mid first century AD by 'Petronius', possibly the same Petronius known to history as a fashion advisor, pleasure-seeker and gen-

eral 'judge of elegance' in the court of the emperor Nero. One of the more famous surviving sections of the work describes a banquet hosted by Trimalchio, a freedman of enormous wealth, but ultimately little taste.

All were now at table except Trimalchio, for whom the first place was reserved … Among the hors d'oeuvres stood a little ass of Corinthian bronze with a packsaddle holding olives, white olives on one side, black on the other. The animal was flanked right and left by silver dishes, on the rim of which Trimalchio's name was engraved and the weight. On arches built up in the form of miniature bridges were dormice seasoned with honey and poppy-seed. There were sausages, too, smoking hot on a silver grill, and underneath, Syrian

2 'UnRoman' interior design: inside the reconstructed roundhouse at the Cranborne Ancient Technology Centre, Dorset

a tray, with a wooden hen in it, her wings spread round, as if she were hatching … At once the orchestra struck up the music, as the slaves also struck up theirs … In the bustle a dish chanced to fall, and when a boy stooped to pick it up, Trimalchio gave him a few vigorous cuffs for his pains, and bade him to 'Throw it down again' and a slave coming in swept out the silver platter along with the refuse. After that two long-haired Ethiopians entered with little bladders, similar to those used in sprinkling the arena in the amphitheatre, but instead of water they poured wine on our hands. Then glass wine jars were brought in, carefully sealed and a ticket on the neck of each, reading thus: 'Opimian Falernia, One hundred years old'.[3]

The contrast between the heroic and violent machismo associated with mealtime in Celtic Ireland and the effete decadence of a Roman dinner party cannot be more striking. But then that's the point. These two texts were chosen deliberately and, if and when cited in works of modern history, are noted without comment as if they were objective statements concerning the reality of ancient life. The Romans were debauched, the Celts aggressively quarrelsome. Of course, that's not the whole story, for selection of alternative texts could have emphasised the dark, violent underbelly of Roman life or the decadent exuberance of the 'barbarian' Celt. The important thing to note here is that both the works cited above were created within well-developed artistic cultures. They are both introspective and, arguably, hugely satirical. They also demonstrate, in very different ways, the great literary heritage of Rome and the 'Barbarian'.

'Civilisation', as we said, is a matter of perspective.

plums and pomegranate seeds … We were in the midst of these delights when Trimalchio was brought in with a burst of music. They laid him down on some little cushions, very carefully … Then going through his teeth with a silver pick, 'My friends' said he, 'I really didn't want to come to dinner so soon, but I was afraid my absence would cause too great a delay, so I denied myself the pleasure I was at, at any rate I hope you'll let me finish my game'. A slave followed, carrying a checkerboard of turpentine wood, with crystal dice and with gold and silver coins instead of the ordinary black and white pieces. While he was cursing like a trooper over the game and we were starting on the lighter dishes, a basket was brought in on

THE NATURE OF CHANGE

In most considerations of Rome in Britain, opinion is divided as to whether the Roman Empire was or was not 'a good thing'. The situation facing the indigenous population of first-century AD Britain is often depicted as if it were clear cut: you were either with Rome or against her. If you sided with the Romans you were either forward thinking, a visionary hoping to participate in a great social experiment and benefit from all the things that a Mediterranean-based civilisation could offer, or a quisling, a collaborator, a turncoat betraying your own people. If you took a stand against Rome, you were either a courageous freedom fighter trying to liberate your friends and family, or a squalid terrorist, living life on the run and in constant fear of arrest.

Things were never, of course, that simple.

In June 2005 a BBC reporter noted, with no little irony, that electricity, rather than self-determination, was at the top of most Iraqi demands in the aftermath of war. In the city of Basra in southern Iraq, residents were lucky if they got more than three or four hours of intermittent electricity a day, far less than they had before the beginning of the American- and British-backed invasion, which had been intended to force regime change on the country and bring about political reform. In the increasingly stifling heat of summer, most Iraqis found that supplies of drinking water were diminishing, whilst their homes and key civic buildings were falling into disrepair. Rubbish was no longer collected; pools of raw sewage were gathering in the streets. Living standards and health were in serious decline.[4] 'A better electricity supply seems to be a higher priority than even security' the piece concluded, leaving the audience, we suspect, expressing some incredulity. Surely security and good

3 'Roman' interior design: inside the reconstructed room at Fishbourne Roman Palace, West Sussex. *Courtesy of the Sussex Archaeological Society*

government are the most important prerequisites for a healthy, happy existence?

No, not really.

People, by and large, crave stability and feel uncomfortable when presented with change, especially that over which they possess very little control. There is always some degree of disruption following a revolution, coup or invasion, sometimes involving loss of life on a tragically epic scale. It is interesting, however, not to say perhaps rather comforting, how quickly those that survive adapt and attempt to continue as before. For the bulk of the population living in Britain through the Roman invasion of AD 43, the Saxon invasions of the fifth century, the Viking attacks of the ninth, the Norman invasion of 1066 or the civil war of 1642-51, the basic rhythms of life, assuming they

4 Traditional view of 'the Briton', here an Iceni warrior. *Courtesy of Sue White*

didn't live right next to a battlefield site, would have continued as normal. Fields were ploughed, crops grown, children and livestock reared. Only the ruling elite of any given time period would understand that the arrival of an enemy or a foreign warband spelt trouble. For those aristocrats on the losing side, the choice would have been relatively simple: continue to resist and possibly die on the battlefield, surrender and possibly die in captivity, stay put and modify outlook and allegiance so as to find a place in the new order, or migrate out of harm's way.

The 'bigger political picture' does not often impinge upon more ordinary lives, unless of course it involves the total collapse of governmental infrastructure. When this happens, at a local or national level, it can trigger a social catastrophe; military commanders, disenfranchised politicians, small-time criminals and businessmen, all previously constrained by a fully functioning justice system, are set free to do as they want. In the early years of the twenty-first century, political deficit in Chechnya, Somalia and Afghanistan gave power to a series of warlords, each claiming their own territory, and a fanatical brand of self-serving acolytes. Warlords form alliances or fight neighbours as and when the situation demands. Sometimes the battle-lines are drawn on the basis of religious, cultural or ethnic grounds; more frequently the divide between various factions is blurred. To an outsider the situation can seem unfathomable, it being difficult to take sides or to determine 'good' from 'evil'. In situations such as this there can be no 'just cause' to support; only continually unfolding acts of violence in a bloody cycle of revenge. Power vacuums unsettle the rhythms of life, sweeping away the familiarity of daily existence. New forces can cause a deep

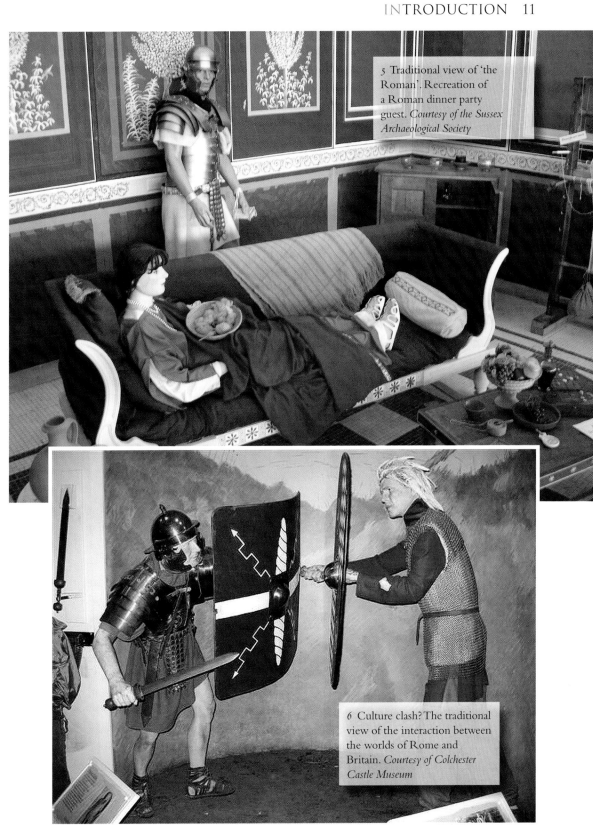

5 Traditional view of 'the Roman'. Recreation of a Roman dinner party guest. *Courtesy of the Sussex Archaeological Society*

6 Culture clash? The traditional view of the interaction between the worlds of Rome and Britain. *Courtesy of Colchester Castle Museum*

7 Captive. Parthian prisoners of war paraded through the streets of Rome on the arch of Septimius Severus

ideas were adopted wholesale by Rome and remade in her own distinctive image. Rome, then, represented the epitome of cultural plagiarism.

Hence, whilst we can speak with some authority about what constitutes Roman art, mosaics, wall plaster, statues, coins etc. the arrival, application and creation of mosaics, wall plaster, statues, coins etc. in areas of the Empire as diverse as Britain and Egypt, was very different. A mosaic, set down inside a Roman town house in Syria, retains many of the cultural tastes, artistic temperament, likes and loves of the Syrian population, whilst a similar mosaic appearing in Britain can (and often did) look distinctively 'British' (or at least 'northern-provincial'). Artistic variation in any given province depended, in the main, upon both the nature of indigenous culture and the art forms that proceeded Roman influence.

Whether 'imperialism' was something which was oppressive and to be feared or a welcome change in lifestyle offering a new life filled with luxury products and opportunity, depended on who you were, what you wanted in life, how much cash you had and what, ultimately, you had to lose. The adoption of Roman culture, customs and fashions was a necessary prerequisite for success within the Empire's provinces and those infected early by Rome were more likely to benefit in the new order. Being Roman gave one the opportunity to directly access a new world of consumerism, personal adornment, prestige and huge opportunities for self-advancement. Those members of a native aristocracy who threw themselves into *Romanitas* (or the Roman way) could hope for a chance to live long and prosper. Those that publicly clung onto the old ways would, at best, have found themselves marginalised, at worst treated with suspicion and contempt.

sense of psychological shock from which it can be difficult to emerge undamaged.

Many people, it would seem, do not ultimately mind too much who is in control of their country, as long as they and their friends and families are fed, housed and generally well-looked after.

On Being Roman

Roman civilisation had spread across Western Europe, North Africa and eastern Asia throughout the sixth to first centuries BC. As Rome the city took control of these areas, making parts of Europe, Africa and Asia 'Roman', so Rome the city itself became more European, African and Asian. Foreign influences, fashions, religions, inventions and

But, then, would they have cared?

Fashion is a curious thing. Many in ancient British society may have been largely unaffected by Roman ideas or fashions, or at least been able to stave off the worst symptoms of the Roman disease, for generations. Few may have seen any benefit in changing their ways of life nor in altering the ways in which they spoke, dressed or behaved. For those living away from the new towns of Roman Britain on rural farms or in villages, any difference in lifestyle before and after the Roman invasion of AD 43 may have been negligible. Taxation, in the form of the presentation of an agricultural surplus, may increasingly have been paid to a more Mediterranean-looking official, wearing Mediterranean-style clothes in an increasingly Mediterranean-style town of brick and stone (rather than a more traditional-looking chieftain in a traditional hillfort), but little else was different. As the Roman academic Richard Reece has noted, a British worker on the farm may only be vaguely aware of the changes occurring in government and fashion 'because he never goes to the tribute gathering, nor do his

9 Longinus, an auxiliary cavalryman, recruited from the Balkans, son of Sdapeze, son of Matycus. *Courtesy of Colchester Castle Museum*

cousins who still have their 50 acre small-holdings, for they have tribute collected by an official, but they had noticed that the official was wearing a silver ear-ring last time he came, and they had no idea at all, well only an unmentionable one, what that was supposed to signify'.[5]

It is safe to say that 'Being Roman' was not a concept that everyone adhered to or even desired. The farmer returning from a new 'Romanised' market may have brought back the odd bronze coin in change, a new style brooch, a wheel-thrown cooking pot or a new form of knife for the kitchen: all things that better facilitated an *existing* way of life but did not, on the whole, threaten to change anything on a dramatic scale. This is passive or permissive acculturation; a form of cultural change that ultimately benefits the consumer but does not overly unnerve them nor unsettle the *status quo*. There may well have been other people, for there always are, who saw new the array of Roman artefacts, lifestyles and fashions on offer in the new towns and marketplaces as a way of bettering themselves and advancing their own social position. In such instances, Rome presented them (and sometimes their families too) with new opportunities and new ways of getting rich.

8 Regina, a Catuvellaunian Briton, freedwoman and wife of Barates, a Palmyrene from what is now Syria. *Courtesy of Arbeia Museum*

10 Tiberius Claudius Catuarus, an enfranchised Celt sponsored for citizenship by the emperor. *Courtesy of the Sussex Archaeological Society*

So what did 'Being Roman' actually mean within the context of first-century AD Britain? Someone who came from Rome? Well yes, to a very limited degree, there were almost certainly some people from the eternal city in the province, exploiting natural resources, overseeing the development of business and looking for a way to make a quick *denarius*. But the term 'Roman' itself was something that stretched far beyond the mere confines of an Italian city. By the first century AD there were probably many millions of people who thought of themselves as being 'Roman' in outlook, lifestyle and thinking, even if few had ever seen the city close up, let alone had relatives or ancestors who lived (or had lived) there.

Can the term 'Roman' then be usefully applied to someone who had been conquered by Rome? Strictly speaking yes: someone captured or enslaved by Rome is owned by the Roman State, having lost all sense of identity and belonging. Such loss of personal freedom, however, is hardly likely to have engendered a desire to actually *be* Roman, let alone to provide opportunities to pursue all that the culture has to offer. 'Roman' as a label makes far more sense when it is applied to a person or persons *influenced* by Rome; someone who wanted to be part of Rome and its institutions; someone who desired either full or partial immersion in all of its fashions, concepts and customs. Of course, in the sense of Rome as an influence, there are multiple degrees of Roman-ness, each of which were ultimately dependent upon circumstances. Who you were, where you lived, and what you did were all just as important factors in determining your degree of Roman-ness as what it was you wanted in life, how far you wanted to go to achieve this, and how important (or not) you were to the State.

For those who made it to the top of the social pile and became fully fledged Roman citizens, rather than mere provincials pretending to be Roman, there were very big advantages, not least of all legal protection and the right to vote (in Rome) as well as various property- and business-related perks. Of course there were disadvantages too, including taxation and military service (which was expected but not always required), but for those with wealth who wished for status and influence, citizenship was ultimately where it was at. *Peregrinae*, or foreign provincials, although they fulfilled the crucial responsibilities within their own cantons and communities, possessed no equivalent civil or legal rights.

TRANSITIONS

Citizenship was not an automatic right. In the first century AD, to be a citizen you would have to have been born into it (not always easy to engineer), served for a minimum of 25 years in the auxiliary army (if you were a man), married a citizen (if you were a woman – although crossing social and class divides in this way was not an easy option), or have had it conferred upon you

11 Hengistbury Head, Dorset, a point of first contact between Britain and Rome

Double Dykes

The Iron Age Entrance to Hengistbury Head

Double Dykes 2000 years ago

Hengistbury Head is internationally important in terms of its archaeology. It has been occupied on many occasions since the early hunter-gatherers of the old stone age, 12500 years ago. Our ancestors camped here as they followed migrating herds of animals. Horse and reindeer provided skins for clothing and shelters, bone and antler for tools and of course meat. At this time the sea was many miles distant and the valley...

12 Hengistbury Head, Dorset. Site of a major Iron Age port

13 Coins. A silver issue of ESV PRASTO, presumably Prasutagus, the pro-Roman king of the Iceni of Norfolk and husband of Boudicca. *Illustration courtesy of Sue White*

by the emperor. In Britain, archaeology has provided evidence for at least three of these four forms of successful social climbing.

From South Shields in Northumberland, at the eastern edge of what became, in the second century AD, the northern frontier of *Britannia*, is the tombstone of Regina, freedwoman and wife of Barates. Barates was a Palmyrene, from what is now Syria, and may have been a serving officer in the frontier army, a veteran or a businessman. Regina, a name which perhaps translates as 'Queenie', is, on the tombstone, recorded as a Catuvellaunian, a native Briton from Hertfordshire. How she ended up a slave, how Barates found or purchased her, when exactly he freed her and whether or not the two were actually in love are, unfortunately, things that cannot be answered from the archaeological evidence itself (although the Palmyrene script, added beneath the formal Latin funerary text, probably by Barates himself, says simply and rather tellingly: 'Barates alas!'). Although damaged, Regina appears serene and elegant, seated, well-dressed and wearing a Celtic torc, or neck

ring, itself a dramatic symbol of power and status. Further evidence of wealth is provided by a large box or casket at her feet, which Regina is leaning forward to open. The casket, decorated with a crescent moon, is protected with a hefty looking lock and was, no doubt, originally filled with jewellery.

A good example demonstrating the initial phases of the native to Roman transition is provided by another tombstone, this time from Colchester in Essex. Here the individual concerned is called Longinus, a fairly generic though perfectly acceptable Roman name. Longinus' father, however, revelled in the very UnRoman, though rather wonderful, name 'Sdapeze, son of Matycus'. Longinus, it would seem, was an auxiliary cavalryman, recruited, so his funerary monument tells us, from an area of the Balkans now covered by Bulgaria. The tombstone shows him in full armour, riding heroically over a naked and rather grotesquely carved barbarian. Longinus died aged 40, some 10 years short of the retirement that would have brought him full Roman citizenship.

The third, and perhaps rather more enigmatic, archaeological find came from excavations at Fishbourne in West Sussex in the late 1990s. The piece is a small but rather splendid gold signet ring, the bezel of which is inscribed, in reverse (presumably so that, if used on a wax seal, it would read the correct way), with a single name: TI CLAUDI CATUARI or 'Tiberius Claudius Catuarus'. In the first century AD, only Roman citizens of the highest rank were permitted to wear gold rings, and only with the explicit permission of the emperor. We do not know who Catuarus was, but his is a fine Romano-British name, Catuarus being an ethnic form derived, quite possibly, from the Celtic term for 'warrior or fighter', hence its appearance in the tribal form *Catu*vellauni (plausibly the 'warriors of Vellaunus'). Addition of the names Tiberius (TI) and Claudius (CLAVDI) to Catuarus' own, furthermore, tells us, rather significantly, that his sponsor for citizenship was one of the members of the Julio Claudian House, in all likelihood the emperor himself; but which one? The issue is not helped by the observation that three emperors, at some stage, all bore the names Tiberius Claudius Nero, these being the second emperor, Tiberius, the fourth, Claudius and fifth, Nero. Tiberius himself can perhaps be discounted, as anyone granted citizenship by him tended to adopt the names 'Tiberius Julius'. Addition of the names Tiberius Claudius to the Celtic 'Catuarus' therefore seems to indicate enfranchisement under either Claudius (AD 41-54) or Nero (AD 54-68).

A significant aspect of citizenship, helping to foster 'a sense of belonging', was derived partly through a defined reward scheme and partly through a public affirmation of loyalty through the swearing of oaths, sponsoring of important projects and the carrying out of public duties. Many nations today advance similar concepts of loyalty affirmation. In Britain, at the time of writing, the 'Citizenship Ceremony' considers an affirmation of fidelity to the sovereign as a key condition to the process of naturalisation. Whether or not existing citizens consider that 'Her Majesty Queen Elizabeth the Second, her Heirs and Successors' have any right to supreme power is ultimately irrelevant, for the key factor in the citizenship ceremony is to present a figure to whom all allegiance can be directed. To the first-century AD Briton, a prominent display of fidelity to the emperor could perhaps help fast-track the citizenship process and, for those that really wanted it, secure a place in the new order.

ROMANISATION

Romanisation is a term which, since it was first coined by the American linguist and lexicographer William Dwight Whitney in 1867,[6] has regularly been applied to the influence and adoption of Roman objects, ideas, language, religion, customs and fashion. Like all processes of cultural change, however, Romanisation was neither uniform nor, ultimately, inevitable. The citizens of Rome had their own term for the spread of their distinctive way of life and ideals across the ancient world: *Romanitas.*

Romanitas can perhaps be better defined as the 'homogenisation' of goods and materials within and beyond the Roman Empire, something which affected different people in different ways at different times and with varying degrees of success. As we have already noted, not everyone in Britain or across the Empire was affected by the process and many of those who were, even partially, seemed to retain much of their own distinctive culture pattern. Purely from

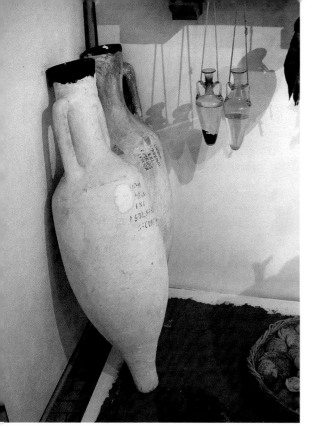

14 Amphorae: Storage vessels designed to transport wine, olive oil and fish sauce to distant parts of the Empire by sea. *Courtesy of Rockbourne Roman Villa, Hampshire County Council*

contained an official title, line of descent, name of the royal seat of power and occasionally carried obvious symbols of wealth and power such as ears of corn, horses, bulls, boars and occasionally ships. In this respect, the coin was a potent symbol of authority, ambition and dynastic intent.

Quite why coins were first adopted by the political elite of Late Iron Age Britain remains a mystery but, by the end of the first century BC, they had rapidly become the propaganda weapon of choice. If the symbols used on the reverse of the coins in question were obviously Roman (perhaps copied direct from Mediterranean originals) or the language used was Latin (such as the use of the term *Rex* for king), this could in turn imply an economic, political or military link with the Roman State. Coins, furthermore, appear in Britain from the early to mid first century BC and seem to have continued in production well after the Roman invasion of AD 43, something that may point towards a degree of continuity in tribal authority within specific parts of the new Roman province.

Another good indicator of early Roman influences at work in certain areas of Britain is the amphora. Amphorae, basically elongated ceramic storage vessels, were designed to transport commodities, such as wine, olive oil and fish sauce, to and from distant parts of the Empire by sea. Like the champagne bottle of today, the amphora was the visible container of status produce and seems to have been greatly prized by elements in the native elite during the final decades of the first century BC and the early years of the first century AD. Associated with the gradual change in eating and drinking habits in certain elite households across southern and south-eastern Britain, as evidenced by amphorae, we also see, from around AD 20, a small but significant

an archaeological perspective, we can see the process of 'Romanisation' at work in Britain from the beginning of the first century BC with the introduction of coinage.

Coins represent one of the most startling of new artefacts to appear within the context of Late Iron Age society. The appearance of coins in the archaeological record however does not mean that Britain had become a monetary economy. Rather coins appear to have been used as a way of using precious metals, given as payment or as a gift, to pass on a political message or a statement of allegiance. Coins represent, in very basic terms, a small fragment of metal (gold, silver or bronze) stamped with the name of a particular member of the local British ruling elite. Sometimes they also

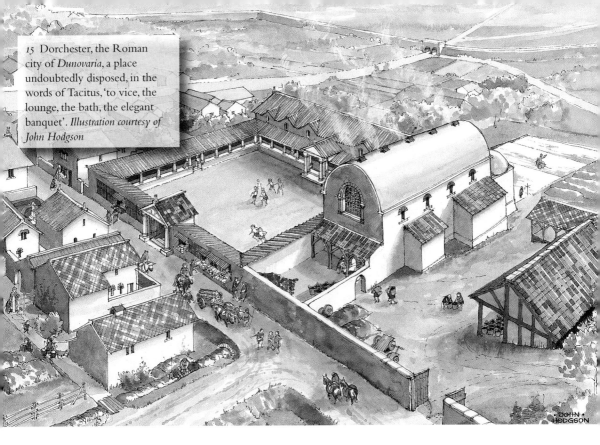

increase in the quantity of pottery imported from places as far afield as Gaul (France), the Rhineland and North Africa. After the invasion of southern England by the emperor Claudius in AD 43, the process of culture change begins to accelerate with the introduction of new gods, urban units, language (at least for official inscriptions), fashion and rural settlement.

'Roman' therefore, at least in an archaeological sense, is a cultural label, used to define things that were more commonly in circulation within the Roman Empire than outside or beyond it. In this sense the terms 'British'/'German'/'Gallic', as used in this book, are ethnic labels, defining origin, background and (perhaps) upbringing. Hence we can use the terms 'Romano-British', 'Romano-Gallic' or 'Romano-German' to describe a person who may have been ethnically British, German or Gallic, but who went into the grave (and therefore the

afterlife) culturally Roman. Longinus, the auxiliary cavalryman whose tombstone has been recovered from Colchester (see above) is one such person who proudly notes his ethnic Balkan background, but who, from his career, name, tombstone and burial status, is culturally very Roman indeed.

Had Longinus not specifically cited his ethnicity within his funerary monument, we would have been none the wiser as to *where* he ultimately derived. Certainly his name is of no use, being as it is a rather generic and commonplace Roman form. Whether Longinus' father, Sdapeze, provided his son with the first step on the ladder to self-improvement by erasing his ethnic heritage and providing him with a solid Latin identity, or whether it was the army, keen to make sure that new recruits dropped all sense of their background (thus increasing loyalty to the State), we will probably never know. What is certain is that had Longinus survived to have children of his own, he would undoubtedly have provided each with a nice new Latin name, eradicating any previous cultural distinctiveness. Archaeologically, people such as Longinus were no longer Iron Age or 'barbarian' provincials, they were well on the way to becoming completely Roman.

An example of the fluid nature of cultural change and, indeed, of the difficulties surrounding its positive identification is the modern term 'Americanisation'. Americanisation is something that, as with Romanisation, means different things to different people. In the United States itself, there is, it is fair to say, no such thing as a uniform type of American culture. As with 'Roman', 'American' makes sense only perhaps as a cultural label; something which covers a familiar range of type-objects, phrases, clothing, music and shared belief-systems. Hence all ethnic groups coming to the USA can ultimately 'dip into' the shared cultural pie, taking from it those aspects that they feel most comfortable with and which best facilitate their own outlook and existence. Of course acculturation is a two-way process and groups can bring aspects of their own ethnic, religious or folk identity to the mix in order to create something wholly new. Today it is not unusual to hear people speak of themselves, not as 'American' per se, but 'African-American', 'Native-American', Irish-American', 'Italian-American' and so on.

At certain times, *Romanitas* appears to have received more than a gentle prod by officials in central government, perhaps desirous of an acceleration in the degree of cultural change, perhaps as a way of increasing stability and hastening economic returns. The end of the first century AD in Britain specifically appears to have been a period in which the State went to substantial efforts to more significantly Romanise key players in the province. New civilian building projects were initiated and increased financial incentives designed.

This process seems to have begun in earnest under the Roman governor of Britain Gnaeus Julius Agricola, at least according to his son-in-law, the historian Tacitus. 'Agricola gave private encouragement and public aid to the building of temples, courts of justice and dwelling-houses', Tacitus tells us, 'praising the energetic, and reproving the indolent … He likewise provided a liberal education for the sons of the chiefs, and showed such a preference for the natural powers of the Britons over the industry of the Gauls that they who lately disdained the tongue of Rome now coveted its eloquence. Hence, too, a liking sprang up for our style of dress, and the toga became fashionable. Step by step they were led to things which dispose to vice, the lounge, the bath, the elegant banquet' (Tacitus *Agricola* 21). The paragraph ends, however, with a typical piece of Tacitean cynicism when he observes that: 'all this in their ignorance they called civilisation, when it was but a part of their servitude'.[7]

The movers and shakers of the developing Roman province seem to have ploughed their money into funding the construction of new urban temples and bathing complexes and, ultimately, developing a whole new series of homes for themselves. Whether this class of *nouveaux riche* sprang from the surviving Iron Age aristocracy, as Catuarus, the gold ring-wearing individual of first-century Sussex may have done, or were simply those who, whatever their ethnic origins, were keen to exploit the province and settle down, we will probably never know for sure. The chances are, however, that a small but significant number were indeed Britons on the make.

Every society throughout history throws up its 'newly rich'; a class of people who generate a substantial amount of money and who then endeavour to spend it as conspicuously as possible. Indeed, the social systems of late first-century southern Britain may have been akin to that of post-Soviet, late twentieth-century Russia where the term *novyi Russkiy*, or New Russian, was frequently applied with contempt to the prominently successful and ultra-rich. New Russians flaunted their wealth through the acquisition of expensive homes and gaudy western status symbols. Often viewed as arrogant, tasteless and lacking in cultural refinement, New Russians were (and are still) frequently treated with suspicion by those who feel that they attained their wealth through dubious, illicit or downright criminal means. 'New Britons' of the later first century AD may well have been thought of in the same way.

INTENT

The intention of this book is to establish a point of view; namely that Britain, although it may have been a formal part of the Roman Empire for nearly 400 years, was never fully Roman.

Roman culture never fully embedded itself within Britain and had no significant impact upon the people and periods that followed. Gaul (France) and Spain were more successfully integrated into the Empire and its systems, but then both had been on the fringes of Roman, Greek, Etruscan and Carthaginian influence for centuries longer than Britain ever had. It is also worth making the point that both Gaul and Spain were devastated after their conquest by Rome, making any resistance to the Roman model of control, adminis-

tration and development far less effective. Gallic society, in 50 BC, was very different to that which had been in existence less than a decade before. Hundreds of thousands of men, women and children had been killed, many more severely maimed, injured or carried off into slavery.[8] What is more, the tribal system was in tatters, all large-scale defended settlements and distribution centres destroyed, religious sites overthrown and trade networks eradicated. There was no such widespread disruption and loss of life in Britain, whose tribal networks seem to have remained in place and in some areas positively encouraged and nurtured.

It is perhaps the high visibility and obvious distinctiveness of Rome's archaeological footprint that has caused disproportionate focus upon things that are obviously more 'Roman' than the more 'normal' aspects that are, to coin a phrase, 'UnRoman'. It is evident that Roman ideas, fashions and customs infected the minds of only a small minority of the British population: the wealthy and the aristocratic elite. It is they, together with the military units, recruited in large numbers from overseas, merchants and officials drawn largely from the Mediterranean world, that were the major users of Roman culture in Britain. As with the whitewashed colonial houses built by British émigrés in India, or the brick-built Georgian Houses of America, many of the palatial villas of Roman Britain may not have been created by (or indeed for) the indigenous population, but for incoming officials, entrepreneurs and pioneers. As with the Roman military installations of northern Britain, the nineteenth-century forts of the American West or the US airbases in Europe or Iraq, may simply have established small pockets of distinctive and (to the garrisons at least) familiar culture in uncertain or hostile territory. Ultimately

such cultural 'bubbles' had little or no impact on the wider native lands beyond.

If Roman culture in Britain was only ever superficially applied, is it any surprise that, even after 400 years of occupation, it had very little lasting impact? If Roman culture only affected the merchants, military and administration, none of whom had any real stake in the province, and the native elite, who may have been suddenly overthrown, gradually died out or simply switched their outlook and allegiance, then is it any surprise that *Romanitas* did not survive into the 'post-Roman' period? Are the majority of books, articles and works discussing 'Roman Britain' ultimately based on a huge misconception: that Britain was a successful and fully integrated member of a Mediterranean-based empire? Was Britain largely an UnRoman element of the Roman Empire throughout the first to fifth centuries after all?

1

POWERGAMES

DURING the Late Iron Age, a mere 2000 years ago, food production, social organisation and human settlement patterns were not 'primitive' but were rather modern in outlook. Land was being intensively farmed, surplus coming under the control of an increasingly affluent and largely non-productive aristocracy. A sustainable surplus meant that it was possible for the elite and their followers to purchase foreign luxuries, fund works of art, garner political support and build military muscle, an important consideration when competing for natural resources. Human settlement was, in the British Iron Age, becoming more centralised; tribal territories were expanding; social spaces becoming more strongly defined.

All this was happening at a time when Western Europe was undergoing a period of significant change: Italy, Austria, Switzerland, Spain, Portugal and now France and Germany having fallen under the dominion of a militaristic monarchy. Millions had died or been enslaved in the process of conquest and assimilation. The battle for Britain was shortly to begin.

FIRST CONTACT

Britain was viewed as a natural target by the power-hungry Roman general Julius Caesar. By 55 BC, Caesar had subjugated much of

Gaul and led troops on a punitive campaign across the Rhine into Germania Magna. In 55 and 54 BC he led invasions into Britain, not, it would appear in order to form the basis of permanent conquest, but in order to capture the Roman public imagination; he wanted to demonstrate his ability to go anywhere and do anything.

Truth be told, the expedition of 55 BC was not a great success, at least in military terms. Trapped on the beach, hemmed in on all sides by the enemy, Caesar could only watch helplessly as his cavalry reinforcements were scattered in a storm at sea, whilst his own transport vessels were dashed to pieces on the shore. A stalemate ensued, the Britons being unable either to eliminate the Romans or dislodge them from their coastal base. The Romans, on the other hand, found themselves unable to break out of the beach positions and attack British targets. Eventually both sides called for peace and the Roman army left in a fleet of hastily repaired ships. Characteristically, Caesar, in his own work the *Gallic Wars*, makes even this sound like a victory.

Within a year of departing, the Romans were back. This time Caesar hoped to obtain a more impressive result: ideally defeating the Britons in a massed battle, capturing a British town (or two) and the acquisition of a considerable number of slaves and booty. Unfortunately for him, the British tribes presented a combined face, electing one of their own, a man called Cassivellaunos, as supreme leader. Although we know nothing about Cassivellaunos, his significance cannot be overstated: he is the first character to emerge from over half a million years of British prehistory; our first identifiable Briton. Caesar portrays him as the villain of the piece, previously intimidating his neighbours by fighting expansionist wars of territorial acquisition across southern England. In the Roman mind, Cassivellaunos was a destabilising influence: his very existence legitimising Roman military activity. Caesar, ever aware of an opportunity for political gain, could claim that armed intervention in Britain was necessary in order to force regime-change, weeding out dangerous warlike elements and bringing peace to the northern frontier of the Empire.

The other British aristocrat that Caesar acknowledges during his campaign of 54 BC was Mandubracius of the Trinobantes (or Trinovantes). The importance of this particular character is that he represents the first Briton to embrace 'the protection of Caesar', a wonderful euphemism. Mandubracius' people seem to have previously fought against (and been defeated by) Cassivellaunos and therefore viewed Caesar as the lesser of two evils. That any deeply held blood feud or clan enmity would at some point destabilise Cassivellaunos' resistance to Caesar must have always been a risk. Given his history, it was likely that certain groups would view the arrival of Caesar as the perfect opportunity to level old scores and destroy a more ancient foe. Whilst Caesar was weak, his troops unable to find food or safe haven, then Cassivellaunos might just succeed. If Caesar looked strong, however, then former inter-tribal enmities could reopen and the Briton's position as warleader of a unified resistance would

effectively be undermined. Cassivellaunos' ultimate failure says more about the politics, squabbles and inter-ethnic tensions of tribal groups in southern Britain than anything else.

At the end of the brief campaign, Caesar left taking a number of British hostages with him. Hostages were traditionally taken by Rome as a way of ensuring the loyalty of conquered peoples. If the children of a defeated monarch were retained in Roman custody, then their parents would be less likely to revolt. Hostage taking also had a more significant aspect to it, however, for, having been taken from their homes, the children of native aristocrats would be brought up within the Roman world and gradually indoctrinated into the Roman mindset. If such Midwich Cuckoos were ever required to return to their people, they would take back a range of new gods, ideas, customs and language: Latin. Having been exposed to a Mediterranean lifestyle from a very early age, they could help fast-track Roman culture within and among the aristocratic classes of their own people.

As well as hostages, Caesar took with him promises of protection money (which he termed 'tribute') and assurances that Cassivellaunos' tribe would 'not wage war against Mandubracius nor the Trinobantes'. Mandubracius was left as a British ally of the Roman State and his tribe as a 'Protectorate'. This Briton was someone who, from now on, would enjoy special trade status and enhanced power. He could, in theory, also rely on Caesar or his nominated officers to provide military assistance in times of trouble. The concept of allied or client kings and queens was one which Rome found particularly favourable, for they provided the State with a degree of security along potentially unstable frontiers. From an economic perspective, client kingdoms also provided Rome with the opportunity to make significant amounts of money through increased trade.

IN CONTROL

A sense of what life was like in Iron Age Britain, at least in political terms, is difficult to achieve. Plans and maps depicting 'Life in the Iron Age' can today create a wholly artificial sense of reality. Sites and artefacts appear in clusters, neatly grouped into discrete tribal zones. Each tribe has a name and possesses, at least on paper, clearly defined borders. Each tribe evidently had its own leaders but we do not know whether such leadership was in any way stable nor whether it brought a sense of unity and identity to the population at large.

Contemporary Roman and Greek authors are of little help, as most simply reinforce the perspectives and prejudices of their own times, depicting the Britons as barbaric and rather backward. 'They are simple in their habits', Diodorus Siculus tells us from the late first century BC, 'and far removed from the cunning and vice of modern man. Their way of life is frugal and far different from the luxury engendered by wealth'. 'The Britons', Tacitus, writing in the early second century AD, tells us, 'were formerly governed by kings, but at present they are divided in factions and parties among their chiefs; and this want of union for concerting some general plan is the most favourable circumstance to us, in our designs against so powerful a people. It is seldom that two or three communities concur in repelling the common danger; and thus, while they engage singly, they are all subdued' (Tacitus *Agricola* 12).

Julius Caesar mentions a series of tribes and rattles off a few aristocratic names in the *Gallic Wars*. Ultimately, however, he leaves his audience in the dark as to the specifics of British society and politics beyond noting that 'the interior of Britain is inhabited by people who claim on the strength of their own tradition to be indigenous; the maritime portion by immigrants from Belgic territory who came after plunder and to make war, nearly all of them being named after the tribes from which they originated' (*Gallic Wars* 5, 12).

Our understanding of society in the British Iron Age is therefore both incomplete and severely limited. We do not know how people were organised or what they thought of themselves or their leaders. The names that we have for the different tribal groups, such as the Iceni, the Atrebates and the Catuvellauni, are those preserved by the Roman State in the late first and early second century AD. It is highly probable that, in establishing this organisational framework, Rome recognised only the larger political groupings and disregarded all others. The real political map of Iron Age Britain was no doubt simplified by Rome who preferred the idea of single tribes occupying single areas under the rule of individual leaders. More likely the names that we have today for the 'tribes' of Britain were no more than the identifiers of particular ruling dynasty or aristocratic lineage. A 'tribe' could simply have been those who owed allegiance to a particular leader and not necessarily always a discrete ethnic or cultural group.

It was the aristocracy, the non-productive elite, holding power through military supremacy, trade, divine right or blood heritage, who decided whether external influences, such as those presented by the Roman Empire, would succeed within particular areas. If the leaders wanted wine and olive oil then it was up to them to negotiate directly with Rome. Any subsequent wid-

17 The legendary ocean, a formidable barrier to Rome, in both physical and psychological terms

Opposite top   18 Roman invasion fleet. A cast section taken from Trajan's Column in Rome showing Roman troops crossing the Danube. *Courtesy of the Sussex Archaeological Society*

19 Devils Dyke, Wheathampstead, Hertfordshire. Possible centre of power of the British king Cassivellaunos, enemy of Caesar in Britain

20 The traditional view of the major Iron Age tribal groupings within the area that was to become the province of *Britannia. Courtesy of Jane Russell*

Mediterranean consumables such as wine may have provided a similar route to the top for prehistoric entrepreneurs in Britain. As with the 'royal' houses of the British Iron Age, the control of business and the organisation of protection rackets in early twentieth-century America increasingly came under the control of a few powerful dynasties.

There was never a chance, in Late Iron Age Britain, that everyone would enjoy the proceeds of trade, exchange and big business. Tempting though it may be to see new Mediterranean imports into Britain as the beginnings of a better, more civilised society of benefit to all, there does not seem to have been much of a 'trickle-down' effect, with those beyond the elite suddenly shaving, bathing, drinking wine and wearing Roman gold. Only those with direct access to the Roman State would benefit from its patronage. Mediterranean contacts and the goods they provided were no doubt jealously guarded by the native elite, keen that the prestige associated with links to the Empire was not diluted by broadening access.

SETTLING DOWN

Across southern Britain, the most representative archaeological type site of the Iron Age is the hillfort. These imposing, contour-hugging enclosures seem to provide confirmation of the warlike nature of Iron Age society which, we are told by Roman writers such as Julius Caesar, was always feuding, brawling, fighting and stealing. Strong hilltop defences must, we assume, imply a very real fear of neighbouring communities combined with the desire to protect house and home from attack. The majority of Iron Age settlements at this time, however, were relatively small-scale; representing close-knit

ening of access to Roman goods, fashions or customs to the wider population would depend on how tightly leaders controlled their followers and how many gifts and favours they ultimately bestowed.

Parallels for the successful development of power through the brutal control of business and the exploitation of family networks can be found throughout human history, particularly in early twentieth-century America. Here, groups operating small-scale urban criminal activities in New York, eventually grew to control significant areas of the city. By the time of prohibition in the 1920s, when the sale and consumption of alcohol was banned across the United States, the manufacture and distribution of bootleg liquor proved the perfect way for aspiring gangsters to further develop and expand their criminal empires. The exploitation of natural resources in return for

21 Cefn Du, Anglesey. Large thatched roundhouses of the Iron Age and Roman periods. *Courtesy of John Hodgson*

22 Cranborne Ancient Technology Centre, Dorset. A recreated Iron Age roundhouse

23 Uffington, Berkshire. A univallate hillfort. *Kite photograph courtesy of Hamish Fenton*

24 Cleeve Hill Camp Iron Age hillfort, Gloucestershire. *Kite photograph courtesy of Hamish Fenton*

farming communities, trading, interacting and existing in a relatively open landscape apparently without ever feeling the need to massively defend or protect.

The roundhouse was the standard domestic unit within most Iron Age settlements. The size of floor varied, but most houses lay within the range of between 10 and 15m in diameter, defined by low external walls and, it is presumed, conical thatched roofs. 'Open settlement' roundhouses tended to cluster in groups of three or more, one structure serving as the main residential unit, others as ancillary buildings, storerooms and, occasionally, shrines. Enclosed farmsteads, comprising a single, enlarged roundhouse set within a bank and ditch defining an area of around a hectare, are also found throughout the British Isles.

Warfare between the various Early Iron Age communities of southern England may well have been endemic, a semi-permanent state of rivalry between clans or farming units; but rarely, if at all, would it seem that any particular group desired the total defeat and/or extermination of the other; this being a more modern concept of war. Conflict between prehistoric societies more often took the form of competition, something which helped foster alliances and enforce allegiances. Competition increased the desire amongst the leaders of particular communities for prestige goods and extreme dress items, and ultimately more visually impressive forms of hilltop enclosure.

Hillforts, then, could have less to do with a permanent state of open war, and more to do with the desire to elaborately define and protect the political heart of a particular clan group. Hillforts were probably where organised gatherings took place at particular times of the year for the purposes of trade,

26 Maiden Castle, Dorset. The north-western slopes of the multivallate hillfort

27 Badbury Rings, Dorset. Patrolling the south-eastern ramparts

exchange, taxation, marriage, food distribution or religion. Hillforts were where the elite resided and where leadership of the tribe was reinforced and bonds of allegiance strengthened. Yes, they represented state-of-the-art prehistoric defensive capabilities; the final word in elite protection, power and prestige (much as the motte and bailey castle was to the Norman lord); no, they did not reflect a fragmented society, barricaded in fear upon the highest and most remote areas of the country. They were not the ultimate symbol of a divided or broken Britain.

In the south and east of Britain, few of the large developed hillforts continued much beyond 100 BC although small enclosed farms and open farmsteads did continue to flourish. As the hillforts faded, a new form of elite enclosure developed. These are called *oppida*, an unfortunate title, derived from a rather vague term applied by Julius Caesar to pretty much every large Iron Age settlement he encountered in Britain and Gaul, regardless of location, size or extent. Annoyingly, Caesar never defines what precisely he thinks an *oppidum* is, but, given current archaeological considerations, the term probably has more valid application in France, Germany and Switzerland where some Late Iron Age sites possess urban planning in the form of street grids, administrative and religious buildings, elite settlement and enclosing walls of stone.

In Britain there is really nothing comparable to the continental *oppida*, though the term 'territorial *oppidum*' is sometimes applied to a discontinuous form of Late Iron Age linear earthwork found in areas where the hillfort seems to have died out. Territorial *oppida* have been identified at a variety of places in Britain including Colchester in Essex, St Albans in Hertfordshire, Silchester in Hampshire and Chichester in West Sussex. These sites possess complex systems of banks and ditches which demarcate, but rarely enclose, vast swathes of land. At Colchester, an area of just over 32 square kilometres was partially defined by multiple series of ramparts. These earthworks would not have proved overly effective in halting a truly determined invasion, but they would have seriously impeded movement from the west, especially if that involved chariots or large numbers of cavalry. They looked pretty impressive too.

The quantity of Mediterranean imports recovered from excavations in and around the Colchester *oppidum* is suggestive of a focus of trade and, ultimately, political control. There have been few extensive surveys of the interior, but it seems clear that few areas to the east of the ditch systems were in any way intensively occupied. At Sheepen, to the west of the later Roman and medieval town, an area of Iron Age settlement associated with industrial activity, coin manufacture and exotic Roman imports, most notably wine and Mediterranean olive oil, has been located, while at Gosbecks and Lexden, to the south-west, a religious complex and major cemetery have been recorded. At Lexden a burial mound, excavated in 1924, produced a wooden chamber containing a wealth of domestic objects, furniture, a chain mail shirt, 17 amphorae and a silver medallion of the emperor Augustus. Pottery finds suggest a date of around 15-10 BC.[9] At Gosbecks a trapezoidal-shaped rampart enclosed a series of impressive roundhouses. The coinage produced under the regional king Cunobelinus in the early years of the first century AD gives us the *oppidum*'s name: *Camulodunum*, 'the fortress of Camulos'.

The sheer cost of constructing *oppida*, at least in terms of labour, must have been immense; the equivalent of hundreds of men, women and children working 10-12-hour

28 Multiple grain storage pits of the Later Iron Age being excavated as part of the Durotriges Project at Bournemouth University in 2010

shifts every day for well over a year. Even if the entrenchments were created in a series of stages over time, their creation must have tied up a considerable body of the population. This was communal effort on an immense scale, which itself implies a well-organised central authority, or at least someone with a grand design and little in the way of local opposition. Clearly *oppida* were required; their presence in the landscape was felt necessary. Whether such sites provided the focus of elite settlement, where a king or queen ruled their people, the centralisation of key resources (such as horses or cows), the spiritual heart of a religious community or the defended limit of a particular tribe, is, however, unclear.

Perhaps *oppida* represented the political formalisation of a particular authority, the defended boundaries of the tribe. Perhaps certain communities simply feared the expansionist tendencies of their immediate neighbours and so were keen to protect their territories in ever more dramatic ways. Historically we know that a number of British kings, including individuals called Tincomarus and Verica, sought shelter in Rome at the beginning of the first century AD, so such a theory may not be too wide of the mark. The fact that many of the hillforts of the Early Iron Age were not being refortified at this time, however, could alternatively suggest that fear of attack and the escalation of hostilities was not a major concern for the bulk of the population. Only those with a vested interest in maintaining good relations with Rome may have felt the need to define the limits of their power

29 Chichester entrenchments, West Sussex. A small section of the 10km-long *oppidum* rampart which remains impressive today

30 Devils Dyke, Wheathampstead, Hertfordshire. The interior of the *oppidum* today: was it originally the focus of elite settlement where a king or queen ruled their people, or simply a place where a 'very large number of men and cattle' were collected?

31 Augustus. Bronze image of the first citizen of Rome *c.25* BC from the Sudan. © *Trustees of the British Museum*

in dramatic new ways. The control of trade with the Mediterranean, and of the profits that ensued, may have led some British leaders to protect their investments better with networks of defensive ramparts backed by displays of intimidation and force.

RISE OF ROME

Following the assassination of Julius Caesar in 44 BC, the Roman world was convulsed by civil war. The conflict finally ended in 31 BC when the combined forces of Caesar's friend, Mark Antony, and his lover, the Egyptian queen Cleopatra VII, were decisively beaten at the battle of Actium by Caesar's adopted son, Augustus. In the aftermath, as first emperor of Rome, Augustus felt that he needed to show the Senate and People that he, like his adopted father

Caesar, was successful in the dual theatres of politics and war, especially against the barbarian nations. Wars brought prestige to Rome. They also delivered swift economic returns in the form of slaves, tribute, booty and the opportunity of taking direct control of a wide range of natural resources. The question was, Augustus may have mused, exactly who could he legitimately pick a fight with?

Early in his reign, it seems that contact between Augustus and a number of prominent British families was relatively strong, trade and tribute binding the 'barbarians' closely to the State. 'At present', the Roman author Strabo tells us, 'some of the chieftains there, after procuring the friendship of Caesar Augustus by sending embassies and by paying court to him, have not only dedicated offerings in the Capitol, but have also managed to make the whole of the island virtually Roman property. Further, they submit so easily to heavy duties, both on the exports to and on the imports from Celtica (these latter are ivory chains and necklaces, and amber-gems and glass vessels and other petty wares of that sort), that there is no need of garrisoning the island; for one legion, at the least, and some cavalry would be required in order to carry off tribute from them, and the expense of the army would offset the tribute-money; in fact, the duties must necessarily be lessened if tribute is imposed, and, at the same time, dangers be encountered, if force is applied'.[10]

Strabo's calculation of the military resources required in order to keep Britain securely under Roman control seems ludicrously small: one legion (around 5000 men) 'at the least' with accompanying cavalry. Presumably Strabo was referring to the area of Britain that Rome knew; the south and east, rather than 'the whole of the island', but then the point is that he is

32 Gold stater from southern Britain bearing the name Commios, possibly the same king of the Atrebates and ally of the Roman general Julius Caesar during his invasions in 55 and 54 BC. Commios seems to have established an 'Atrebatic' kingdom in Britain, one which became closely affiliated with Rome. *Courtesy of Chris Rudd. Cat. No. 534*

providing his audience with the justification *not* to attack Britain. The embassies of these unnamed British chieftains were in Rome 'paying court' to Augustus and dedicating offerings in the most holy of Roman sanctuaries. Those who wanted to ensure that their neighbours in Britain did not gain the upper hand were actively pursuing the emperor and he was only too happy to advertise the fact. Conquering the Gauls and Germans was one thing; having the Britons emerge from the very edge of the known world in order to pay homage to the Roman people was quite another.

Augustus was happy to meddle in the internal affairs of tribes that bordered his empire. This, of course, was nothing new, for Rome had for many centuries interceded in the internal politics of other nations, suggesting alliances, overseeing a disputed succession or overthrowing an unfriendly government. Regime change through diplomatic means was preferable to direct military intervention, although, from a Roman perspective, force of arms could always be portrayed rather more heroically on coins and in statuary. The unilateral imposition of Augustus' will upon British or German tribes through a display of military might would, however, have been costly, both financially and, if things did not go to plan, politically. As Augustus was to discover, client kingdoms, 'buffer' states at the margins of Empire, could be manipulated in far more subtle ways than by mere military intimidation.

None of Augustus' own policy statements survive, but a clue to his methods and motives may be provided in the writings of the second-century imperial biographer Suetonius, who noted that: 'except in a few instances he restored the kingdoms of which he gained possession by the right of conquest to those from whom he had taken them or joined them with other foreign nations. He also united the kings with whom he was in alliance by mutual ties, and was very ready to propose or favour inter-

marriages or friendships among them. He never failed to treat them all with consideration as integral parts of the Empire, regularly appointing a guardian for such as were too young to rule or whose minds were affected, until they grew up or recovered; and he brought up the children of many of them and educated them with his own'.[11]

A key element in traditional Roman society was the institution known as *clientela* (clientage). This ran on the principle that a *cliens* (client) was obligated through a debt of loyalty to repay favours (gifts, financial aid, employment, protection etc.) received from a benefactor or *patronus* (patron). The patron acted as a father-figure to his clients, taking a personal interest in their businesses and financial and legal well-being. In return the client could offer financial, political, legal and, occasionally, even military support to his patron. The more clients a patron possessed, the greater his support-base and social standing. The system worked tolerably well at a personal level, but at an institutional level, when entire families, clans, cities or tribes became *clientes*, it all became a little more complicated.

In such a situation, British monarchs could feel obligated to supply 'gifts' of slaves or metal ore, pay tribute or tax or provide fighting men for the armies of Rome. They may also have been required to surrender their children to the emperor, partially as a way of ensuring their continued loyalty to the Roman state but also in order that their offspring could receive a 'good education' and mix with the great, the good and the politically influential. Once 'educated', former hostages could be returned to their people, now fully conversant with the ways and systems of Empire. Thus Rome could minimise potentially destablising events by returning their own preferred candidate to a position of supreme power.

By the mid first century AD, Britain and the Britons were evidently well known to those within the inner circle of the emperor. Rome had been trading with certain Britons on a regular basis and interfering with their internal affairs for some time. A situation of calm stability was good for all parties. In peacetime, the Romans benefited from cheap metals, foodstuffs and slave labour, whilst some British aristocrats grew fat on the proceeds of trade, beginning to dominate the lands of their immediate neighbours. One such British magnate was called Cunobelinus, whom the Roman historian Suetonius refers to as 'King of the Britons'.[12] We possess no description of Cunobelinus, although there is a large number of coins, produced under his authority, that carry realistic-looking portraits. Can any of these represent the great king? Possibly. If the coins are indeed of him, they show the monarch dressed and styled as a Roman ruler, clean-shaven in a tunic and with a laurel wreath. Perhaps more likely is that the image was intended to represent either the emperor Augustus or his successor Tiberius. By copying the face of the emperor on his own coin, Cunobelinus may have hoped to flatter his Roman counterpart. Perhaps he was merely indicating the debt of loyalty (the obligation of service) that he, as a client, owed to his patron.

Cunobelinus was an important figure in the Late Iron Age of southern Britain. He would appear to have been king of either the Catuvellauni (based at St Albans) or the Trinovantes (at Colchester) and, at some stage in the AD 30s, was minting coins with the place name CAM – *Camulodunum* (modern-day Colchester). As his coins also possess the name VER – *Verulamium* (St Albans), it is possible that Cunobelinus was fighting a low-level conflict and spreading his influence through eastern and southern Britain. Cunobelinus was in all probability the Iron Age equivalent of a Mafia godfather: dangerous, strong, politically powerful and in control of all economic and financial transactions for his region. Certainly the area around *Camulodunum* appears, in the last decade before AD 43, to have been the premier importer of Mediterranean and exotic consumables. He was also, judging by the images appearing on his coins, an ardent supporter of Rome and may well, like other client kings of the period, have sent his children to Rome to be educated under the protection of the emperor.

Archaeological evidence, in the form of both finds and features, suggest that elements of the Roman army were in Britain, at Fishbourne near Chichester in Sussex and Gosbecks at Colchester in Essex, during the early decades of the first century AD.[13] The thinking behind the placement of Roman troops within territories beyond the frontiers of Empire was something that was entirely consistent with imperial policy elsewhere. In fact the strategy is neatly summed up by Julius Caesar when discussing the placement of troops in Egypt, at that time outside the remit of the Empire, during the 40s BC. Here soldiers of Rome were embedded within the Egyptian royal court so that they may 'support the authority of the king and queen, neither of whom stood well in the affections of their subjects, on account of their attachment to Caesar, nor could be supposed to have given any fixed foundation to their power, in an administration of only a few days' continu-

34 Recreation by Karen Hughes of the Winchester Late Iron Age hoard as it may originally have been worn. © *Trustees of the British Museum*

35 Cranborne Ancient Technology Centre, Dorset. A recreated set of Roman timber buildings. Structures such as these were constructed within the Roman fort at Fishbourne prior to the invasion of AD 43

ance. It was also for the honour and interest of the Republic that if they continued faithful our forces should protect them; but if ungrateful that they should be restrained by the same power'.[14]

Under such circumstances, and with such precedents, it would perhaps be more difficult to argue why Rome would *not* have been active in Britain: protecting British aristocrats and establishing military bases in order to directly protect Roman trade interests. Given the relative wealth of Britain and the high levels of commerce evident across the south and east, it would be hard to believe that the Senate and People would have left the Britons well alone. The British garrison may have been tiny, but it was important. Whether such troops were billeted here in order to protect friendly British kings from outside aggression or to intimidate them, it could be that a low-level provision of troops was thought of as the first stage in a greater plan: the acquisition and eventual conquest of the island.

By the late 30s and very early 40s AD the situation in Britain appears to have been unravelling. One of Cunobelinus' sons, at least according to Suetonius, left Britain to seek the protection of the emperor. The year was AD 40 and the emperor in question was Caligula: third emperor of Rome and borderline psychotic. Our sources for Caligula's campaigns against the Germans and the Britons are overtly hostile, all desperate to establish that Caligula was in some way delusional. A major achievement of his actions in north-western Europe, in fact the *only* one according to Suetonius, was 'to receive the surrender of Adminius, son of Cynobellinus king of the Britons, who had been banished by his father and had deserted to the Romans with a small force'.[15] Adminius is probably a later garbling (or mistranslation) of AMMINVS, a name appearing on coins within eastern Kent and issued by a British king at around the same time Caligula was in power (or at least between the late AD 30s and early 40s).

The death of king Cunobelinus, at some point after AD 40 but before AD 43, probably left a great political void in which many British leaders fought for dominance. We hear of at least two rivals, the surviving sons of the great king Caratacus and Togodumnus, but there were probably more. Some British leaders may, like Amminus before, have decided to flee to the relative safety of the Roman imperial court, something that provoked additional unrest, the historian Suetonius observing that Britain was 'in uproar at the time as a result of the Roman refusal to return certain fugitives'.[16] Later, Dio Cassius says that in or around AD 41 'a certain Berikos' was in Rome, complaining about the British situation to the newly installed emperor Claudius. Berikos, usually equated VERICA, a descendant of Julius Caesar's Celtic friend Commios, had 'been driven out of the island as result of an uprising'

37 Stone relief from Aphrodisias, Turkey. Propaganda image showing the emperor Claudius as a nude hero, about to deliver the death-blow to the prostrate Amazonian figure of *Britannia*. *Massingheimer Collection*

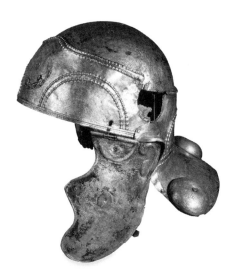

36 Roman cavalry helmet of the first century AD from Ely, Cambridgeshire. Traditionally such military artefacts are thought to relate to the invasion of Britain in AD 43, but they could also indicate a low-level Roman military presence in Britain prior to the emperor Claudius. © *Trustees of the British Museum*

and was in Rome in order to persuade Claudius 'to send a force there'.[17]

The circumstances that had deprived Berikos/Verica of power are not set out in any detail by Dio Cassius, but it may be instructive to note that this particular king's coins appear to concentrate around Silchester, in northern Hampshire, as well as the coastal zone of West Sussex. If the distribution of these indicate the extent of Verica's power, then whatever the unrest or 'uprising' entailed, it was presumably happening in central southern Britain.

INVASION

On the morning of 24 January AD 41, Tiberius Claudius Nero Germanicus became the fourth emperor of Rome fol-

38 Fragment of the inscription originally forming part of the triumphal Arch of Claudius in Rome proclaiming the surrender of 11 British kings to the emperor

lowing the assassination of his predecessor Caligula. Aware that he was no great politician with no claim to military prowess, Claudius desperately needed a distraction; in short he needed a war.

Britain was a land of opportunity, as previous emperors Augustus, Tiberius and Caligula had all understood. From Claudius' perspective, annexing the island made a great deal of sense, for assuming that the propaganda could be spun correctly, it could be said that Julius Caesar, greatest warrior of Rome, and now officially a god, had failed to establish a lasting conquest, despite intervening in British politics on two separate occasions. If Claudius could not only win a victory in Britain but more critically establish a province under direct military control, he would have demonstrated that he was

greater than Caesar and therefore, by inference, greater than a god.

Whatever the reality of Rome's former relationship with Britain, it was evident that by AD 42 there were two prominent Britons, Amminus and Verica, in Rome together with their supporters. Such important political players offered hope that an expedition to Britain could actually succeed, unlike the brief forays of Caesar nearly a century before. Importantly, as everyone in Rome would be aware, Britain was rich in metal and grain whilst slaves would come in great numbers in any war. Direct military intervention would not only make political sense, but could also be made to sound economically viable. Whatever the bulk of the population in Britain felt, they were about to become a part of one of the largest empires of the ancient world.

The invasion, when it came, seems to have been relatively swift. Irrespective of where forces actually landed,[18] within months Claudius was in Colchester receiving the surrender of 11 British kings, 'defeated without reverse' as an inscription set up in Rome would later proclaim. Claudius could now celebrate his triumph over *Britannia*, something that he continued to do throughout the remainder of his reign. Southern Britain, or at least that part previously belonging to the Iceni, Trinovantes, Catuvellauni, Atrebates and the various tribes of Cantium (Kent), was now formally part of the Empire, having been 'liberated' from a potentially messy civil war.

It was clear, however, that the larger conflict was not over, however much the emperor's public relations machine said otherwise, for despite the submission of so many British aristocrats to Rome, Caratacus, leader of the British resistance movement, remained at large.

2

MAKING THE CHOICE –
RESISTANCE OR ALLIANCE?

IN the later AD 40s, the Roman army moved into, what was for them, the relatively unknown lands of the west (the Cotswolds, Devon and Wales) chasing both the fugitive Caratacus and the greater mineral wealth of Britain. In their absence, the long-term stability of land acquired by Rome in the central south and east of England appears to have been guaranteed by the acknowledgement of client states, kingdoms maintaining a semi-autonomous existence under the watchful eyes of Rome. In the immediate aftermath of the invasion, four tribes in particular seem to have benefited directly from Roman patronage to a lesser or greater degree: the Iceni, the Brigantes, the Atrebates/Regini and the Catuvellauni. It is worth examining the relative situation of all four of these broad tribal groupings and contrast this with the major loser in the establishment of *Britannia*, the Trinovantes of Essex.

ATREBATES/REGINI

Of all the relatively fluid tribal groupings identified in Britain, the Atrebates are probably the easiest to identify and categorise. Their political centre seems to have been established at Silchester in Hampshire, where the Roman town of *Calleva Atrebatum* was later constructed directly over its heavily Romanised Iron Age predecessor. This embanked *oppidum* was specifically named on the coins of the British king Eppillus as *Calleva* (which may loosely be translated as the 'town in the woods' – a name that perhaps echoes the densely wooded British *oppida* that Caesar describes in his *Gallic Wars*). The name Atrebates is used by a tribe in Belgic Gaul and it may be that together these two clusters originally represented either two halves of the same ethnic group or that the British tribe was formed from a migration to the island, possibly led by the Atrebatic king Commios, a friend and ally of Caesar during his long campaigns across Gaul and Britain.

The Roman town of *Calleva Atrebatum*, established as a *civitas* or tribal capital, covered, in its final phases, a polygonal area of just over 40ha, its shape being largely defined by the position, form and nature of the pre-Roman *oppidum*. Evidence retrieved during excavations across the interior of the Roman town, in the late twentieth and early twenty-first century, have shown that the Late Iron Age settlement comprised substantial timber-framed buildings set in a semi regular street grid.[19] Artefacts include large quantities of imported northern and central Gallic pottery (which is what one would perhaps expect from a tribe whose ethnic background was Gallic/Belgic), amphorae (originally full of wine, oil and

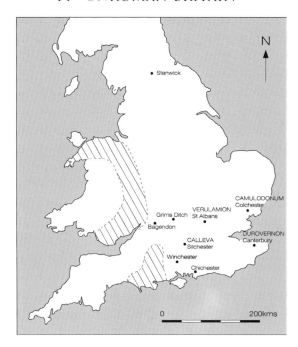

N

• Stanwick

CAMULODONUM
Colchester

VERULAMION
Grims Ditch   St Albans
• Bagendon

DUROVERNON
Canterbury

CALLEVA
• Silchester

• Winchester

• Chichester

0   200kms

39 The territorial oppida *of southern Britain, indicating the possible form of their original pre-Roman names, and the 'hillfort dominated zone' to the west (shaded).* Courtesy of Jane Russell

preserves) and oysters (something the ethnic Britons seem to have otherwise avoided).

By the mid first century AD, with the establishment of the Roman province, *Calleva* hit the big time. A new street grid was imposed and surrounding structures remodelled, most notably the prestige forum, the baths, some of the brickwork being stamped with an official die proclaiming the involvement of NER(o) CL(audius) CAE(sar) AUG(ustus) GER(manicus), and a number of prominent temples and shops. Large quantities of ornate stonework, including Corinthian capitals recovered from the foundation levels of the main phase of the Roman town, suggest that there may well have been a palace or high-staus aristocratic house at the approximate centre of the earliest town.

To the south-east of *Calleva* lay the Roman town of Chichester, on the West Sussex coast. Two versions of the *Geography*, the *magnum opus* of early second-century mathematician, astronomer and geographer Claudius Ptolemaeus (Ptolemy), record that the ancient name of Chichester was *Noeomagum* or *Noeomagus*, and that it was the capital of the Regni. *Noeomagum* or *Noviomagus* (the 'new town' or 'new market'), if it served as a tribal or *civitas* capital in the Roman province, means that the second element of the name, *Regentium*, should represent tribal affiliation. The problem is that *Regentium* is sufficiently close to the Latin term *Regnum*, meaning 'kingdom', something which could mean that the full name of Chichester was originally *Noviomagus Regnensium:* 'the new market town of the people of the Kingdom'. Given the relatively large number of early civilian building projects discovered across eastern Hampshire and Sussex,[20] it is indeed possible that the 'Regini' were not a distinct *people* but instead a discrete *kingdom* established within the lands previously occupied by the Atrebates or were themselves a sub-sect of the Atrebates.

The land of the Regini/Regni, incorporating eastern Hampshire and much, we may assume, of West Sussex, contains a significant number of prestigious civilian building projects, notably the substantial temple complexes of Hayling Island and Bosham and the extravagant palaces of Fishbourne, Southwick and Pulborough. Fishbourne is justifiably one of the more famous Roman sites in Britain comprising, in its main phase, a large central courtyard, with formal gardens, a public range containing a large entrance hall and aisled basilica, an impressive apsed *triclinium* (dining room), a private range and a guest wing arranged around a series of discrete apartments. It also contains some of the earliest and most lavish examples of mosaic and decorated wall plas-

40 Silver unit of Verica, king of the Atrebates, proclaiming his descent from the king and former ally of Julius Caesar, Commios. *Courtesy of Chris Rudd. Cat. No. 597*

ter to be found in the UK. The Southwick palace, although on a smaller scale, mirrored the architectural form of Fishbourne as, apparently, did the building complex at Pulborough. Fishbourne palace, constructed in the latter years of the first century AD, replaced an earlier Mediterranean-style courtyard house, built in the mid 60s AD during the reign of Nero.[21]

Two ethnic Celts, presumably British in origin, have been mentioned in relation to the Fishbourne palace: Tiberius Claudius Togidubnus and Tiberius Claudius Catuarus. Togidubnus is cited from an inscription in Chichester, where he seems to have been referred to as 'Great King of Britain'; Catuarus from a gold ring found close to the palace. If we accept that building work for the Sussex palace did not commence much before AD 90 (at the earliest) and that both men were ethnic Britons who owed their position and status to either the emperor Claudius, for service to Rome during

the events of AD 43, or Nero, for service during the revolt against Roman power by the British queen Boudicca in AD 60/1, then the palaces seem the perfect reward to them or their descendants. Alternatively they may represent the homes of Roman administrators, brought in to carve the client kingdom up following the demise of either Togidubnus or Catuarus. Given that we possess no firm idea as to who lived within the palaces, nor whether they were ethnically British (although they were clearly culturally very Roman), we cannot know for whom these building projects were intended.

It is tempting, however, to consider the Sussex palaces as homes or powerhouses designed for members of the pro-Roman native elite, some of whom may have been brought up in Rome as hostages. If the sites were the product of a brief but considerable expenditure of cash, an extravagant attempt to spend new wealth in as conspicuous a way as possible, rather than a part

41 Fishbourne, West Sussex. Fragments of an imposing Corinthian capital from the proto Palace phase, *c*.AD 65. *Courtesy of the Sussex Archaeological Society*

of imperial policy, creating houses for the new administration, then it is interesting to see how long they lasted. By the beginning of the second century AD, possibly less than two decades after their completion, the palaces of Fishbourne and Southwick were in a state of contraction and decline. At Fishbourne a great aisled hall, designed as an enlarged audience chamber, was extensively remodelled, a bath suite being unceremoniously inserted through one end. The formal gardens at the centre of the site were abandoned and the 'state apartments' broken up. At Southwick the public ranges were down-sized and subdivided, whilst the bulk of the eastern and southern wings were demolished.

The severe restructuring of both palaces indicate the first serious attempt to escape the constraints of the unitary floor plan and move towards more discrete units of occupation. This is perhaps unsurprising, given that these grand sites represented imperial-style architectural statements, artificially transplanted into Britain. Unlike the later villas of southern England, places of wealth production, the palaces of Sussex were centres of wealth *consumption*: buildings within which the owners spent their money swiftly and conspicuously. It may be that the palace owners did not possess ways of sustaining such flagrantly high levels of expenditure. Perhaps their money ran out too quickly. Possibly, much like the Icenian elite of Norfolk (see below), the owners found, after throwing themselves so enthusiastically into the Roman way of life, that their financial accounts had been suddenly frozen and their loans recalled, after

The likely line of the
Roman road to Chichester
1 mile away

42 Fishbourne, West
Sussex. Footprint of the
main palace constructed
in the late first century
AD. *Courtesy of the Sussex
Archaeological Society*

43 Fishbourne, West Sussex.
Coloured mosaic from the late
first century palace. *Courtesy of
the Sussex Archaeological Society*

44 Bloodgate Hill, South Creake, Norfolk, a roughly circular, single entrance enclosure. *Illustration courtesy of Sue White*

a change of government strategy back in Rome. Perhaps a review of imperial fiscal policy led to a decrease in the viability of grand palatial apartments in Britain and of the political will to maintain them.

The palace of Fishbourne represents the ultimate high visibility piece of *Romanitas* in Britain. It is tempting to see it and believe that this was the sort of home that all Britons could aspire to. This was the main reason why 'Being Roman' was desired and was felt to be important. This was why the Roman life was so much better than that of the barbarian. Unfortunately, of course, the palace at Fishbourne was not an open access facility for all to enjoy; neither was it an 'ideal home' exhibition that everyone could see and aspire to. Fishbourne was a powerhouse, a private residence constructed for an important individual; a base of opera-

tions designed with the dual purpose of luxury and comfort, but also, perhaps more importantly, for the effective governance of a kingdom. As such, the building lasted probably as long as the client kingdom itself. When the kingdom was dissolved, presumably in the early second century AD, Fishbourne was dissolved with it: premium space being sold off and restructured for the new owners.

Ultimately, none of the early palatial buildings created in this part of Britain appears to have had much impact upon the wider British population. The nearby Roman town of Chichester was, after the creation of urban infrastructure, never a great success and no great adventures in rural Roman architecture were to occur here for at least a century. Native settlement patterns along the Hampshire and Sussex coast continued largely without interruption. The palaces of Sussex were a flash of *Romanitas* that flared brightly for an instant, before dying out completely.

ICENI

The Iceni are probably the most famous of all British tribes thanks to the revolt led by their queen, Boudicca, in the early 60s AD. The tribe seem to have been based within an area of eastern England roughly corresponding to Norfolk and parts of Suffolk and Cambridgeshire. From their rather distinctive coin series, we can say with some certainty that they called themselves the Eceni, although as the modern academic convention is to refer to them as the Iceni, this fiction will be maintained here for consistency's sake.

The Iceni seem to have been left largely to their own devices as the Roman military moved westwards in the late 40s and early 50s AD. There appears to have been no significant disruption or alteration in native settlement patterns. A series of medium to large enclosures (given the landscape of Norfolk it seems somehow wrong to call them hill forts) are known, at South Creake, Thetford, Warham, Holkham and Narborough, although none has been comprehensively dated. Bloodgate Hill at South Creake is a roughly circular, single entrance enclosure, measuring just over 200m across. Geophysical survey suggests ordered, symmetrical planning. At the Fison Way in Thetford, Norfolk, an early to mid first-century AD site was found to comprise two rectangular ditched enclosures, the smaller set within the larger, the space between the two being filled by eight concentric palisade, wooden fence or tree bedding trenches. The smaller ditch surrounded an area measuring just over 220 by 170m and contained, at its westernmost end, at least five round,

45 Thetford Castle, Norfolk. Iron Age ramparts

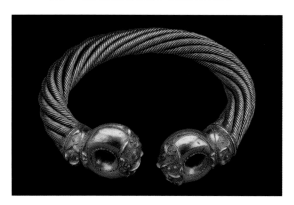

46 The Great Torc, a gold neck ring from
Snettisham, Norfolk. © *Trustees of the British
Museum*

post-built structures. The excavators of the
site have argued that the well-organised
system of internal planning, 'excessive' numbers of enclosure systems and lack of any
clear defensive nature, especially around
the entrance, when combined with the
near total absence of any 'normal' domestic
debris, make the sanctuary interpretation
by far the most plausible.[22] Perhaps this was
the spiritual hub of the local clan group, the
Iceni/Eceni; a tribal centre, meeting point
or place of assembly.

The material culture of this region suggests that some of the Iceni elite benefited
from Roman contact. Many of the torcs
(neck rings) and other decorative dress
items recovered from hoards of the period
indicate that the raw material necessary
to manufacture such jewellery was, in all
probability, derived from Roman bullion.
Analysis of the metallic content shows that
these 'native' forms contain a very high proportion of silver, something which compares
extremely favourably with early first-century AD Roman coins.[23] Could it be that the
raw material necessary to create such Celtic
works of art was ultimately derived from
imported Roman bullion, coins or ingots,
given as a gift by the emperor Claudius and

the Roman State in order to ensure the
long-term loyalty of Icenian aristocracy? It
is interesting to note that, of all tribal groups
in Britain, it was the Iceni who seem to have
been allowed to retain certain native culture
patterns and continue manufacturing distinctive neck rings and minting coins.

It is the coins that perhaps provoke the
most interest as their continued presence,
and the fact that the tribe appears to have
been allowed to continue minting them,
implies a substantial degree of autonomy
within the new political system. The facial
image depicted on the last of the series,
that of a man whose name contained the
element 'PRASTO', is intriguing: the real-
istic portrait of a clean-shaven young adult
with a very distinctive Roman hairstyle of
long, individually parted locks and curling
sideburns. This could easily be the face of a
British aristocrat, depicted as a Roman citizen wearing the latest fashions and sporting
the most up to date of hairstyles. If so, this
would represent a genuine contemporary
image of a Briton depicted as he would
like his people to see him: a model Roman.
Unfortunately, as with the face on the coins
of king Cunobelinus already described, the
image could just as easily depict a rather
'garbled' depiction of the then emperor, the
youthful Nero, whose face was so prominently placed upon the British king's coins
as a way of officially confirming tribal loyalty to the State.

PRASTO (plausibly Prasutagus or
Prastotagus) is famous for another reason:
as the husband and partner of the most cel-
ebrated and renowned of British aristocrats,
queen Boudicca. Boudicca exists only in
the written word of her bitterest enemies,
there being no independent verification of
her in the coins of the Iceni, although given
that the PRASTO coins of her husband
were among the last Celtic issues minted in

Britain, this is hardly surprising. After the death of Prasutagus, there was probably no desire amongst the Iceni to emulate slavishly the cultural markers of Rome and they may well now have rejected the coin, the ultimate symbol of *Romanitas*.

The death of Prasutagus created immediate problems for the Iceni and their special relationship with Rome. The Roman historian Tacitus says that the British king had cited the young emperor Nero his heir, together with his two (unnamed) daughters, 'an act of deference which he thought would place his kingdom and household beyond the risk of injury'.[24] This perhaps highlights the unusual legal nature of client states within the developing province, as well as the highly uncertain status of the client him/herself. Prasutagus had made his peace with Nero's predecessor Claudius, but had he renegotiated the deal with the new emperor? Did the peace accord still stand, and if it did, was it on the same terms as before, once Claudius was dead? So into Nero's reign, the Briton had steered the Iceni through times of honourable peace, ensuring that their status and position remained intact. It had probably not been easy; some aspects of the relationship had undoubtedly been humiliating, but the Iceni had survived and thrived. Roman bullion had poured into the pockets of the tribal aristocracy, much of it being melted down and reformed into the kind of Celtic power statements that the native Briton preferred: torcs, brooches and equestrian equipment.

The problem was that Nero, or at least his delegated officers in Britain, felt that the finer details of the king's last will and testament were irrelevant once Prasutagus was dead. Tacitus notes that, within days of the king's demise: 'his kingdom was pillaged by centurions, his household by slaves; as though they had been prizes of war. As a beginning, his wife Boudicca was subjected to the lash and his daughters violated; all the chief men of the Icenians were stripped of their family estates, and the relatives of the king were treated as slaves'.[25] To add clear insult to injury, another Roman historian, Dio Cassius, tells us that the Roman administration decided at this point to target the finances of the Icenian elite, a demand being made for all financial aid provided under Claudius to be paid back immediately. Nero's advisor, Seneca, further compounded the problem as 'in the hope of receiving a good rate of interest, had lent to the islanders 40,000,000 sesterces that they did not want, and had afterwards called in this loan all at once and had resorted to severe measures in exacting it'.[26]

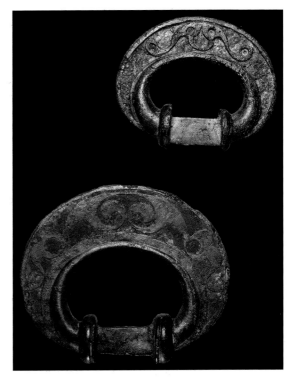

47 Enamelled bronze terrets, or reign-holders, from Westhall, Suffolk. © *Trustees of the British Museum*

An unexpected recall of all loans, which certain members of the British aristocracy may previously have perceived as gifts, presents to do with as they saw fit (such as recasting the precious metal into jewellery), would have suddenly crippled the ruling, pro-Roman classes within the Iceni. All their accounts were now frozen and all royal assets could legitimately be seized by the emperor's debt collectors, co-ordinated through the *procurator* (finance minister) for *Britannia*. The ruling and religious classes within the tribe now found themselves at the mercy of the Roman State and, where money was concerned, the State had no qualms about getting what it felt it deserved. The rough treatment meted out to the Iceni was conducted as if they had been the enemies of the Roman people, not their allies and friends. Now, as their houses were torched, their possessions and land taken and their bodies punished, many of the elite must have reflected that it may have been better to have stood up against Rome during the events of the AD 43 invasion.

Dio Cassius echoes these sentiments in a speech that he gives to Boudicca, on the eve of her final and ultimately (for her) disastrous battle against two Roman legions.

> You have learned by actual experience how different freedom is from slavery. Hence, although some among you may previously, through ignorance of which was better, have been deceived by the alluring promises of the Romans, yet now that you have tried both, you have learned how great a mistake you made in preferring an imported despotism to your ancestral mode of life, and you have come to realise how much better is poverty with no master than wealth with slavery. For what treatment is there of the most shameful or grievous sort that we have not suffered ever since these men made their appearance in Britain? Have we not been robbed entirely of most of our possessions, and those the greatest, while for those that remain we pay taxes? Besides pasturing and tilling for them all our other possessions, do we not pay a yearly tribute for our very bodies? How much better it would be to have been sold to masters once for all than, possessing empty titles of freedom, to have to ransom ourselves every year! How much better to have been slain and to have perished than to go about with a tax on our heads![27]

Although these are the words of a British noble filtered through the cultural perspective of a Roman, rather than being accurately copied by a journalist on the edges of the battlefield, they are worth noting, if only to provide an alternative perspective to life in a client kingdom of Rome.

TRINOVANTES

The Trinovantes were evidently the losers of the Roman invasion and its immediate aftermath. Their leaders had, it would seem, formed the primary resistance to Claudius' army and it was they who had been singled out as the key enemies of Rome. With their aristocracy broken and their liberty restricted, the Trinovantes had also lost their capital, the *oppidum* of *Camulodunum*, modern-day Colchester.

Camulodunum was the main focus of the Roman advance under the emperor Claudius following the destabilisation of the south-east during the AD 40s. Having served as the centrepiece for Claudius' victory in Britain – it was here that the emperor received the surrender of the British kings – the *oppidum* was heavily garrisoned by the *XX Valeria* Legion who established their fortress at its vacated centre. With the transfer of the XX Legion to the western front in AD 49, the fortress was rebuilt, not as a *civitas* or tribal town, but as a *colonia*. *Coloniae*, or 'colony towns' were founded in freshly conquered enemy territory. Their purpose was to act as a model town (to help Romanise the natives) but also to act as a military reserve, premium space within the *colonia* being allocated to soldiers approaching retirement age. *Camulodunum* was therefore now rebranded, its old tribal name of *Camulodunum* being rejected in favour of *Colonia Claudia Victricensis*: 'the city of Claudius' victory'.

Colonia Claudia Victricensis seems to have been provided with all the luxuries expected for a classical city, including an organised street grid, established directly over the earlier internal road network of the legionary fortress, a forum (the prestige market centre), basilica (the focal point of local government authority), a theatre, shops and baths. It also had a temple complex, a large religious building, later dedicated to the deified emperor Claudius. Nothing of the temple superstructure survives, though the foundations suggest a substantial building set within a large sacred precinct. It was, according to Tacitus, a 'citadel of an eternal tyranny' whose priests, chosen by the State from amongst the native aristocracy, 'were bound under the pretext of religion to pour out their fortunes like water'.[28] Possible members of the native elite who, in Tacitus' view were being bled dry by the necessities of State religion, were found at Stanway. Most of the burials here appear to post-date the AD 43 invasion and pre-date the Boudiccan revolt of AD 60. Finds included a spear, shield, surgical kit, ink pot, gaming board, exotic pottery, copper strainers and the ubiquitous amphorae.[29]

Whether the main residents of the town, the retired soldiery, appreciated their new-found 'friends' and their new surroundings is unclear. Most of the new city-dwellers may have lived in the fort whilst still on active service. Now they were being 'rewarded' by the State with property built within incompletely demolished military buildings. Worse, they were being encouraged to live in peace with the very people whom, only a few months or years before, they were killing, imprisoning and generally lording it over. 'The veterans', so Tacitus tells us, 'were acting as though they had received a free gift of the entire country, driving the natives from their homes, ejecting them from their lands'.[30] It is clear, in retrospect, that the experimental 'model-town' of *Colonia Claudia Victricensis* served only to fuel the fires of resentment within the native population.

CATUVELLAUNI

The treatment meted out by the Roman State to *Verulamion* (St Albans), an *oppidum* of the Catuvellauni, is in marked contrast to that of their eastern neighbours, the Trinovantes, whose centre at *Camulodunum* (Colchester) was treated as a conquered city. According to the Roman historian Tacitus, the Romanised form of the *oppidum*, *Verulamium*, was accorded the status of a *municipium*, a discrete, self-governing community in which the magistrates were granted Roman citizenship. The disparity between the treatment of the Catuvellauni and the Trinovantes in post-conquest Britain seems to have had its origins in the way their respective leaders approached the arrival of Rome. Caratacus, on behalf of the Trinovantes, fled to the west and actively campaigned against the Roman army, later being pursued through the mountains of North Wales and hunted down in northern England. For the Catuvellauni, however, their leader's acquiescence with Rome

48 St Albans, Hertfordshire. The foundations of post–Boudiccan shops fronting Watling Street

49 St Albans, Hertfordshire. The foundations of the second-century theatre

50 Balkerne Gate, Colchester, Essex, originally a free-standing monumental arch, possibly erected around AD 50 in the final years of the emperor Claudius

51 Stanwick, North Yorkshire. The ramparts of the Brigantian *oppidum*

52 Stanwick, North Yorkshire. Equestrian
equipment, including a bridle bit and two terrets,
from the Stanwick hoard. © *Trustees of the
British Museum*

seems to have been well rewarded by both
the emperors Claudius and Nero.

Verulamion comprised an impressive
series of earthworks covering an overall length of seven miles (compared to 12
at *Camulodunum*). The main commercial
centre seems to have been close to the River
Ver, where archaeological evidence has suggested the metalworking combined with
the manufacture of large quantities of pottery, coins. To the north-west of the Ver, at
Folly Lane, the cremated remains of a man
were found in a wooden chamber together
with the smashed remains of domestic pottery and wine amphorae, equestrian kit,
parts of a disassembled chariot and a folded
shirt of chain mail. Pottery dates the deposit
to around AD 55. Whoever was buried here
was probably a chief negotiator for his tribe
during the years following the Claudian
invasion, possibly even helping to negotiate the status of the *municipium* and client
kingdom.[31]

Construction on the town of *Verulamium*
seems to have begun in around AD 49/50,
timber-framed, tile-roofed shops lining the
main streets and a stone structure, either the

first forum or, just possibly, a royal palace, was
constructed near the centre. A bath house,
painted inside with scenes from classical
mythology, was built to the north-east of the
speculative forum. Given the planned street
grid and setting out of civic amenities, with
evident signs of personal wealth, it is probable that the followers or supporters of the
pro-Roman Catuvellaunian monarchy were
accorded high status in the *municipium* of St
Albans. There were, almost certainly, a large
number of provincials, drawn from a variety
of locations around the Empire, also living
in the new town, keen to exploit the emerging markets and develop contacts with the
emerging Romano-British population.

In the lands to the immediate east, the
Trinovantes, originally operating from
Camulodunum, Colchester in Essex, had
become a subject people possessing no official status within the new political system.
When, in AD 60, a revolt exploded within
the lands of the Trinovantes and the Iceni
against the Roman authorities, *Verulamium*
was an obvious target.

BRIGANTES

In the late 40s and early 50s AD, the northern limits of the newly establishing Roman
province needed to be secure as the military moved westwards into the 'barbarian'
unknown. Stability was ensured, for a while
at least, by the establishment of good relations between local government and the
Brigantes. The Brigantes tribe apparently
covered an immense territory, centred on
Yorkshire but stretching from the Peak
District to Newcastle. The Roman historian Tacitus was quite vague concerning the
proper application of the tribal name, and it
is possible that the word 'Brigantes' itself was
a generic one meaning, in Celtic, something

like 'the upland people'. Given the wide expanse of land involved, together with the identification of additional (smaller?) potential tribal groups within Brigantia, such as the Carvetti (of Carlisle), the Latenses (around Leeds), the Gabrantoviccs (of East Yorkshire) and the Tectoverdi (in southern Northumberland), it is also entirely possible that the Brigantes were not a single, coherent 'tribe' as such, but a confederation of social groups coalescing under a single leader. In the mid first century AD that leader was Cartimandua.

Much as with the Iceni of Norfolk, the Brigantes under queen Cartimandua seem to have had a special relationship with Rome that involved a broad agreement of peace, probably in return for donations, paid in cash, to the native aristocracy. Such an arrangement would have been politically expedient for the Roman government, allowing the majority of military forces on the island to co-ordinate their advance into Wales and the west without having to bolster a second front to the north. The agreement paid dividends when Cartimandua surrendered the British warlord Caratacus to the Roman State in AD 51, following his defeat in North Wales. Cartimandua, as a pragmatist, may have realised that wherever Caratacus went he brought trouble, the Roman army snapping at his heels. Permitting the resistance leader to operate freely in her lands could have disastrously destabilised her realm, potentially weakening any control that she had over the geographically dispersed population.

The most substantial monument of the period, and probably the political centre of the 'tribe', is the earthwork system recorded from Stanwick in North Yorkshire. Unlike the territorial *oppida* of the south and east of England, Stanwick, which comprises a series of discrete phases of construction,

fully encloses a block of land some 300ha in area. Excavations at the site have confirmed its status as a premier importer of Roman goods, wine amphorae from Rhodes and olive oil amphorae from Spain 'rubbing shoulders' with Neronian period samian ware, flagons and other decorated vessels.[32] As with the Iceni of Norfolk, there does not appear to have been any substantial restructuring of society in the area of Yorkshire during the first century AD, with much of the material assemblage and recorded settlement pattern suggesting continuity rather than change.

Intriguingly, high-status objects of Celtic art found in the area of Stanwick, and usually taken to represent a broad resistance to Roman fashions, seem actually, on examination, to have been facilitated by the Roman State. The Melsonby hoard, for example, discovered in 1845, comprised at least 140 separate objects, mostly equestrian gear: horse harnesses, bridle bits and chariot decorations. The most famous artefact in the hoard is the so-called 'Stanwick Horse', a small model of a horse's head made from a single, thin sheet of bronze. The head is a masterpiece of highly stylised Celtic art, and had probably originally been fixed to a wooden object, such as a bucket or container used in a funerary or feasting context. The key thing about the piece is that it, and the majority of objects in the hoard, were made of a zinc alloy or brass. As brass was not used prior to the arrival of Rome, and due to the subsequent intensification of extraction and processing activities, it would appear that, as with the 'Celtic' torcs and coins of the Iceni, these items are consistent with material supplied as a gift from (or the product of trade with) the more Romanised south in the AD 50s or early 60s.[33] Just as happened with the Iceni, however, the retention of such native traditions, leaders and culture patterns, albeit with the gradual introduction of Roman goods and money, meant that there was no obvious desire within the elite to 'Be Roman'. This, when combined with an almost complete disinterest, on behalf of the new Roman provincial administrators, to reorganise the political or economic infrastructure of the Brigantes, to make it more amenable to Romanising influences, or to offer the aristocratic classes some incentive to 'join the party', seems unsurprisingly to have led eventually to problems.

Civil infighting destabilised the Brigantine confederacy during the mid 50s AD and, with no internal placement of Roman troops to aid her, Cartimandua's position gradually became tenuous. The revolt was led, so Tacitus tells us, by the queen's ex-husband, a man called Venutius. 'Venutius summoned help and with a simultaneous revolt on behalf of the Brigantes themselves forced Cartimandua into a very tight corner. She in turn appealed to the Romans for help, and after a number of indecisive engagements our cohorts and cavalry squadrons managed to extricate the queen from her dangerous situation'.[34] It was clear that the privileged status that the Brigantes had up to this point received was at an end. 'Venutius was left with the kingdom', Tacitus notes, 'we the war'. In AD 71, the new governor of Britain, Petilius Cerialis, launched a major assault on the Brigantes. 'There were numerous battles', Tacitus says, 'some of them bloody, and a large part of Brigantia was either annexed or overrun'.[35] Cerialis had brought with him a legion that was new to Britain, the II Adiutrix. This unit seems to have been placed at Lincoln, whilst the IX Legion was advanced northwards to York and a network of auxiliary forts established across Brigantian territory. Any hope that the favoured status previously enjoyed by the aristocrats of the Brigantes would

return was over. From now on the tribe would be ruled as a conquered state and, although villas developed in the third and fourth centuries, they were small in number and modest in size, their mosaics portraying a very 'provincial', or lively, style. A *civitas* for the Brigantes was established at Aldborough (*Isurium*), but it was never hugely successful.

CONSEQUENCES?

The differential status of the five main tribal players in southern, northern and eastern England in the years immediately following AD 43 appear clear enough. The Catuvellauni and Atrebates/Regini were all provided with the infrastructure of local government in the form of towns; Silchester, St Albans and Chichester all possessing evidence of early street grids and bathing complexes. St Albans and Silchester may well have had high-status domestic structures established for their ruling elite within the area of the new town, whereas Chichester had one close by at Fishbourne. The native elite in these areas were favoured in the new system. They retained their positions of power, spent their new cash and generally showed off in extravagant and very Roman ways.

The Iceni and Brigantes, occupying the lands at the north and north-eastern extremities of England, Norfolk and Yorkshire, also seem to have had a privileged existence, forts being largely absent in the early years from their lands. The ruling aristocratic elite within the two tribes received large cash donations (or loans) from central Roman government in order to keep them happy. The trouble is that, in either case, there was no desire amongst the elite to be more Roman, using their cash like the elite of the Atrebates and Catuvellauni, in order to buy into the Roman way of life. Similarly there was little or no attempt on behalf of the new government to push towards a more Roman lifestyle through the creation of new Mediterranean concepts, like planned towns. The Icenian and Brigantian elite were permitted to retain critical aspects of their native culture patterns, namely Celtic jewellery, Celtic coins, the refurbishment of traditional enclosures and the retention of their monarchs (Prasutagus in the east and Cartimandua to the north). When Prasutagus of the Iceni died and Cartimandua of the Brigantes was finally ousted from power in a 'palace coup', the Roman State tried to wrap the respective client kingdoms up. In both instances, the clear absence of *Romanitas* beyond the native elite, other than at a very low level, made a bad situation very much worse.

In Essex, the Trinovantes enthusiastically joined the Iceni uprising against the provincial government. They had a similar set of grievances to the Iceni, namely the loss of status, land and possessions, but they had been a conquered nation for considerably longer than their immediate neighbours. The chief target of their hatred was the city of *Colonia Claudia Victricensis*, the Roman colony town that had been transplanted deep into the heart of their former capital *Camulodunum*.

Colonia Claudia Victricensis lay undefended; the rampart surrounding the old legionary fort had been levelled, the ditch filled in to make way for housing. Apart from the retired soldiers, some of whom may have (illegally) retained armour or swords, there was, according to Tacitus, only a 'small body of troops' in the town. An appeal to the *procurator* (the provincial finance administrator), Catus Decianus in *Londinium*, resulted in the arrival of less than 200 men 'without proper weapons'. There was no preparation

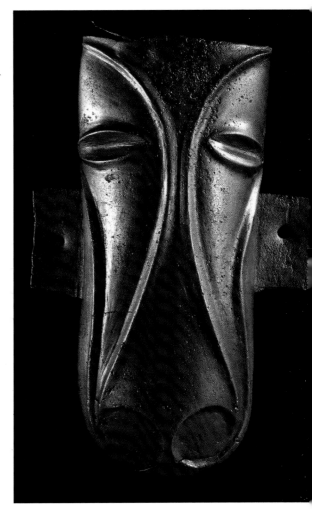

53 Stanwick, North Yorkshire. Bronze model of a horse's head from the hoard. © *Trustees of the British Museum*

made within the town, bemoans Tacitus, no creation of defensible positions, no mass evacuation of women and children. When Boudicca's army of disaffected Icenian and Trinovantian nobles and their warriors descended upon the city, those with any sense fled to the temple of Claudius, where they held out for two days. No quarter was given; no prisoners taken.

Evidence for the destruction is not hard to find; the thick deposit of charcoal, baked clay and burnt earth beneath the modern

54 Boudicca, instigator of the great revolt that brought the client kingdoms of southern Britain to their knees. Nineteenth-century statue on the Thames Embankment, London

city of Colchester is clear enough. Within the charcoal can be found smashed fragments of burnt, high-status pottery, molten lumps of metal and glass, food remains, furniture and collapsed wall plaster.[36] To the west of the city, one of the cemeteries also seems to have been desecrated, tombstones thrown over and vandalised. Further afield, evidence of burning detected at a number of early villa sites in Essex and Cambridgeshire may indicate the murder of landowners, most of them probably ex-soldiers and officials, and the destruction of their rural estates.

London, the Roman boom town constructed on the northern shore of the Thames, was next. Here there were riverside wharves, the warehouses and store rooms of provincial commerce, the shops, markets and prestige emporia as well as the banks and offices of the provincial tax collector. With no military support, *Londinium* fell swiftly, Tacitus noting crisply that 'the enemy neither took captive nor sold into captivity; there was none of the other commerce of war; he was hasty with slaughter and the gibbet, with arson and the cross'.[37] It came as no surprise that the next target for the native uprising was *Verulamium*. That tribal grievances could survive and fester for over a century, from 54 BC and the time of Julius Caesar to Boudicca in AD 60, may seem incongruous, but sadly modern experience in areas as different as Northern Ireland, Iraq, Bosnia-Herzegovina, Georgia and Afghanistan demonstrate, almost on a daily basis, that events occurring many generations earlier can impact upon the present in very real and terrifying ways.[38] Blood feuds, betrayals, tribal loyalties and clan memories can resonate for centuries; each new generation being taught the concept of hate.

Verulamium may well have been deliberately targeted because of deep-seated tribal tensions between the Catuvellauni and their neighbours; Icenian and Trinovantian payback for decades of hurt. The fact that it was an obvious centre of *Romanitas*, proudly displaying its newfound status, was of course another good reason to eradicate it. Tacitus chides the British rebels for 'their relish for plunder and wish to avoid hard work' which ensured that they 'steered clear of the forts and military garrisons and made for places rich in spoil but unprotected by any defending force',[39] but this strategy made sound sense. Those facing the might of Rome in open battle ended up dead; those who employed guerrilla tactics, ambushing troops, burning crops and attacking soft targets, avoiding well-defended military installations in the process, could wear down the Roman resolve.

The insurgency appears to have spread. At Winchester, examination of Roman levels during the 1950s and early 1960s found evidence that was broadly consistent with that recorded from London and Colchester, suggesting that *Venta Belgarum* (or at least bits of it) may have been hit by a catastrophic fire around the middle of the first century AD.[40] Similarly at Silchester, fieldwork conducted in 2008 found widespread evidence of fire, dated to between AD 50 and 75, accompanied by the blocking of wells and demolition of buildings. Following the fire, the town street grid was re-laid on a completely different orientation, suggesting that the entire early phases of the town had been swept away.[41] As Silchester was *Calleva Atrebatum*, a *civitas* designed to serve the Atrebates, a key pro-Roman power in the region, one has to wonder, as with the destruction of *Verulamium*, whether such targeting was opportunistic or ethnically inspired.

The uprising of AD 60/61 had resulted in the deaths of many thousands of citizens, soldiers, provincials and natives. The whole of Rome's investment in Britain had been at stake and, had it not been for the swift action of the governor, Suetonius Paulinus and his army, combined, we may presume, with aid from those tribal groups still wedded to the Roman system, then the loss of the province would have been inevitable. If the revolt had succeeded, then the political fallout for Nero and his advisors would have been severe, especially as the key grievance of the rebels had been the rapaciousness of both emperor and his delegated officials.

The social dynamics of clientage, bringing the native royal families into the web of loyalty and debt obligation, had catastrophically failed. A new phase of *Romanitas* was required if Britain could be kept under Roman control and finally turn in a profit.

3

A ROMAN FACE FOR BRITAIN

THE client kingdoms had failed; the carrot and stick diplomacy of defining friend and foe within the native elite had brought catastrophic results. What the Boudiccan revolt of AD 60/61 had clearly demonstrated to the imperial government was that the native elite could not be relied upon to keep the peace. From now on Britain had to function as a province, just like any other. The big question was, the new provincial government must have pondered, would more of the population, apart from just the aristocratic classes, really start thinking, acting and living as Romans? Would the concept of 'Being Roman' successfully extend beyond the wealthy to more layers of British society?

TOWNS

We have already seen that the concept of 'towns' was not entirely alien to Britain prior to the arrival of Rome. *Oppida* and hillforts were central places, social, economic and administrative anchor points in the landscape. When you look at them from an archaeological perspective it is clear that most possessed a political heart, areas of religious activity, storage facilities, industrial workshops, elite housing, street networks and circuits of defensive wall. In short they were towns; at least in everything but name. They were not, however, part of a Mediterranean politico-economic system. They did not look like, nor did they function in the same way as, Greek or Roman towns. If you were to wear down the old tribal system in Britain and erase the Roman State's over-reliance upon the native aristocracy to keep the peace, you had to impose a new system of doing things. The native elite could survive, but they would thrive only within a more organised and controlled system of urban planning. Kings, tribute, cattle raiding and tribal law was out. Magistrates, taxation, civic pride and Roman law were in. The Britons could retain a sense of self-government, but it was a government which followed a Roman pattern and one which would only work under the careful supervision of Rome.

Establishment of towns was therefore essential if the people of Britain were to be fully integrated into the Roman Empire. The people of the 'tribes' had to work within the imperial system if the province were to function efficiently and effectively. To help achieve this aim, the Roman State established a more formal system of *civitates*, or cantons. This was a form of government by devolution: the rather vague tribal identities of before were now rigidly formalised, a new Mediterranean-style urban unit being created at the centre of each. All the major tribes identified by Rome in southern

55 Dorchester. Recreation of the forum and basilica of *Dunovaria*. *Courtesy of John Hodgson*

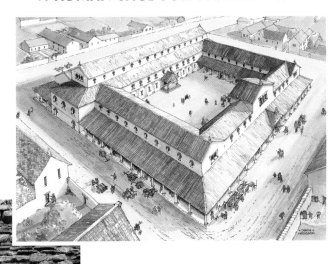

56 Leicester. Surviving section of the monumental public bath house of *Ratae*

57 Dorchester. Recreation of the amphitheatre of *Dunovaria*. *Courtesy of John Hodgson*

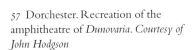

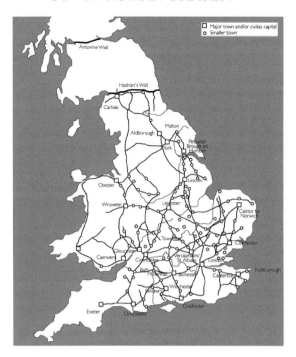

58 Map of Roman Britain

Britain would be allowed to retain a certain degree of self-determination, but their place of regional assembly would now no longer be the hillfort or *oppidum*, but the town. Anyone wishing to climb the greasy pole of self-advancement would have to do it within an exclusively Roman system.

If they functioned in the same way as a 'normal' classical city, each *civitas* or tribal capital would have had its own council (*ordo*) or regional assembly. To begin with, every *ordo* would theoretically have comprised elements of the native elite, an attempt perhaps to ease the transition from tribal authority to Roman. In the classical city, membership of the *ordo*, limited by adherence to a strict property qualification, was restricted to 100, all of whom were male. Members, known as *decurions*, were eligible for a variety of official positions, the most prestigious of which was that of magistrate. Each year two magistrates, known as the *duoviri iuridi-*

cundo, were elected to preside over judicial courts, organise religious festivals and supervise the running of the *ordo*. Magistrates were assisted by *duoviri aediles*, whose job it was to deal with public works and services, *quaestores*, who dealt with finance (including tax collection) and *censitores*, who managed the official documents of the canton, including all census records. Some individuals using such titles have been recorded from inscriptions in Britain, but it is not known just how vigorous the take-up of the Latin career structure was nor how widespread was its application.

Some towns had already been established in Britain by the latter half of the first century AD, albeit on a seemingly rather ad hoc basis. Most of these needed some form of reconstruction following the revolt of queen Boudicca. Other urban units required extreme modification to get them to an acceptable level of *Romanitas*. Others still needed to be built from scratch.

The first stage of creating a classical-style town would have been to set down the basic skeleton: a regular grid of streets, intersecting at right angles. At the central point of this new grid, where the two main highways, the *Cardo Maximus* and the *Decumanus Maximus*, crossed, the first buildings associated with local government, the forum and basilica, were established. The urban forum was essentially a large open courtyard surrounded by a covered walkway or colonnade. This was designed to act as the economic heart of the town, the region and the tribe that claimed authority over it. It was the prestige market centre, the place to do business, to gather to hear proclamations and announcements and where tribal and civic identities could be subtly fused. The forum would contain all the key symbols of *Romanitas* including images taken from the Roman pantheon of gods (especially

Jupiter) and portraits of the current head of State (or his honoured ancestors).

The basilica, which adjoined the forum, comprised a massive apsidal-ended, fully covered rectangular hall, and was designed to act as the focal point of local government authority. If the forum was the economic heart of the tribe, then the basilica was its brain. As a key element in defining civic pride, the basilica was designed to impress. In Britain, where few buildings had previously risen much above a single storey, the architectural impact of such a grand and monumental structure must have been dramatic. The basilica created an ordered space in which the town council (*ordo*) could meet, where Roman (and tribal) justice was dispensed, rates of taxation calculated, the effectiveness of public services discussed and where the records, documents and legal papers relating to the region were ultimately stored. The blueprint for the forum and basilica complex, with its open courtyard backed by a covered administrative hall, can be seen in the *principia* or headquarters building found at the heart of all first- and second-century Roman forts. This would seem to indicate that the design and initial layout of all new towns in Britain was overseen and co-ordinated by the military.

Once the army surveyors had set out the areas associated with the infrastructure of regional government, it was theoretically up to the newly established urban authorities to get the civic arteries pumping and flesh out the street-based skeleton with private houses, public baths, shops, inns and other centres of social interaction. Every Roman town would have had at least one major public bathing amenity, which, in the absence of public drinking dens, night clubs and/or casinos, would have acted as the foremost place of social interaction within the city. Roman bath houses followed the same basic design throughout the Empire; a range of rooms of varying temperatures which functioned in much the same way as a modern Turkish bath or Swedish sauna.

Theatres, amphitheatres and circuses housed the prestige spectator events within the Roman town. The amphitheatre was not just a place where gladiators fought or wild animals were hunted – both forms of sport were expensive and the bill would almost always have landed at the feet of the presiding magistrates for the year – but where the townspeople could see wrongdoers receiving the full penalty of law. In the absence of an effective criminal justice system, the punishment of those who had transgressed the law, as decreed by the *ordo* or town council, would have taken place in the arena. It was important not just to entertain the masses, but to convince them that justice triumphed in the end. Amphitheatres, by the nature of the events that they staged and the potential risk of violence (between spectators) and danger (if the condemned man or wild beast were to escape), were usually placed beyond the limits of the town. Although most towns possessed an amphitheatre, few had theatres. Theatres, if they are to be found at all, are usually close to the centre of the town, adjoining a temple; religious plays or events may have played a key part in the determination of performance. Curiously, despite the alleged love that the Britons had for equestrian activities, the circus or chariot racing track has been found at only one site in Britain, at Colchester in Essex.

Away from the grandeur of the main civic buildings, comparatively little is known about everyday domestic activity in the towns of Roman Britain. Excavations conducted in the interior of most British towns have often been of relatively restricted size and scale, Roman levels frequently being disrupted by later urban development. The

59 Cirencester. Amphitheatre of *Corinium* today. *Courtesy of Hamish Fenton*

60 Caistor St Edmund. Remains of the third-century defensive circuit defining *Venta Icenorum*, a largely unsuccessful *civitas* implanted within the territory of the Iceni

first non-monumental urban buildings appear to have been constructed primarily of wattle and daub, timber and thatch and, as a consequence, have rarely left a clear footprint in the archaeological record. Most of the earliest domestic units comprised long, relatively narrow buildings fronting directly onto the street. In some instances the street frontage itself was occupied by a shop, with living quarters above and basic manufacturing areas behind. Throughout the second, third and fourth centuries, many timber structures were rebuilt on a grander scale, sometimes with inward-facing rooms set around an enclosed courtyard; a classic Mediterranean-style house form. It is on such substantial houses, with obvious evidence of Roman lifestyle, in the form of mosaics, hypocausts and wall plaster, that most archaeological attention has focused.

Intent, with regard to urban planning and civic administration, is one thing, the hard reality, however, is often very different. The Britons may have been provided with new

markets; some members of the elite, *nouveaux riche* or desperate social climbers, may
even have been encouraged to live and work
within them. But did the urban life actually
work? Compared to other provinces of the
Roman world, Britain possessed few towns
and those that did exist were hardly in the
same league, as far as architecture, organisation, density of occupation and artistic
flourishes were concerned, as those of Gaul,
Spain or the Danubian provinces. Few of
the civic amenities created for the population early on within the new towns seem to
have been well used, maintained or, in their
final stages, used for the function for which
they were built. The fora of Silchester and
Caerwent, for instance, were being used for
industrial activity, including metalworking,
by the mid third century AD. London's prestige forum, which may never actually have
been finished, was being demolished by the
late third century. Bath houses were often
modified for different use altogether. Away
from the prestige civic centre, towns such
as Dorchester (*Dunovaria Durotrigum*) and
Wroxeter (*Viroconium Cornoviorum*) have a
very rural feel to them, as if the countryside,
in terms of house structure, food production
and general day-to-day activities, had been
invited in.

   Few Romano-British towns could be
judged as a success in Greco-Roman terms,
Britain never becoming a fully urban-
ised society. What the *civitas* towns of the
province seem to show is, in a sense, broad
continuity from the Later Iron Age. These
were tribal centres which, in some instances,
were run by surviving elements of the native
elite to whom Rome had delegated authority, in very tribal ways. These leaders oversaw
the implementation of the justice system
and heard disputes about property and land;
they decided who lived, who died and how
much tax everyone paid. Towns were centres

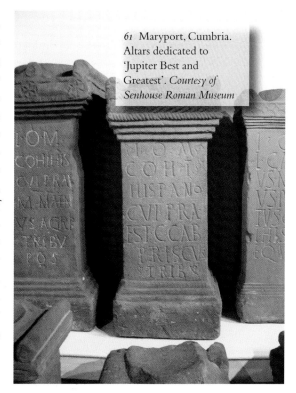

61 Maryport, Cumbria.
Altars dedicated to
'Jupiter Best and
Greatest'. *Courtesy of
Senhouse Roman Museum*

62 Bath, Avon. The Great
Drain for the hot spring
of Sulis Minerva

of trade and commerce; places where the old gods continued to be worshipped, albeit in new structures of stone, brick and tile. This was where the wealthy and powerful lived in their big houses; where agricultural produce was brought, bartered and stored. This was where various industries and trades were practised and where the people defined the limits of their settlement behind large defensive walls, even if there was no perceived threat to life or the security of everyday existence. The Britons had been provided with the skeleton of urban life by the State, but it is fair to say that they fleshed that life out in very UnRoman ways.

RELIGION

Religion and religious belief infused every aspect of Roman life from business to leisure, travel to home life, marriage to war. The chief deities of the Roman world were collectively known as the pantheon, each individual god or goddess having clearly defined roles and uniquely distinctive attributes. This meant that a particular request, prayer or dedication could be directed to a specific deity.

Jupiter, as head of the Roman pantheon, was considered to be the most powerful of gods, father of the human race and ultimate protector of the city of Rome itself. Jupiter was, perhaps not unexpectedly given his attributes of strength and power, highly popular within the Roman army and many altars set up outside forts on the frontiers of the Empire are dedicated to *Jupiter Optimus Maximus*, literally 'Jupiter Best and Greatest'. As well as being the chief god of Rome, Jupiter was worshipped together with the goddesses Juno and Minerva in a group known collectively as the 'Capitoline Triad'. Juno, Jupiter's wife, was the foremost female

63 Bath, Avon. Bronze head of the goddess Sulis Minerva, a super deity created from the fusion of Roman and native religions. *Otto Fein Collection*

deity, principally associated with childbirth, whilst Minerva, their daughter, was the goddess of warfare, crafts, wisdom and (quite usually) healing. Beneath the top three came a variety of other important deities including Mars, Mercury, Neptune, Venus, Diana, Apollo, Ceres, Vesta, Saturn, Vulcan and Janus.

Unfortunately, in comparison to classical forms of religion, the precise nature of Iron Age religious practice is unclear. British religion was not recorded in any great detail by Roman and Greek historians, most of whom viewed it as being wholly alien to their audience's classical sensibilities. Julius Caesar, a first-hand witness to prehistoric society in Britain and Gaul, did not produce any radical insight into the nature of native belief. Perhaps this is unsurprising, for Caesar, as we have already noted, was writing for a Roman audience and much of what he does tell us is infused with racial prejudice. Hence he speaks of headhunting, cannibalism and bloody human sacrifice in sacred groves. These are emotive issues even today, for mutilation, decapitation and the eating of human flesh are activities which, when reported by the media, are guaranteed to shock, terrify and repulse. The reality of Iron Age religious practice has, unfortunately, been lost somewhere in Caesar's text.

One term in particular that Caesar uses in relation to Iron Age religion that has resonance today is that of 'Druid'. The word druid is powerful and emotive, conjuring up a wide range of diverse images within modern popular culture. Caesar does not, however, provide a description of what the term druid actually means and for most people today it has become a catch-all phrase for priests, seers, teachers, shamans and holy men or women. Infuriatingly, despite witnessing the priestly or druid caste in Gaul, Caesar supplies no information on belief systems (other than in very general terms) or the mythology surrounding certain deities. More dauntingly, especially for those anxious to demonstrate that druidism was firmly enmeshed within the British Isles, Caesar mentions only once, and almost in passing, that 'it is thought that the druidic system was invented in Britain and thence imported to Gaul'.[42]

Generally speaking, Rome was happy to tolerate all belief systems that it encountered during its campaigns of expansion, incorporation and conquest. The absorption of local, non-Roman cults, gods and goddesses into the imperial system was conducted primarily because of the deeply superstitious nature of the Roman mind, in which it was felt important to get the indigenous spirits of conquered peoples on the side of the new government. Toleration was also useful from the practical viewpoint that a society whose religious beliefs are not persecuted is far less

likely perhaps to rebel. The only notable occasions where the Roman State objected to a particular religion is when the practice in question was monotheistic, belief in the one god providing a clear impediment to the acceptance of the Roman pantheon. Belief in a single, all-powerful deity also meant that those who followed a monotheistic faith, rejected both the earthly powers of the emperor and the concept that he may have had divine ancestors. Faiths such as Judaism and Christianity were therefore judged to possess a political dimension and, at times, were ruthlessly persecuted.

The non-acceptance of indigenous religion has always proved a major sticking point in processes of domination and cultural change. A conquering power must, if it is to prove successful and maintain control, accept all local religions, or modify them only gently. The founders of European empires carved out in the Americas, Australia and Africa were largely intolerant of the indigenous faiths that they encountered and repeatedly attempted to either

64 Barkway, Hertfordshire. Third-century 'temple hoard' containing a votive silver leaf dedicated to 'Mars Toutatis', a fusion of Roman and Celtic deities. © *Trustees of the British Museum*

65 Making a dedication at the grave of Carinus, a Romanised citizen of Dorchester. *Courtesy of John Hodgson*

the goddess of the hot spring which bubbled up to the surface.

Conflation with classical gods and goddesses is often the only process through which the particular names of Iron Age deities have survived to the present day. Unfortunately the Britons did not write the names of their gods on altars, on walls or on the countless pieces of metalwork they deposited in springs, bogs and other watery places. They did not record the nature of their religious practice and neither did they build, as far as we can tell, monumental temple structures in which particular deities could reside. It is only through later Roman altars and religious dedications, all inscribed in Latin, that we encounter the unfamiliar-sounding Celtic names of indigenous gods, goddesses and spirits of the place. Hence at Lydney, in Gloucestershire, we hear of Mars Nodens, a Romano-British god of healing, whilst at Colchester in Essex we find Mars Medocius and in Carlisle Mars Belatucadrus.

Mother goddesses were also popular figures within the native belief systems of Britain, Gaul and Germany, being specifically associated, we may assume, with fertility. The *Deae Matres* usually, though not exclusively, appear in triplicate and in sculptured form are often to be seen nursing young children or holding baskets bursting with fruit. Dedications to mother goddesses occur throughout Britain, and are to be especially found within the chief cities and frontiers of the province. The concept of dedicating to the mother goddess appears to have generally been related to the Celtic world beyond Rome, although examples exist elsewhere through the Empire.

eradicate them or at least replace them with the standard European perspective on divinity. This often led to varied forms of resistance (both passive and aggressive), revolt and protracted war, the effects of which can still be seen in some areas of the world to this day. In its tolerance and acceptance of indigenous practice, the Roman State often successfully managed to absorb pre-Roman deities and combine them with, what was in its mind, more acceptable Mediterranean examples. Thus in the city of *Aquae Sulis* (Bath) we hear of the goddess Sulis Minerva; Minerva being the Roman deity associated with wisdom, craft, war and healing, whilst Sulis, it would appear, was her local Iron Age equivalent:

Unlike Roman State religion, there does not seem to have been a universal family of gods and goddesses within Iron Age Britain and north-western Europe. Rather deities

66 Vindolanda, Chesterholm, Northumberland. The foundations of a Romano-Celtic temple

67 Jordan Hill, Weymouth, Dorset. Foundations for a Romano-Celtic temple

68 Lancing Down, West Sussex. The small, roughly square pre-Roman shrine. *Courtesy of the Sussex Archaeological Society*

may have been specific to particular tribes, clans or family groups. Spirits were furthermore, as far as it is possible to tell, probably associated with natural features in the landscape, such as a spring, river, mountain, hill or forest. The process of acceptance into the Roman world would therefore have meant that any local Iron Age deity could receive a brand new stone-built house within which the spirit of the place could reside. Such houses or temples would have been sited on or close to the point at which earlier practices had been conducted. Discovery of Iron Age deposits (metalwork, pottery, and cremation burials) beside or beneath a Roman temple building could therefore imply the presence of a significant focus of earlier worship.

Aside from the key urban statues, temples and monuments, many of the gods and goddesses of the Roman pantheon appeared to the British upon the coins in daily circulation. Images of the gods would also have appeared in the mosaics of well-to-do town houses and rural villas. The use of a particular deity or classical legend within the interior décor of villas may, however, have indicated nothing more than the owner's desire to be seen and acknowledged as a fully integrated member of Roman society, rather than that a particular deity was actively being worshipped at the site in question.

Although the gods and goddesses that comprised the Roman and Romano-British pantheon could ultimately be worshipped anywhere, altars, statues and mobile shrines being established wherever it was thought appropriate, more permanent specific temples, or houses of the god, could be established in towns. Temples, dedications and altars, specifically to Jupiter, Juno, Minerva, or the Capitoline Triad as a whole, are commonly found at the centre of new urban developments across the Roman world, though other temple buildings can be found on the margins of towns, outside forts, close to ports or alongside prominent highways.

Classical temples were generally built to a standard design throughout the Roman world, with an enclosed room or *cella* that contained the cult statue of the deity in question. The *cella*, which was built according to the principle that its length should not exceed one and a quarter times its width, was normally approached through a double door surrounded by an ornate set of columns which in turn supported a highly decorated pediment. Temples were where members of the public could travel in order to make a dedication or prayer directly to their god or goddess. Usually the public did not enter the *cella*, for worship in the early Roman Empire was not a congregational activity, the focus of religious fervour being at the front of the building, which explains why so many classical temples possess ornate façades. Temples were usually set within their own *temenos*, or sacred precinct, something which helped further distance the holy building from the real world beyond. Upon approaching a temple, the request, gift or prayer was either left on the main altar in front of the building, or passed directly to a priest who would then convey it inside. The *cella* therefore acted as a sort of celestial telephone, a hotline connecting the priest to the heavens above.

Few classical temples have been recorded from the British Isles. In Colchester, the Roman town of *Colonia Claudia Victricensis*, a temple was dedicated to the deified emperor Claudius and, though nothing remains above ground, the foundations of the great podium are still preserved beneath the Norman castle. In Bath, the foundations to a classical temple have been found, whilst significant amounts of the temple pediment, sawn up for use in later building projects, have also been discovered. Although not proven, it seems likely that the temple at Bath was first established in the late first century, possibly by Tiberius Claudius Togidubnus, the Romano-British king recorded from a dedicatory inscription found in the town of Chichester, West Sussex.[43]

The central pediment of the temple at Bath originally contained a startling image: a craggy, moustachioed face with snaking hair and a penetrating gaze. Closer inspection shows that the snaky hair is literally that, a writhing mass of serpents. Some writers have attempted to identify the face with the Roman sea deities Neptune or

69 A carved stone head, possibly representing a Celtic or Romano-British deity, from Piltdown, East Sussex. *Courtesy of the Sussex Archaeological Society*

Oceanus, but the wings evident in the hair, just behind the ears, make the identification of the figure certain: this is Medusa, albeit a male, moustached Medusa. Perhaps the sculptor commissioned to generate the Bath temple pediment was unfamiliar with the iconography of the Gorgons and wrongly provided the unfortunate Medusa with male attributes. Given the prominence of the piece, however, this seems perhaps unlikely. More probably we are seeing a deliberate fusion between Neptune, god of the sea, and Minerva to create the Medusa of popular legend. Anyone seeing the face should, theoretically, have made the

connection; the head of Medusa appearing here as an early form of brand or logo, advertising the temple of Minerva. Those who did not automatically make the association were provided with additional attributes of Minerva on the pediment, namely an owl, together with symbols of Victory including a Victor's wreath.

One particular type of structure that appears to be intimately associated with religious practice in north-western Europe (and specifically in northern Gaul, Germany and southern Britain) is the so-called Romano-Celtic temple. The main defining characteristics of this category of building are a central room, usually, though not exclusively, square, with a concentric corridor, walkway or ambulatory (*porticus*) creating the effect of 'a square within a square'. As with more classical forms of temple structure,

it is assumed that the central room was a form of *cella* containing the cult statue and was therefore off-limits to all but the professional religious specialists. In such a scenario, the encircling ambulatory would have been for more general access, providing a form of shelter from the elements, a secluded walkway for processions or a sacred space for meditation and the deposition of offerings. The area directly in front of a number of Romano-Celtic temples appears to have been set aside for an altar, upon which specific offerings and dedications could be left and prayers made.

At Lancing Down in West Sussex, the excavation of a Romano-Celtic temple building in 1980 revealed evidence of Late Iron Age religious practice in the form of a small, roughly square-shaped, timber building, set within a shallow, oval-shaped enclosure gulley or *temenos*.[44] Around the temple, to the south and west, a series of Iron Age and early Roman cremations, together with a single inhumation, were also located. The timber structure, which clearly dates to the Later Iron Age, was very similar in basic form, albeit on a vastly smaller scale, to the later Roman temple, something which probably suggests continuity in religious practice from late prehistory to the Roman period. Whether structures like the small square Iron Age building (which may be interpreted as a shrine) found at Lancing Down would have been used in a manner reminiscent of a late Roman temple, with a priest conducting ceremonies outside and conveying prayers, messages and requests to the cult statue within the sacred, non-public inner space, is unknown. Given the size of the Lancing structure it is, however, unlikely that this would or could have functioned as a place of congregational worship; more likely it was a building designed to house a particular idol, entity or religious identity.

At Uley, a stone-built Romano-Celtic temple was found at the apparent centre of a large settlement.[45] The temple itself measured 12 by 14m and comprised a central room or *cella* surrounded by an ambulatory. Unfortunately there is little evidence for interior activities or features, a central pit perhaps representing the remains of a water-filled pool into which dedications to the deity could be placed. The Roman phase structure overlay a distinct Later Iron Age area of activity comprising two timber buildings set within a sub-rectangular ditched enclosure. Pits containing a range of presumably votive offerings, including pottery, coins, infant burials, iron spears and brooches, were found within the timber structures. No evidence as to the nature (or name) of the pre-Roman deity worshipped at Uley was found, although 'curse tablets',

inscribed sheets of lead with requests and prayers, were found with dedications to Mercury and Mars, whilst images of Sol (the Sun) and Bacchus (wine) were also discovered on the site. A larger male head carved from Cotswolds limestone seems to have originally been that of the main cult statue; his features, including the distinctive short-cropped curly hair, identify him as Mercury. Presumably he had originally fused together with an Iron Age equivalent in order to create a super-deity akin to Sulis Minerva at Bath.

Another excellent example of a native cult centre preserved beneath the remains of a later Roman religious complex may be seen at Hayling Island, in Hampshire. The primary phase of construction at Hayling Island appears to have been a round structure, measuring over 10m in diameter, defined by settings of internal posts and external gullies, possibly during the middle of the first century BC.[46] The building, which resembles the form of a native domestic 'roundhouse' structure, was set within a roughly square enclosure, the ditch of which had been filled at specific places with a range of artefacts which seem to reflect the accoutrements of a prominent Iron Age warrior and his chariot. Other assemblages included pottery vessels (possibly containing offerings), the bones (and meat) of sheep and pig and a wide range of Iron Age coins. Extensive cross-Channel contacts with central and north-eastern Gaul are evidenced from the coins, whilst the British series seem to emphasise links with Hampshire and Dorset. In the late first century AD, at about the time of the great developments at Fishbourne and in Chichester just over the water from Hayling Island, the site was redeveloped, the stone foundations of the new complex following the same basic plan of its predecessor (a

71 Lead ingot from Hints Common, Staffordshire, stamped in AD 76 with the name and titles of the emperor Vespasian. © *Trustees of the British Museum*

circular building within a square enclosure), albeit on a significantly grander scale.

The deliberate fusion of Iron Age deities and spirits of the place with their Roman counterparts probably meant that, for many Britons, the worship of the old gods continued broadly as before, albeit within the more substantial masonry structures built under the new administrative order. At sites like Hayling Island and Lancing Down, not only do religious structures of the Later Iron Age lie directly beneath their Roman counterparts, but the form taken by the later buildings appears to represent a more monumental version of the original prehistoric structure. Romanisation of native belief systems therefore probably meant little more than the deliberate reshaping of the primary shrine using more permanent building materials. No doubt altars and cult statues were also added and deposition of artefacts continued, with coins, objects and animal remains now derived from a much wider geographical area, but for the bulk of the population, the process and nature of worship remained substantially unchanged.

Away from the civilian south, the militarised north rigidly maintained its adherence to the State faith. Key Roman deities predominate, as one would expect in an area

where allegiance to the State was paramount. Certain native gods and goddesses are acknowledged, ensuring that local deities and protecting spirits were kept happy, but generally the religions practised by the Roman military reflect the 'culture in a bubble' aspect of frontier life.

From the early third century AD, a variety of exotic deities from the eastern provinces of the Roman Empire (chiefly Egypt, Syria and Judea) and beyond, started to make their appearance within Britain. Amongst the Roman army the most popular eastern deity was the Persian god Mithras, though within non-military social circles other religions, such as that based around the figure of Jesus Christ, were starting to develop. The popularity accorded to the majority of Eastern cults, Christianity included, was due to the fact that they gave hope of a salvation and of a continual war between the forces of good and evil in which good would prevail. The chief difference between Christian and non-Christian doctrine, however, was that the cult of Christ was open to all levels of society, regardless of status, wealth (or lack of it), sex, social standing (free or slave) or ethnic origin. At a time when the Roman Empire was undergoing severe stress from economic turmoil, internal political conflict and mass population pressure from beyond the frontiers, Christianity offered redemption and peace to everyone. Mithraism offered salvation, but only to the freeborn males initiated into the faith.

The key distinctive aspect of Eastern cults was that their places of worship were essentially congregational. To pray at a Mithraic temple or early Christian church meant to enter the building and communicate directly with a higher power, unlike the classical or Romano-British style temples where, it would appear, only the professional priest could enter the innermost sanctum of the divine. Congregations were composed of adherents and believers who had been admitted into the faith through teaching, baptism or some other initiation rite (which in some of the more extreme examples could include castration). Christianity was, for much of its early history, an underground religion, persecuted by the Roman State for a variety of reasons, chief among which was the belief that as monotheists, Christians refused to acknowledge both the divine nature of the early imperial families and the pantheon of deities revered across the Empire.

It is not known what impact Christianity had upon the population of late Roman Britain. Certainly the religion was practised by some in the province (see Chapter 7), as both the archaeological (artefacts, wall paintings and mosaics) and historical sources (such as the martyrdom of Alban in the third century) clearly demonstrate. Evidence recovered from a variety of non-Christian religious sites in Britain, however, shows that, although Christianity became the State religion of Rome from the early fourth century, rural 'pagan' temples in Britain flourished well on into the latter half of the century.[47] The final decline of non-Christian centres of worship in the later fourth century AD may indicate that interest in the old gods was fading as new faiths from the Roman East and also the Germanic north began to make their appearance felt in Britain. Perhaps the cost of maintaining and repairing distant rural shrines simply became too expensive; centres of worship devolving to the towns or other forms of tribal centre. Perhaps, in the absence of an organised State structure, religion became a matter for personal belief.

TRADE AND INDUSTRY

There was, throughout prehistory and the Roman period, a huge network of trade and exchange across southern Britain, exporting goods to northern France, Belgium and The Netherlands, whilst simultaneously importing continental goods, ideas and people. For many thousands of years the English Channel represented a vital link to the continental landmass of Europe. It is sometimes difficult to appreciate that for much, if not all, of later prehistory, the Channel was the primary trade corridor to the outside world, sea fare being far more reliable and dependable than transportation of goods inland. In the days before an organised road, canal, rail or air network, the best way to move goods from A to B was by water, along the rivers, across the tidal estuaries and over the open sea. In the Iron Age, those communities living on the southern coast of Britain would probably have had far more in common with those living on the opposite side of the English Channel than those living 40 miles or so inland. Language, religion, fashion and general outlook towards life would all have been closely similar; only in recent years has the desire to create fixed, impermeable boundaries helped to create segregated national identities, stalling the natural development of language and culture. The Channel was an important trade link and it is in areas situated close to the sea that we find our best evidence for the importation of foreign artefacts in the Late Iron Age and Early Roman period.

A good early indicator of the success of trade with Rome, and of the impact that contact had upon the population of Britain, comes from the discovery of a distinctive form of pottery container known as the amphora. Amphorae are outwardly rather strange-looking objects, comprising a long

72 The State Highway: Jeffery Hill, Lancashire. *Courtesy of John Hodgson*

thin neck, prominent handles, a slightly globular body and pointed base. Amphorae are singular items and were distinct from anything that had appeared in Britain before. The impact of such vessels upon Late Iron Age society should not be underestimated, for whoever had an amphora in their possession, house or grave was evidently someone of great wealth and power. They would also be seen to possess a certain degree of prestige, for whomsoever possessed an amphora could claim wider links with the world of the Mediterranean.

It is not the vessel itself that was important of course, though its distinctive form evidently helped, but the contents. Like the champagne bottle of today, the amphora was the visible container of Mediterranean status produce, in this case wine, olive oil and fish sauce (known as *garum*); evidence that a few well-off members of the native population were accessing prestige consumables. Amphorae containing previously unknown luxury commodities were brought to Britain by people seeking to exchange them for personal profit and, later on, for materials to help bulk out the official coffers of the Roman State. A list of the major trade items available in Britain is mentioned by the Greek historian, geographer and philosopher Strabo in his work the *Geography*, a 17-volume treatise covering all aspects of the known world in the early years of the first century AD. With regard to Britain,

Strabo observed that the principal exports were agricultural and mineralogical.[48]

The possibility that certain Britons grew rich on profits generated by the slave trade should also not be discounted. The trafficking of people represents one of the worst forms of criminal activity, a major violation of human rights which sadly remains a common practice in certain areas of the world today. In the Iron Age, slaves were undoubtedly generated through war, prisoners being deprived of all freedoms and exported directly into the developing world of Rome. The Roman economy was fuelled by slave labour and, when the Senate and People of Rome were not directly involved in conquest, large numbers of slaves could still be acquired through trade with societies based beyond the frontiers of Empire. Despite this, we do not know the extent of such activity in Late Iron Age and Early Roman Britain, for it did not leave much of an impact in the archaeological record.

Metals were one of the earliest of British exports and, by the time the Roman Empire was spreading through Gaul, the mineral wealth of the island was well known, Julius Caesar noting that the Britons used bronze or gold for their coins as well as 'iron bars with a fixed standard of weight'. 'Tin is found inland', he added rather vaguely, and 'iron on the coast, but in small quantities'.[49] Strabo noted that 'gold, silver, and iron' were exported by the Britons together with grain, slaves and hunting dogs.[50]

The main areas of extraction had probably already been identified by the Roman State at the time of the Claudian invasion, something which probably explains the need to get the armies westwards into the Mendips, Derbyshire, Cornwall and West Wales as swiftly as possible. Taking direct control of the exploitation of mineral deposits in Britain was vital, for production needed to intensify if the resources of Britain were to feed the insatiable hunger of the Roman State. Gold and silver was required for bullion, bronze for coinage, lead for pipes and waterproofing, iron for tools, armour and weapons.

Theoretically, all minerals were the property of the emperor, their identification, extraction and exportation under the remit of his delegated official, the *procurator metallarum*. In practice, however, the emperor only took direct control of the exploitation of precious metals, other forms of mining and extraction being left in private hands in return for substantial payments. It is likely, therefore, that the lead and iron industries of southern Britain were, by the mid first century AD, largely in the hands of private companies. Metal production was a major source of income for some, and no doubt corruption and profiteering, at least for those not actually working in the mines, was rife. Whether the indigenous population (or even the aristocratic elite) ever benefited from any of the profits generated by the mines is debatable. Given that the mines were probably in the hands of the State and its delegated officials, it does not seem likely. The native Britons were probably never as fabulously wealthy as the twentieth-century leaders of Saudi Arabia and Kuwait who grew rich on the sale of 'black gold' to the west.

Examples of successful individuals (*conductores*) and limited companies (*collegii*) within the world of metals and mining can be found from an early date across Britain. In the latter half of the first century, for example, a private company, known as the *Socii Lutudarenes*, seems to have prominently established itself in the Peak District, whilst at the same time a certain Tiberius Claudius Trifernus was striking out in the lead-rich area of the Mendips. Given Trifernus' first names, it would seem likely that he was either a newly enfranchised citizen who owed it all to the emperor Claudius, as per Catuarus and Togidubnus in Sussex (see Chapter 2), or perhaps a freedman (ex-slave) of the imperial family who reached Britain in the hope of making his fortune. Another entrepreneur and probable freed-man, Gaius Nipius Ascanius, is known from a lead ingot found at Carmel in Flintshire, whilst others from the same area have been found bearing the name DECEANGL, the Deceangli, a tribe known to have inhabited this part of Wales. This raises the question as to whether or not the native population in any way were able to oversee exploitation of the resource (although the general absence of status artefacts or houses within the tribe makes that seem somewhat unlikely), or whether use of the name was merely an aid to help the State identify the geological source of the material.

Within a few years of the invasion, lead from the Mendips was being extracted and removed. We know this because the earliest ingots found to date were stamped with the name and titles for the year of the relevant emperor under whose authority the metal was removed, as well as the place of origin. Hence an ingot found in the Mendips bear-ing the text TI CLAVD CAESAR AVG P M TR P VIIII IMP XVI DE BRITAN ('Tiberius Claudius Caesar Augustus, High Priest, holding tribunes power for the ninth time, hailed commander in the field 16 times – From Britain') tells us that the piece was manufactured either very late in AD 48 or (more likely) in AD 49, Claudius holding the position of Tribune of the plebs for the ninth time for a year from December AD 48. Soon the ingots were flooding back into the Empire, Pliny the Elder noting, prior to AD 79, that 'in Spain and the whole of Gaul,

lead is extracted with considerable effort; in Britain however, it is so abundant within the upper layers of the earth that there is a law forbidding its production beyond a cer-tain amount'.[51]

Exactly how the exploitation of gold, tin, lead, copper and iron was organised in the wake of Roman absorption remains unclear. Some areas may have been controlled by private businesses, civilian entrepreneurs who used the new road network to export their product to the markets in London and beyond, whilst in others the *Classis Britannica*, or British Fleet, seem to have taken direct control of production, for their stamped tiles are found in abundance across the iron fields of Sussex, Surrey and Kent.

The presence of the fleet here may under-lie the perceived importance of iron, for the *Classis Britannica* was less of a 'navy' in the modern sense, its role being more in terms of providing support rather than represent-ing an effective fighting force. In the Weald, the fleet was presumably a crucial part of the transport infrastructure, moving mate-rial from the extraction areas to the more secure depots on the Kent coast. From there, iron could be directly exported into Gaul, and the heart of Empire, or taken north-wards to the frontier outposts of Britain. We do not know how directly, if at all, the military involved themselves in the day-to-day administration of mining and smelting activities. At areas such as Beauport Park, where some 1,600 stamped tiles belonging to the fleet were found from the on-site bath house, the *Classis Britannica* may simply have been involved in the construction of major works and the shipping out of the finished product rather than overseeing production.[52]

At Dolaucothi in Carmarthenshire, an extensive gold-mining area has been uncov-ered and surveyed, although much of the Roman-period workings have, unfortu-

73 The State highway: Stane Street, West Sussex. *Courtesy of the Sussex Archaeological Society*

nately, been erased by more recent mining activity. A range of open cast pits, adit mines and deep shafts with galleries, some descending to depths in excess of 44m, are known.[53] A system of aqueducts over 11km in length could have brought, it has been calculated, some 13.5 million litres of water to the mine area every day. Large tanks and reservoirs pooled and stored water for use in scouring the hillside (looking for ore deposits), washing crushed ore (separating out gold particles in the process), fire-setting (when the rock face was heated by the direct application of fire then cooled instantly with water in order to shatter it), feeding the bath houses (an important factor for officer morale at least) and, possibly, the powering of waterwheels and trip hammers. The mines lie close to an auxiliary fort at Pumpsaint, something that presumably added a vital level of security to the proceedings and the transportation of the end product.

In Cornwall, few of the tin-mining zones are known in any detail, as with Dolaucothi, later extraction pits having erased the Roman phase activity. In most instances, the presence of pit workings are only hinted at by milestones. Milestones, basically upright pillars of stone carrying distance information such as the relative mile number, were established along all the major State-financed Roman highways, linking military garrison, agricultural estates, metal fields, mines and centres of civilian population. Distance along these main roads would have been calculated in miles (*milia passuum*: literally '1000 paces'), the Roman mile being shorter than its modern equivalent. British stones were often simply inscribed with the names of emperors, under whose patronage or authority (we may assume) repairs were conducted.

Roads were important in order to keep the peace, but they also ensured the economic viability of the new territories. The designers and builders of Roman roads were not hindered by concerns of where to place their highways. In order to function effectively, central government needed a network of direct, reliable thoroughfares linking all the major mining zones, towns, forts, harbours and farms. Road developers therefore aimed for straightness. Modern worries about the environmental impact of major building works were not shared by the ancients and neither was the Roman State really all that concerned about the location of existing settlements, for farms and villages could all be relocated. It was undoubtedly the army that set the pace and direction of the first road network in Britain, linking their forts with the emerging towns, farms and areas of metalworking, creating the supply lines necessary to maintain order in the new province, and the army was not to be questioned.

Lowland Britain was, and remains, a fertile land for agriculture, and food production must have been one of the major factors in the economy of the region during the Roman period. Aside from farming, other key elements in the economic infrastructure of the area which have left some trace in the archaeological record were the production of salt, the manufacture of pottery and tile and the quarrying of stone. Large amounts of stone were apparently quarried from British sources for incorporation in the large-scale State-funded building projects of the first and second centuries, most notably the towns and forts, although there is, as yet, no clear understanding of the circumstances under which such material was obtained. Presumably there were many well-organised centres of extraction in existence throughout the Roman period, but little detailed work has yet been conducted upon the identification and analysis of such an industry. The open cast pits, adit

mines and shafts which must have existed have either been destroyed by later workings or still lie undiscovered and forgotten.

We can probably say a bit more about pottery manufacture within the province of Roman Britain, given that so much evidence has, comparatively speaking, been found. The initial impetus for large-scale indigenous production of Roman-style pottery forms was undoubtedly the army. The frontier garrisons of Britain were major users and consumers of ceramic vessels and, wherever they were, local pottery production increased dramatically. Pottery does not travel particularly well, at least long distance transportation of vessels in the ancient world was not recommended, and so the need of the army was fed by more regional forms of supply. A good example of this is Black Burnished Ware, a distinctive kitchenware manufactured in the area of Wareham and Poole Harbour in Dorset and shipped directly, in considerable numbers, to the military frontiers. It is almost certainly one of the most common ceramics to be found in Britain, the big explosion in the market seemingly occurring in the early second century AD.

Black Burnished Ware was a product manufactured on an apparently local level prior to the arrival of Rome, but, following the incorporation of southern Britain into the Empire, someone, possibly a local (or group of locals) with an eye to business, expanded production and signed a contract with the Roman military. Other regional potters also seem to have benefited from a link to the army, as well as to those civilians seeking a Roman lifestyle or the simple convenience of good quality ceramics, with fine wares being manufactured in large numbers in Oxfordshire, Cambridgeshire and Surrey. When supply to the military ceased, in the political turmoil of the later fourth century

AD, the manufacture of Black Burnished and other wares declined. Neither the demand for Roman-style ceramic forms, nor, apparently, the technological ability to manufacture it and transport it in large numbers extended beyond the collapse of the Roman administrative system in Britain.

ART

When we think of Roman culture, one of its most obvious elements is Roman art. We think of statues in the Graeco-Roman tradition, we think of classical statues perhaps or mythological mosaics, we think of wall paintings or classical mouldings. By contrast when we think of pre-Roman British art we think of geometric and swirling designs on metalwork, of enamelling, of mysterious, staring faces.

The swirling, abstract forms that are found on certain pieces of metalwork, such as swords, shields, mirrors, brooches and horse gear, are perhaps the most characteristic, as well as the most archaeologically durable, of the period. These strange designs in their ultimate form are both distinctive and unique to the non-Roman world of mainland Europe. As a consequence they are known as 'Celtic Art'. Such startling designs were, it would appear, mainly for the social elite, and less for consumption within the mundane and everyday world of more 'ordinary' people. These were forms of art that may have been placed upon specific metal artefacts in order to design or enhance display and status-defining activities (such as fighting, raiding, hunting and horse ownership). Stylised, abstract examples of Celtic Art may well, therefore, have been in some sense symbols of tribal control that emphasised a particular form of social domination, far removed from their use today as icons of peace, tranquillity and relaxation.

By the end of the first century BC, Roman influence was starting to make itself felt on British design values. This is most noticeable in the coinage of the period. With two tribal groupings in particular, the Catuvellauni/Trinovantes and the Atrebates, in a matter of decades, coin designs were transformed from the almost purely Celtic to the almost purely classical via a number of stages in between which represent a mixture of the Celtic and the classical. It is a dramatic transformation that says something hugely significant about the attitude of the tribal rulers, in these tribal groupings, to Rome.[54]

However, two things need to be pointed out about this dramatic transformation. Firstly, it is restricted mainly to the Catuvellauni/Trinovantes and the Atrebates (and the Cantii, a more minor tribe in close contact with these two tribes). Three other tribes, the Iceni, the Dobunni and the Corieltauvi, show some signs of classical influence in their late coinage, but the other British coin-issuing tribe, the Durotriges, only shows signs of classical influence on a tiny number of coins. The second point is that the classical coinage of the Catuvellauni/Trinovantes and the Atrebates represents merely the culture of the elite. As discussed previously, there are Roman items being imported into Britain in the pre-Roman period in some quantity, but they seem to be mainly in use by the upper echelons of society, not by the average Briton.

And to some extent similar factors continue to apply after the invasion. In the west and north of Britain, Roman culture and art never took hold very strongly among the British population. By contrast, in the central, south and east of England, the rich and powerful among the Britons seem to have enthusiastically latched on to the idea of displaying their wealth and power by buying luxury imported goods in classical

Above: 74 Romanising British pre-Roman coin. Coin of Cunobelin, with his name shown on one side in its Roman form, in Roman letters Cunobelinus, and on the other side a strictly classical figure in classical garb. *Courtesy of Chris Rudd. Cat. No. 2746*

Left: 75 Celtic design on British pre-Roman coin

styles and by employing craftsmen, some of them also imported, capable of producing designs in classical styles. Fishbourne, possible palace of the British king Togidubnus with its amazing mosaics and other items of classical art, is one of the most startling examples of this. It even includes distinctive first-century black and white geometric mosaics. Other well-known examples are the two portrait busts, carved from Pentelic marble probably in the Mediterranean, and found carefully buried at Lullingstone villa. However, throughout the Roman period (with the possible exception of parts of the third century) there are examples of rich and powerful patrons spending, presumably, large amounts of money on building for themselves a life surrounded by classical artworks whether in towns or in the coun-

tryside. In the fourth century, for instance, the great villa at Chedworth shows spectacular mosaics featuring mythological scenes including satyrs and maenads, and more than 50 mosaics can be dated to the fourth century alone.[55]

This patronage of classical art by rich and powerful Britons went to some extent hand in hand with the patronage of classical art in Britain by official Rome, by the civilian administration and by the military. A large proportion of classical sculpture in Britain, in the sense of sculpture close enough to its Roman antecedents to be viewed as distinctly Roman rather than Romano-British, is either directly linked to the civilian administration or the military, or at least comes from towns with a strong official and/or military presence. A visit to

76 Marble sculpture from Lullingstone. *Otto Fein Collection*

77 The pediment from the temple at Aquae Sulis, Bath. The central figure has significant classical elements but a Celtic feel. *Otto Fein Collection*

the museums along Hadrian's Wall produces numerous examples of carvings and inscriptions in classical style.

A further segment of British society found patronising classical art is civilian immigrants from more Romanised parts of the Empire. There is again a certain cross-over with official Rome here, because such immigrants tended to be found either in military areas or in large cities with a significant official presence. The tombstone of a Catuvellaunian woman, Regina, commissioned by her husband Barates from Palmyra and set up at South Shields, is an excellent example of this. The figure is strongly classical, as is the setting inside an architectural niche featuring classical detailing.

Finally, because the towns were, in many ways, the most Romanised part of Roman civilian Britain, ordinary townspeople in general could be expected to have some of the trappings of the Roman lifestyle, but the poorer they were, the fewer these would be.

There was little pre-Roman tradition of monumental sculpture in Britain and none of such arts as mosaic-making or intricately carved architectural stonework, so inevitably the Celtic influences are less here than on such items as brooches where there was a much stronger pre-Roman tradition. However, even among works commissioned by the elite and in military zones there are differences from the tradition of classical sculpture. Sometimes these differences have been attributed to provincial craftsmen failing fully to grasp the skills of classical sculpture, but today, in an era where the classical sculptural depiction of the human form is generally out of fashion, it is easier to accept that many of these differences are attributable to genuine aesthetic choice, rather than just lack of skill. The huge face from the pediment of the temple of Sulis Minerva at Bath, for example, con-

78 Carving showing a classical theme with Celtic styling. *Courtesy of Chesters Museum*

79 Mosaic from Rudston. The designs are based on classical originals but the ultimate depiction is non-naturalistic. Some would argue the mosaicist was just unskilled, but the figures have a Celtic, or even modern feel, reminiscent of some Picasso figures. *From a painting by David S. Neal. Courtesy of Hull and East Riding Museum*

80 Head from Corbridge, Northumberland, possibly of a local deity, showing very little Roman influence. *Otto Fein Collection*

81 Head of Antenociticus from Benwell. A classical head carved with a distinct Celtic flavour. *Courtesy of Great North Museum*

flated probably from depictions of Neptune and a Gorgon, shows a face that, with the swirling patterns of its hair and with its staring eyes, has a very Celtic feel. The mosaic of Venus at Rudston, for instance, shows a Venus and figures around her that owe far more to Celtic traditions than they do to classical ones, and some of the carvings from the Hadrian's Wall area, such as the head of Antenociticus from Benwells, show staring, unsmiling faces that again look essentially more Celtic than classical. Note again on the Antenociticus the use of the hair to create swirling, almost abstract patterns.

Outside towns, military areas and the houses of the rich, there is far less evidence of classical art. In the Romanised part of Britain, such signs tend to be restricted to

the small, cheap features of classical culture, small personal items, small moulded statuettes perhaps, and most frequently pottery. Roman pottery does appear extensively on sites across Britain, but even here the extent to which it can actually be regarded as Roman is sometimes overstated. Some types of pottery, like Samian, can be properly regarded as classical. However, other types, the product of the huge Black Burnished Ware industry based in Dorset, show strong signs of continuity in terms of design and production from pre-Roman times. It could be argued that these are basically non-Roman products produced under Rome.

It's hard to be entirely certain, but there is some evidence of a distinctively British

82 Head from a late fourth-century British buckle

element remaining within classical art in Roman-period Britain and beginning to strengthen again as Roman power in the country faded.

In the fourth century official and military art virtually ceases in Britain. Classical culture does, however, continue in the large villas and in the late fourth century, ostensibly Roman mosaics show stylistic differences that seem to be linked to tribe/ *civitas* boundaries.[56] The styles are basically Roman, but some experts see something distinctively British about a number of these mosaics.[57] Some of the military/paramilitary/official buckles and other belt fittings manufactured in Britain in the late fourth century may also show signs of reviving Celtic influence. Some of the buckle plates carry complex geometric designs that may have Celtic overtones, and mysterious staring heads, in which delineation of the hair seems to be a key feature, also reappear on some of the buckles.[58]

Certainly at the end of the Roman period and in the post-Roman period, Celtic art traditions re-emerge strongly in western and

northern Britain. Penannular brooches with enamelled terminals appear[59] and hanging bowls decorated with discs that carry bright, swirling enamelled patterns.[60] The origins of these bowls are still controversial but they seem to have links back to late Roman examples and maybe even further back. The Staffordshire Moorlands Pan, probably of second-century date, has, for instance, a number of features in common with later hanging bowls.

COSTUME / PERSONAL ADORNMENT

We choose our clothes today through a mixture of basic practicality (what does the job of keeping us warm, dry etc.), easy availability (what's in the shops) and the fashion element (what cultural messages we wish to project).

The inhabitants of Britain during the Roman period would have made costume choices on a similar basis, though obviously, with very different options, the results were very different.

When the Romans arrived in Britain they found people who in many ways looked different to the Roman norm. Certain features of costume in Britain and Gaul obviously struck them as distinctively UnRoman – in particular the wearing of trousers by men, the way men stripped off and decorated themselves for battle, and the way they shaved their chins but left a moustache and wore their hair long. However, there were also similarities, in particular the wearing of the fibula, and Roman styles of dress were no doubt already making some impact among the elite of the more Romanised parts of the south and east of Britain. A medallion carrying the head of Augustus was, for instance, found in the Lexden burial, and it seems reasonable to assume that the extensive Roman stylistic influences displayed on the coinage of the Atrebates and Catuvellauni must have echoed at least some Roman influence on the costume worn by the elite in these areas.

Inevitably as Roman culture spread through south, central and eastern England after the Roman invasion, some elements of Roman costume and personal style were adopted by many, for the same range of reasons that other aspects of Roman culture were adopted. For some, it was a way of showing off, a way of identifying with the dominant power in the country and assimilating some of that power's perceived attributes. Tacitus mentions the sons of chieftains wearing the toga as a result of Agricola's attempt to Romanise them.[61] For others, it was a case that some of the mass-produced items available did the job better than what had been available before, and for others it was simply a case of what was in the shops. As we know from the world around us, assimilating costume items from a particular culture need not necessarily imply huge affection for that culture. Western clothes, for instance, particularly for men, are

83 Sculpture from the Great North Museum showing local dress. *Courtesy of the Great North Museum*

found all round the world today, worn by many people who may see the West as powerful and to be emulated in some ways but who, for instance, also reject many current Western social and religious values and who certainly do not aspire to a Western political identity.

The adoption of specifically Roman costume in Britain, though, may have been limited. There are only two clear depictions in Britain of people wearing togas.[62] Outside the Romanised areas and military areas, clothing may have changed little during the occupation, and even in the Romanised and military areas, if civilian fashion did develop, it seems to have done so in a non-Mediterranean direction. A basic item of clothing for men and women was the so-called Gallic Coat, a loose-fitting tunic worn without a

84 Dragonesque brooches

85 Celtic-influenced Roman military metalwork

belt.[63] Trousers may have been worn under this, at least in wet or cold weather, and in addition a cloak, sometimes a long hooded cloak, something like the original duffle coat, could also be worn over the top. This is seen in carvings and is probably also the type of item mentioned as a *Birrus Britannicus* in an edict on prices at the beginning of the fourth century. The origins of the Gallic Coat are slightly obscure. It seems to have been worn in Gaul by men from the Claudian period at least, right through to the fourth century AD (though increasingly being supplanted by a slightly different tunic, the Dalmatic). It may have had its origins in the pre-Roman costume of ordinary Celtic men. Its use in Britain may therefore represent some form of continuation of Celtic tastes. Its increasing adoption by British

women in the second and third centuries AD may reflect a new development influenced by its use by women in the military areas of Britain.[64]

Possibly associated in some way with British costume during the pre-Roman period were button and loop fasteners. These seem to continue in widespread use, particularly in the north, well into the middle of the second century and many of them show a strong Celtic heritage in their designs.[65]

The most widespread archaeological evidence for personal appearance during the Roman period, though, comes in the form of brooches and they tell an interesting story. In the first century, many of the brooches have non-Roman forms and there is even, in a number of cases, some evidence of different types of brooch being found in different tribal and regional areas.

Two-piece Colchester brooches, for instance, are found most frequently in eastern England,[66] while the Polden Hill type of brooch occurs most regularly in Dobunnic and Cornovian territory.[67] In the north, the dragonesque style may, in origin, have been from Brigantian and Parisian territory.[68]

There is a particularly strong Celtic design influence on these dragonesque brooches. They are basically shaped like an 'S', but incorporate characteristically Celtic swirling shapes and designs and the vivid use of brightly coloured enamel.

Brooches seem to have become slightly less common in the third century, a development perhaps to be linked to an increasing adoption by women of the Gallic Coat, but even in the later period, there are some clear links to Britain's Celtic design heritage. Enamelled brooches continue to be worn, and the so-called Horse and Rider brooches seem to continue in production, well into the fourth century and may be some of the latest brooches in production in Roman Britain. It has been suggested that they have ritual significance and are linked to a British cult.[69] Certainly they seem rather UnRoman. As with dragon-esque brooches, we again have the same use of vivid enamels and swirling shapes, and the modelling of the riders in particular seems more Celtic than Roman. In addition, penannular brooches which were common in pre-Roman and early Roman-period Britain seem to make something of a comeback.[70]

Interestingly enough it is worth noting that not all the costume influence taking place in Britain, and other Celtic areas, during the Roman period was all one way. The hooded cloak from Britain and Gaul came into more widespread use across the Empire in the second and third centuries. Button and loop fasteners are found in military areas of Roman Britain in the first and second centuries (as are dragonesque brooches). In addition, in the second and third centuries, a particular style of Celtic-influenced military metalwork, perhaps influenced by northern British workshops, is seen particularly widely in the form of belt and strap fittings and became common both in Britain and in mainland Europe.[71]

IDENTITY

When the Romans invaded Britain, there may have been no Britons, except to Roman eyes. The Britons would not have seen themselves as part of a nation of Britons. They would have seen themselves primarily as members of an individual tribe.

In a pre-literate society, tribal identities may not have been quite as solid as modern national identities. Nobody had a birth cer-

tificate stating which tribe they were born into, and tribal entities probably evolved over time, changing names perhaps, or forming a confederation with a neighbouring tribe, or splitting off from one tribe to form a new tribe. Alliances bringing a number of tribes together seem to have been feasible but probably only in the face of an unusual outside threat, such as the invasions by Caesar and Claudius, and these large-scale alliances seem to have been highly unstable and short-lived.

The names we have for the tribes, like Catuvellauni, Brigantes, Dobunni etc., mainly come from Roman sources, and we have no way of knowing if these are the names the Britons originally used, but it seems likely that most of the names have some kind of genuine British heritage. In one case, that of the Iceni, we may even have independent British evidence of that. Some of the coins of this people carry the legend ECEN, which is often thought to be a reference to the name of the tribe.

We are very used today to having layers of identity. Someone, for instance, may be a Londoner at one level, who is also English on another level, British at a further level, and now even European on a fourth level. Different people, at different times and in different contexts, will place more emphasis on different layers of their identity.

From the start the story of identity in Britain is one of multiple layers. The Romans based their civilian administration in Britain on tribal identities, so for a start each person had a tribal identity. On top of this the Romans imposed a British identity. To the Romans, all the inhabitants of this island were Britons (or alternatively, the diminutive and slightly insulting *Brittunculi*, used a bit like 'Argies' instead of Argentines, in the Falklands War era)[72] no matter what tribe they belonged to, in much the

RECORD OF BUILDING WORK BY THE civitas
OF THE DUROTRIGIAN PEOPLE
OF LINDINIS (ILCHESTER)

RIB 1672

CAWFIELDS

B263
CH267

86 Inscription from Hadrian's Wall recording the presence of a squad from the civitas *of the Durotriges.
Courtesy of Chesters Museum*

same way that Victorians often referred to Africans, without being more specific about ethnic identity. Some no doubt of this attitude would have been adopted by the most Romanised elements in British society. Then on top of the British identity came a Roman identity. From the final imposition of Roman control, the Britons became in some sense part of the Empire. From very early on, small numbers of Britons would have been made part of the Empire in a more significant way, as Roman citizens, with the rights and privileges that entailed. And from 212, all free Britons became full Roman citizens thanks to an edict passed by the emperor Caracalla. The vital question then becomes, of course – what value did

Britons put on these three different layers of identity?

Inevitably it's hard to be entirely sure about this, but the evidence seems to suggest that the tribal layer of identity remained significant throughout the occupation, in many cases, probably more significant than the other two layers. The habit of putting up personal inscriptions in Britain was never that strong and eventually pretty much died out. However, up until that point, Britons in inscriptions about themselves where they refer to their origins at all (they would be less likely to do so in their own territory since it would be understood) tend to refer to themselves by their tribal identities. Thus a sandstone base at Colchester carries a dedication from *Similis Ci(vis) Cant(iacus)*, a citizen of the *civitas* of the Cantii to the south of Colchester. An inscription from Hadrian's Wall records one Tossodio, of the '*civitate Catuvellaunorum*'. Again, one Aemilius, who had served with the *Classis Germanica*, is recorded on a tombstone from Cologne where he is mentioned as '*civis Dumnonius*', 'a citizen of the Dumnonii'.

There are some inscriptions that simply identify people as Britons, but these tend to be from Europe, where British tribal identities would mean little to the locals. Gildas, a British cleric writing in the sixth century, does refer to Britons, but he also talks about a land divided into different British kingdoms, and his use of the term Britons may simply be a sign of his Latin education or an attempt to develop a united British identity in opposition to an Anglo-Saxon identity.

It is also quite possible that most Britons may never have fully seen themselves as Romans. Unlike their Gallic counterparts, there is little sign that the British elite ever got involved in mainstream imperial politics, or ever wanted to, and even in the fourth century people in mainland Europe still seem to have seen Britain as a far-off, very UnRoman place. Claudian, a fourth-century poet, refers to *Britannia* wrapped in furs and with tattooed cheeks,[73] while the late fourth-century Gallic poet Ausonius finds it amusing that a British poet, the only one of whom we know from the period, is called Bonus (Good) because in his eyes, being British and being good was an impossibility.[74] Gildas too, for all his Latin education, draws a clear distinction between Britons and Romans in his brief description of history during the occupation. In Gildas' account, the Romans come and the Romans go, while the Britons remain through the occupation and are still there after the Romans left.

In fact, there are perfectly good reasons why tribal identities should have remained strong throughout the occupation. As already indicated Roman local administration in Britain was based in the tribes. It is likely, judging, for instance, from the frequent building of high-status villas in the same locations as high-status pre-Roman sites, that many of the same aristocratic families in power before the Romans stayed rich and powerful under Rome. Dynastic cults, such as those probably going on at Hayling Island (where a Roman-period temple possibly linked to the Atrebatic royal family was built on top of a pre-Roman temple of identical design) and Folly Lane (where a cult site surrounding the burial

87 Dedication to Brigantia from South Shields. *Courtesy of Arbeia Museum*

88 Latin inscription in Roman script on pre-Roman coin. On one side it says 'Camuloduno', i.e. minted at *Camulodunum*/Colchester. On the other side it carries an abbreviation of the king's name, Cuno, short for Cunobelin. *Courtesy of Chris Rudd. Cat. No. 2764*

of a presumed Catuvellaunian royal of the mid first century AD continues in operation into the third century),[75] and, perhaps, other sites, would probably have helped maintain tribal identity, as would tribal cults, such as the Brigantian cult of Brigantia, and specifically tribal expressions of cults with a wider geographic following. There is also a certain amount of evidence to indicate a continuing tribal element to the organisation of economic activity, with, for example, some pottery industries probably located on tribal boundaries to give access to the markets of more than one tribe,[76] and with, as already discussed, different schools of mosaic makers operating in different tribal areas.[77] There is also the fascinating find of lead ingots, bearing the names of the *civitates* of the Iceni and the Brigantes, discovered on a shipwreck site off the coast of Brittany.[78] Who was taking the load of ingots to where is not at all clear; however, the names of the tribes on some of them do seem again to indicate some kind of commerce organised along tribe/*civitas* lines and interestingly

the wreck may well date from the second half of the fourth century (as some of the mosaics definitely do), thus perhaps suggesting that this tribal/*civitas* element of commerce remained strong until the end of the Roman period.

Even in more Romanised Gaul, there is plenty of evidence of tribal identities surviving into the fourth century and beyond. A Gallic orator addressing the emperor Constantine in the fourth century, where he might be expected to stress his Roman identity, instead tells the emperor about the proud history of his people, the Aedui.[79] A number of fifth-century Gallic writers mention details of their tribal backgrounds. And at the end of the Roman period, many Gallic tribal capitals, where occupation continued, lose other elements of their Roman-period names but retain the name of the tribe as their name. Thus, for example, we have Paris from the Parisii, Soissons from the Suessiones, Trier from the Treveri.[80] If tribal identities could survive like this in more Romanised Gaul, it is likely that they survived even more strongly in less Romanised Britain.[81]

LANGUAGE AND LITERACY

Pre-Roman Britain seems to have been a basically non-literate society. In both Spain and Gaul there is some evidence of the population in pre-Roman times developing and using writing systems to express their language. The evidence is rather more extensive in Spain than in Gaul, but even in Gaul it is there.[82] By contrast, in Britain the only pre-Roman inscriptions that have survived are those on coins issued in the decades prior to the Roman invasion. These are in Latin letters and it is generally assumed that they mostly represent nothing more ambitious than names of rulers or, less frequently, the names of towns where the coins were issued (*Calleva*, *Verulamium* and *Camulodunum* or their British equivalents all appear in abbreviated forms on pre-Roman coins), and in the one case mentioned above (ECEN for Iceni), probably a tribal name.

It is quite possible that the elite were becoming literate in these last few decades. It was a common Roman policy to educate the children of friendly kings in a Roman fashion, to help ensure their continuing friendliness to Rome when they grew up, and it has been suggested that such a policy existed in regard to Britain.[83] However, the coin inscriptions on their own can't be used to suggest anything more than a tiny percentage of pre-Roman Britons being literate.

Frustratingly, because the inscriptions largely seem to consist of names, they can't really be used to demonstrate anything too much about what language or languages were being spoken at the time in Britain. The names largely seem to be of Celtic origin and because of this, because of Tacitus' comment that the Britons spoke a similar language to the Gauls,[84] and because of the survival in the west of such languages as Cornish and Welsh, it seems best to assume that the majority of Britons in what was to become Roman Britain did speak some form of Celtic language. We can't, however, know to what extent the languages spoken by the different tribes were mutually understandable. It has also even been suggested that in the far east of Britain there may already have been Germanic influences on the language spoken, hundreds of years before the arrival of the Anglo-Saxons.[85]

Inevitably once the occupation was firmly in place, there would have been a tendency for both literacy and the use of Latin to spread. Latin after all became the language of power and Roman administration was based on documentation. The garrisoning of Roman soldiers in Britain would also inevitably help spread both Latin and literacy. The Vindolanda tablets, of course, offer particularly striking evidence of this – it's particularly worth noting the large number of different hands found among the tablets.[86] Latin was the language that bound the disparate ethnic groups that comprised the Roman army together, much like English was later the unifying force in the 'native' regiments serving within the army of the British Empire.

Ultimately, though, it's extremely hard to be sure how literate, and how Latin, Britain was during the Roman period.

We have almost no literary evidence concerning the spread of literacy and Latin in Britain. Tacitus asserts that by the late first century AD, Agricola had the sons of British chiefs learning Latin, which seems entirely likely.[87] As we have already seen, the sons of some British kings may, in fact, have been learning Latin long before this. Then

89 Graffiti on a tile from Bignor villa, West Sussex. *Reproduced with kind permission of the Tupper Family*

towards the end of the period, there is evidence, already mentioned, of a single British poet called Bonus and the emergence of a small number of British theologians, like Pelagius. None of this, however, indicates literacy and Latin outside aristocratic and, in the later period, church circles.

The archaeological evidence such as it is, is inconsistent and unclear. The habit of rich locals setting up public inscriptions to commemorate their good works never seems to have taken off in Britain in the way that it did in other Roman provinces, perhaps because so few of the locals could actually have read them, and by far the largest proportion of stone inscriptions generally from Roman Britain are linked to the military and the military community. It is estimated that 87 per cent of epigraphy from Roman Britain comes from the militarised zones.[88] Overall, among the western provinces, Britain has one of the lowest rankings on an epigraphic chart, down there with other marginal areas – *Raetia*, inland Spain, and *Mauretania Tingitana* – with less then 10 inscriptions per 1000km^2. By contrast, central and northern Gaul is in the less than 20 inscriptions per 1000km^2 category, while southern Gaul is way up there in the less than 100 inscriptions per

1000km² bracket.⁸⁹ Inscriptions in mosaics in Britain are also very rare.⁹⁰

Graffiti in Roman Britain again tends to be mostly found in military areas or major towns. Of 151 sites producing graffiti on Samian ware, almost half were military sites.⁹¹ Rural graffiti often consists of numbers and it's worth bearing in mind that functional numeracy may often have been more useful to many of the inhabitants of Roman Britain than functional literacy.⁹² The collections of lead curse tablets from places like Bath and Uley, detailing grievances for which someone sought divine help (such as items of clothing, or money, believed stolen), shed an interesting light on literacy levels among the wider population. Many of the Bath lead tablets were either written by scribes or those who were barely literate, which doesn't seem to indicate high levels of Latin literacy. The badly blundered and often illegible legends on locally produced copies of official coins in the third and fourth centuries similarly suggest a society where literacy was very limited. Finds of seal boxes and styli on villa sites probably indicate a certain level of literacy among the rural British middle and upper classes, but need not indicate anything much more than that.

In more Romanised Gaul there seem to have been significant pockets of people speaking a Celtic language even in the very late Roman period. Jerome notes that the language of the Treveri was similar to that of the Galatians, another Celtic language. It is worth noting here the large number of Celtic names listed in the Bath tablets, names like Brigomalla, Deomiorix, Riovassus and Vinidorix, with almost half being Celtic even in the late Roman period.⁹³ Plus, of course, there is the fact that Welsh and Cornish are Celtic languages. Welsh has significant numbers of Latin loan words; however, it has been suggested that some significant Latin-influenced changes on the phonology of Welsh, and particularly Cornish, occurred in the post-Roman period.⁹⁴

The best guess we can perhaps make is to say that Latin was probably spoken among the middle and upper classes, and in towns. It was less widely spoken in the countryside in the Romanised part of Britain, though, no doubt, its use would have spread with time. However, in the west, its use was most likely restricted to the rich, to the military, to officials and to the Church, with the rest remaining with their original Celtic languages but absorbing some Latin loan words. The pattern of literacy was probably rather similar, but a little more restricted.

4

THE LIMITS OF EMPIRE

THERE was not, in the later years of the first century BC and the early years of the first century AD, any real concept in the Roman mind of a limit to Empire and conquest. Rome was in a state of continual expansion, its frontiers spreading in all directions. Britain, at the north-western edges of the known world, beyond the mythical Ocean, represented one such zone of economic and military potential. Caesar had invaded and Augustus traded. Caligula had pontificated, waving his fist and threatening from the coast of Gaul. Claudius had 'liberated' the tribes of the south and east. Under the fourth emperor of Rome, certain designated tribal officials had been allowed to stay in power whilst the army of Rome moved westwards, annexing the agriculturally wealthy lands of the Cotswolds and the mineral-rich highlands of Cornwall and western Wales.

As they moved out of southern and eastern England, the Roman army encountered more hostile terrain, more dispersed forms of settlement and a population with little or no experience of the Mediterranean world. Things became difficult very quickly. For the first time since they had arrived in Britain, the Roman army started suffering significant losses.

Wales, it is fair to say, caused Rome some major problems. First, chasing the errant king Caratacus, leader of the British resist-ance, into South Wales in the late 40s AD, the Roman State found itself embroiled in a campaign that proved both difficult and time consuming. Caratacus himself was finally captured, after transferring the theatre of war into North Wales and thence into the north of England, in AD 51, but the Silures fought on. 'There were frequent clashes', Tacitus notes, 'more often than not in the form of skirmishes in woods and marshes, occasioned by individual chance or gallantry, some by accident, others by design, some out of hatred, others for plunder, sometimes under orders, sometimes without the knowledge of commanders'.[95] The situation was not helped, in Tacitus' eyes, by the fact that the Roman governor, Ostorius Scapula, had apparently made the statement that, in his view, the Silures 'should be totally eradicated … or transported to the provinces of Gaul'.[96]

As it was, the Silures were not exterminated, but they were defeated, finally, in AD 74, some two decades later, by the governor Julius Frontinus. The keystone of military subjugation of the tribe was to be the permanent legionary fortress of Caerleon (*Isca*) with its numerous outlying auxiliary bases, whilst the winning of hearts and minds was conducted within *Venta Silurum*, the *civitas* of the Silures, underneath modern-day Caerwent, and Carmarthen (*Moridunum*), the *civitas* of the Demetae to the west. Caerwent

90 Caernarfon, Gwynedd. Interior of the Roman fort first constructed in the late AD 70s, with Anglesey in the distance

91 Tomen-y-Mur, Gwynedd. Amphitheatre adjoining the Roman fort first constructed in the late AD 70s

92 Richborough, Kent. Foundations of the monumental arch erected by the emperor Domitian in around AD 85 to commemorate the total conquest of Britain

was never a successful town, covering an area of less than 18ha, although it was provided with the essential civic infrastructure of a forum basilica, shops, baths and a range of temples. An inscription found in the town, commemorating the life and works of an ex-Legionary general called Paulinus, was set up by 'the community of the Silures' at the 'decree of the local senate' (EX DECRETO ORDINIS RES PVBL CIVIT SILVRVM); something which suggests that certain members of the tribe were keen to immerse themselves in the apparatus of the State. Carmarthen, the most westerly town in the province, at 12.5ha, has the air of a pioneer shanty-town of the American Wild West.

Following the final military pacification of North Wales in AD 78, there was no attempt to Romanise the area with the creation of new civic authorities such as those established at Caerwent and Carmarthen in the south. North and central Wales were to remain under military control. A legionary base was created at Chester (*Deva*) and a network of auxiliary 'policing' forts, connected by roads and harbours, spread out to the west.

Wales was to prove economically important to the Roman State due to its highly prized mineral resources, in particular copper and gold, but the nature of its dispersed, decentralised population, combined with the mountainous terrain, meant that it could also prove hugely expensive to maintain. By the mid to late second century AD, only a handful of forts across North Wales remained in occupation at Caernarfon, Caerhun, Caersws, Forden Gaer, Leintwardine, Castell Collen and Brecon Gaer. Perhaps the perceived levels of security threat had, by then, been downgraded, the scattered mountain communities no longer being thought of as a risk to the economic investments of Rome. Whatever forts remained active in the second century each provided a small but significant enclave of the Roman machine; a militarised administrative framework which, in the absence of towns, held the population together.

A similar policy of low-level military intervention combined with social and political non-interference seems to have prevailed in south-western England. Here, the *civitas* town of Exeter (*Isca Dumnoniorum*) in Devon was constructed over the remains of a legionary fortress sometime around AD 75. Few forts were established to the west of Exeter, known examples being recorded at Calstock, Restormel Castle, Lostwithiel and Nanstallon, leaving Cornwall largely clear of military activity. As with areas of Wales, Cornwall was rich in mineral resources, especially tin, which seem to have been exploited from the later half of the first century AD. A network of roads, although largely invisible on the surface today, are known thanks to a series of milestones, commemorating third- and fourth-century repairs, found in the area of Tintagel and Redruth. Presumably these connected areas of tin exploitation directly to the sea.

Cornwall / West Devon and mid to North Wales occupied curious positions with regard to the developing province of *Britannia* for, whilst both areas were economically exploited by Rome, it would not appear that the aristocratic elite of either area was at any time ever fully integrated into Romano-British society. Certainly there is no radical change in settlement type from the first century BC to the third century AD (see Chapter 5). The low level of forts in each territory appears to indicate that neither area was perceived to be a threat to the security of the province, and could, presumably, be effectively contained. Perhaps there was some form of dependency agreement drawn up between the natives and the Roman government, binding indigenous groups to the State without the need for a more complete form of military occupation or civilian Romanisation.

TOTAL WAR

The mandate for the total conquest of Britain was given to the governor Julius Agricola in AD 77 by the emperor Vespasian, who was no doubt keen to see the completion of a project that he himself had been involved with way back in AD 43/44. Agricola was to hold office for nearly seven years, an unusual but not unheard of posting at a time when the standard length of time given to most provincial governors was three to four years.

The details of the northern British campaigns, discussed in detail by Tacitus' son-in-law, the historian Tacitus in his work the *Agricola*, need not detain us here. Suffice to say that between Agricola's arrival in Britain (late in AD 77) and his recall to Rome (in AD 83/44) we are told that Roman troops under his command crushed resistance in North Wales, advanced through northern England and up the eastern seaboard of Scotland, destroying the last British army thrown against them in AD 83 before circumnavigating the British Isles by ship later in the same year.

93 The Hadrianic frontier at Cawfields milecastle, Cumbria

94 The Hadrianic frontier
(from the outside) recreated at
Vindolanda, Northumberland

Tacitus' account of his father-in-law's campaign climaxes at the battle of *Mons Graupius*. Unfortunately for us, Tacitus fails to provide a detailed description of either the battlefield or an exact placement for the war, but then the historian was not interested in geography, only the human drama. *Mons Graupius* is presented as the culmination of the seven-year campaign, the last, futile attempt by the Britons to gain their freedom. It was the final gasp of a people who did not yet realise they were beaten. The battle is given significant space in the *Agricola*, taking up nearly a full fifth of the total word count. Whether the battle itself was as significant as Tacitus makes out, or whether it was merely a small skirmish that has been inflated to more important status, is unclear. Certainly Dio Cassius, writing in the third century and our only other source for the campaign, doesn't mention it, but then he is more interested in the Roman fleet's circumnavigation of Britain than the minor detail of the war itself.

The human cost of the conflict is, perhaps unsurprisingly, not given by Tacitus, whose work provides a relatively straightforward account of adventure in the far north. The reality on the ground – a difficult advance through mountainous terrain against an enemy that possessed no large centres of population (to besiege), fixed resources (to attack) or large field armies (to fight) – does not figure at all in the published version. The *Agricola* only hints at the severe difficulties faced by Roman troops when fighting a protracted campaign against a guerrilla army with nothing to lose, when it notes the reluctance of the enemy to attack secure positions, which it puts down to cowardice, and their curious strategy of moving 'their wives and children to safety' which it ascribes to arrogance. Only once does Tacitus directly acknowledge the success of the barbarian strategy, observing that, after one particular attempt at ambush was driven off, Roman troops were unable to press home the advantage, 'marshes and woodland providing cover for the fleeing enemy'.[97]

A clearer idea of the difficulties faced by a well-equipped professional army stuck in a hostile country with no one to fight is provided in the later accounts of the emperor Septimius Severus who, in AD 208, launched a spectacularly disastrous invasion of Scotland. 'Once the army had crossed the rivers and earthworks on the frontier of the Roman empire', the historian Herodian says, 'there were frequent encounters and skirmishes with the enemy in which they were put to flight. However, it was easy for them to escape and to disappear into the woods and marshes because of their knowledge of the terrain, but all this hampered the Romans and dragged out the war considerably'.[98]

Were the 'underhand' barbarian tactics of an army resorting to guerilla warfare the main reason why the Agricolan war had lasted quite so long? It is certainly possible; Agricola's unusual seven-year posting perhaps being due not to his successes, but because the British employed tactics that ensured that swift victory and face-saving retreat were impossible. The further Roman troops advanced into Scotland the more isolated individual groups became, proving easy targets for a British army well acquainted with the hostile nature of both landscape and climate.

Agricola had been given the job of finishing the conquest of Britain by Domitian's father, the emperor Vespasian, but, seven years on and with little economic gain evident from the protracted fighting, Domitian probably had a different set of priorities, not least on the Danube frontier where barbarian hordes were threatening Roman interests. Agricola may (or may not) have smashed the Caledonian armies sent against him at the battle of *Mons Graupius*, but the campaign itself was clearly not over. Forts and roads needed to be built and garrisons initiated before northern Britain could effectively become 'Roman'. The highlands of the north possessed no great *oppida* or equivalent native centres that were found in the south. There were no great kings akin to Cunobelinus or Togidubnus with whom the Roman State could do deals, society here seems to have been decentralised and largely dispersed. Worse, there was no history of Roman contact through long-established trade and relations; the highland elite had not been sending their children to Rome for an education in the classical arts. Things also looked serious from an economic perspective, the highlands being better suited to pasture than crop production and, as far as Rome was concerned, there were no known mineral reserves.

Perhaps the State felt that it was better that the conquest of the north could, at least on coins, monuments and other propaganda instruments of the State, be hailed as complete, allowing the army to retreat back to a more secure position without a humiliating loss of face. At the port of Richborough on the Kent coast, a major harbour facilitating access into Britain, a huge four-way triumphal arch was built to commemorate the total *conquest* of Britain at the point where the road network of the province officially began. The monument, which may have stood over 25m in height, was draped in Italian marble and ornamental bronze work. Towering over the arch was, in all probability, a victorious image of Domitian himself.[99]

On the ground, things appear to have been rather less triumphant. Many of the newly placed military installations, established by Agricola along the eastern seaboard of Scotland as the first stage of conquest, were now abandoned. At Inchtuthil, Tayside, a 21.5ha legionary fortress was systematically dismantled, presumably in order to prevent anything falling into the hands of the enemy. Glass and pottery wares were smashed and pounded to dust; over a million unused iron nails were dumped into a pit; timbers were forced apart; drains blocked; the bath house and ramparts demolished.[100]

ESTABLISHING THE FRONTIER

Unlike the emperor Domitian, his imperial successors Nerva and Trajan (in AD 96 and 98 respectively) seem to have had little interest in distant *Britannia*. The conquest of the island had been the pet project of the Flavian family, under Vespasian and Titus, and had reached its climax under the recently deceased, and now discredited, Domitian. Nerva and Trajan may possibly have tried to distance themselves from any association with Britain, fearful of being tainted with anything overseen by Domitian. More realistically, perhaps, as the province was now officially 'subjugated', they felt their energies could be more usefully directed elsewhere. Trajan, in particular, craved military victories and there were none to be won for him in Britain. The energies of the emperor, as well as a large amount of the military reserves of the Empire, were now to be directed against the Dacians (across the Danube in modern-day Romania) and Parthians (in the East).

Britain, following troop withdrawals to supplement Trajan's campaigns in the East, seems to have been left largely to its own devices. By now, the northern frontier was stabilising along a line running between Carlisle and Newcastle (the Tyne-Solway isthmus), all previously acquired territory to the north having now been abandoned. The

95 Simulated courtyard of a Roman headquarters building (*principia*) at Wallsend, Northumberland

legionary bases at Caerleon (in South Wales), Chester and York were all rebuilt in stone at this time, suggesting a general acceptance of the *status quo*: that these were now the permanent military strong-points in the province. New *coloniae* for retired soldiery were established at Gloucester and Lincoln, possibly in the final years of Domitian's reign or in the early months of Nerva's.

In AD 122, however, the situation in Britain demanded the immediate presence of the then emperor Hadrian. We know little about what was going on in Britain at the time, although the historian Fronto, writing in the AD 160s, noted that under Hadrian 'what great numbers of soldiers were killed by the Jews, what great numbers by the British'.[101] The Jewish wars we know about, but the number and extent

of British losses remain unknown. Fronto's reference must presumably relate to a significant event, memorable for all the wrong reasons, otherwise why would he have mentioned it? Given that it is discussed at all, the disaster probably involved a legion (or legions), for auxiliary losses would not have generated much imperial concern. Such a traumatic loss may well have occurred early in Hadrian's reign for the *Augustan History*, compiled in the late third century AD, notes that when he took over in August AD 117, Hadrian discovered that 'the Britons could not be kept under Roman control'.[102]

This reference is usually taken to mean a war, possibly defensive, stemming from a barbarian invasion of Roman-held territory. More likely perhaps, given the phrasing that 'the Britons *could not be kept under Roman* control', the reference is to a rebellion or uprising within existing, possibly even long-held, Roman teritory. Certainly the anonymous author of the *Augustan History* does not mention an invasion *per se* and neither does he refer to barbarian involvement (although to be fair the reference is hardly detailed). It seems reasonable then, given the phrasing, that the Britons *who could not be kept under Roman control* were operating within the province of *Britannia*.

The tribal leaders of northern and western Britain, although within the orbit of Rome for some significant time, had never been as completely affected by Mediterranean culture as their more southern colleagues. The relationship between tribes such as the Silures and Ordovices of Wales and the Brigantian tribal confederation, whatever its full extent and organisational nature, of northern England and the Roman government had never been easy. The Brigantes, in particular, had proven difficult to deal with, riven as the tribe was with multiple internal disagreements; pro- and anti-Roman factions. It would perhaps seem natural to assume that, if the troubles cited by the *Augustan History* had stemmed from within the province, it was either the Brigantes, or their immediate neighbours, or the tribes of Wales who were ultimately responsible.

It is worth pointing out that, although no tribal area or geographic zone is mentioned with regard to the troubles, and, although generally placed in the north, the 'Britons' of the *Augustan History* could, in the absence of secure archaeological evidence, just as plausibly have been causing problems for the Roman administration, disrupting communication, trade, taxation and lines of supply, in the south. In this respect, the severed bronze head of the emperor Hadrian himself, recovered from the River Thames, near London Bridge, in 1834, is not without

interest. The piece, which has been removed from a full statue with some degree of force, was deposited (or simply dumped) in the river. This could represent later iconoclasm or troubles surrounding the collapse of central government in the fourth or fifth century. However, the violent removal and subsequent deposition of an imperial head into a river is paralleled by the decapitated portrait of a young man (Claudius or Nero) from the River Alde in Suffolk. The Alde piece is plausibly associated with the Boudiccan sack of Colchester in AD 60, but the Hadrianic portrait is unassociated with any such event, unless of course there was a period of social instability afflicting London early in Hadrian's reign. It is worth pointing out that archaeological evidence further suggests that significant areas of London were destroyed by fire early in the second century. Whether these fires were started by accident or design, however, is unknown.

Whatever the situation in Britain, Hadrian thought it demanded his immediate presence. In the summer of AD 122, he arrived on the island, whereupon 'he corrected many faults and was the first to build a wall, 80 miles long, to separate the Romans and the barbarians'.[103] Two fragments of a single inscription found near Jarrow seem to confirm that the wall had only been built 'once [the barbarians] had been scattered [and] the province of Britain [recovered]', a reference possibly alluding to more significant military operations. Once peace had been restored, the northernmost limits of *Britannia* were set down in the most monumental of terms.

The wall that Hadrian designed for Britain, measuring in its early stages 3.5m in thickness and around 6m high with patrolled gateways every one Roman mile (1.48km), was only part of an extremely complex barrier designed to both define and protect the edge of Roman administrative

control. It may also have had a further function: the establishment of a permanent
militarised zone keeping Brigantian territory, and the Brigantes themselves, separate
from non-Roman influence; keeping any
disaffected elements of the tribe from those
external forces that might offer military
support. From now on, at least from the
perspective of imperial spin, everything to
the south was 'Roman', everything to the
north 'Barbarian'.

KEEPING THE PEACE

Of course the land to the immediate south
of the Hadrianic frontier was Roman only
in that it was held by Rome, there being
little in the way of civilian settlement to
suggest a change in political emphasis or
focus. The most common form of native
settlement during the Roman military
phase is the small farm, comprising oval
or roughly squared enclosures of drystone
wall set around a handful of roundhouses
(usually 1-3) built upon a roughly cobbled
yard.[104] The majority probably represent
the homestead of a single, albeit extended,
family group. Roman towns were established within the broader militarised zone,
between the wall and the legionary fortress
of *Eboracum* (York) to the south, most notably at Carlisle (*Luguvallium*) and Aldborough
(*Isurium*), but these did not generate the
same high levels of *Romanitas* as those urban
centres recorded in southern England.

As the continued presence of the Roman
army disrupted and effectively retarded
the native social growth in the north of
England, it was the army itself that provided
the focus for Romanised life. Many long-
term forts had civilian settlements, known as
vici, adhering to them. The *vicus* served the
garrison of a fort, providing a range of needs,

services and forms of entertainment (not all
of it entirely salubrious). In some cases it was
the *vicus* that housed the wives and families
of soldiers, although legally speaking in the
early Empire troops were not permitted to
marry. Certain forts, such as Vindolanda, at
Chesterholm to the south of Hadrian's Wall,
possessed substantial *vicus* developments,
which sometimes grew to be larger than the
fort itself. It is possible, given the needs of
a garrison and the desire to avoid travelling
great distances for the purpose of supply,
that settlers were actively encouraged by the
military authorities to establish themselves
around a fort.

Until fairly recently, *vici* represented a
largely overlooked aspect of Roman settlement, but new fieldwork and geophysical
survey in the area of Hadrian's Wall has
better demonstrated the size, scale and nature
of the average *vicus*. Archaeological evidence
recovered to date demonstrates that, rather
than just supplying the specific needs of the
nearby garrison, *vici* became major zones of
habitation, providing considerable evidence
of trade, exchange, burial, agriculture and
industrial production. The *vicus* sat at the
margins of a fort, in a landscape filled with
all the natural resources required to successfully sustain an industrial and agricultural
economy. The position of the fort itself was
also critical, for these were established at or
along major highways, often at a point in
the landscape where they intersected with a
river. Could it be that *vici* grew to fulfil some
of the objectives of the *civitas* to the south,
namely as administrative, judicial and market
centres for a civilian population? Such
sites may have been established to provide
facilities, resources and refreshment for the
troops, as well as protection for their families, but, by the later second century AD at
least, many were spawning successful, semi-
autonomous communities.

We possess little written evidence for life in the average fort or *vicus* from the perspective of Roman historians, whose interest lay elsewhere. Thankfully, however, a wealth of relevant information has been found from at least one British site, the frontier fort of Vindolanda in Northumberland. Here, a wealth of original official documents, relating to garrison life between the years AD 90-105, have been recovered. Much of the information is, as one may imagine, fairly monotonous, detailing lists of supplies, resources, garrison strength etc., but others provide a tantalisingly rare insight into the bubble of *Romanitas* that existed within an average frontier fort.

One of the most well-known letters from the frontier was from Claudia Severa to Sulpicia Lepidina, wife of the commanding officer Flavius Cerialis: 'Claudia Severa to her Lepidina, greetings. On 11 September, sister, for the day of the celebration of my birthday, I give you a warm invitation to make sure that you come to us, to make the day more enjoyable for me by your arrival, if you are present. Give my greetings to your Cerialis. My Aelius and my little son send him their greetings. I shall expect you, sister. Farewell, sister, my dearest soul, as I hope to prosper, and hail'.[105] Another, from Cerialis himself to Aelius Brocchus, husband of Claudia Severa, notes, 'If you love me, brother, I ask that you send me some hunting-nets',[106] whilst an anonymous writer records the sending of 'pairs of socks from Sattua, two pairs of sandals and two pairs of underpants'.[107] Other fragments of text include quotations taken from the *Aeneid* and the *Georgics*, two works of the first-century BC poet Virgil. The fact that one of the lines contains a mistake, combined with the observation that Virgil was often used for teaching purposes, may indicate that these pieces of text preserve a moment of

96 Underfloor heating system in the commanding officer's house, Housesteads, Northumbria

elementary instruction in Latin, possibly for the children of the fort commander.

The only time that the indigenous population impinges upon the very Roman world of the tablet writers is in a fragment recording their apparent lack of fighting skills: 'The Britons are unprotected by armour. There are very many cavalry. The cavalry do not use swords nor do the wretched Britons mount in order to throw javelins'.[108] Intriguingly the word used for the 'wretched Britons' is '*Brittunculi*' as mentioned earlier, a contemptuous, and no doubt rather racist, term of abuse.

Rome had, in northern England (and indeed in North Wales and Cornwall /

Devon) reached the limits of its power. As we have seen, the Empire could not successfully control by might alone, it needed the support of an organised native elite, upon whom it could devolve certain administrative powers. Outside of central southern England, the combined effects of a dispersed society and mountainous terrain meant that native society was decentralised and comparatively small scale. In order to conquer and effectively maintain territory, the Roman government needed large proto-urban centres to attack or influence and well-organised states with whom it could successfully negotiate. North Wales, south-western England, northern England and southern Scotland possessed neither of these features. Ironically, perhaps, the longer the army remained in power within northern England, the more its presence suppressed elements in the indigenous elite (who represented a potentially destabilising factor within military-held lands), preventing any chance that native power might gradually coalesce.

Overall, therefore, it has to be said that the Roman invasion of Britain ended, on some level, in strategic failure. The normal Roman way was to occupy a region, suppress opposition and when the area was finally peaceful, remove the army to serve elsewhere. Rome's ultimate failure to realistically 'conquer' Scotland, given the logistical, social and political problems identified, combined with the fact that it never even seems to have seriously considered a conquest of Ireland, meant that the Roman army could never leave Britain and the province remained a frontier country, an exposed outpost surrounded on three sides by tribes beyond Rome's control.

5

REJECTING *ROMANITAS*

THE establishment of an efficient inland communications network, coupled with the development of new urban units close to former centres of the native elite (such as the hillfort or *oppidum*) and the placement of forts, must have had a profound effect upon certain members of the indigenous population. To those who craved social advancement beyond the limits of the new towns, a basic lifestyle choice would have presented itself: continue the basic rhythms of life as before, unaffected by the imposition of Roman central government, or adapt and adopt the trappings of the new social elite. It was essential that those who wished to succeed and thrive under Roman rule had to display their wealth in new and more complex ways. In short they needed to become 'Roman'.

The physical manifestation of *Romanitas* in the countryside, and indeed the most well-known and popular aspect of Roman Britain today, is the villa. Some archaeologists and historians have noted their dislike of the term 'villa' due to its connotations of 'luxury holiday' or 'retirement home' combined with its apparent inappropriateness when comparing British sites with those grand Roman villas found across Italy and the Mediterranean. The trouble is, that's just what most Roman villas appear to represent. A villa in the context of Roman Britain was a place where the *nouveaux riche* spent their hard-earned cash.

The majority of villas in Britain were at the centre of a working, successful agricultural estate it is true, profits generated from the selling of farm surplus presumably providing the necessary cash for home improvement, but a villa is as far away from a 'normal' working farm as one could expect.

Villas possessed elaborate bathing suites, ornate dining rooms and a generally high level of internal décor. Farms possessed more basic, functional accommodation with easy access to pigsties, cow sheds and ploughed fields. In this respect, the earliest Roman villas of lowland Britain can perhaps be better compared with the grand estates, country houses and stately homes of the more recent landed gentry of England, Scotland and Wales. These houses represented monumental statements of power designed to dominate the land and impress all who passed by. As the home of a successful landowner wishing to attain a certain level of social standing and recognition, the stately home or country house was the grand, architectural centrepiece of a great agricultural estate where the owner could enhance his or her art collection, develop business opportunities, dispense the law and dabble in politics. In this respect the Roman villa was probably little different.

Villas are useful components in the archaeological database of Roman Britain, for they can potentially provide an indicator of the relative success of Roman culture in the province. These were not structures created by the State for ease of administration (towns) nor subjugation (forts); they were not forced upon the native population, rather they were developed by those who were, or who wanted to be, Roman. They were all about show and showing off. Given that the population of Britain at this time was predominantly rural, the distribution of villas across the British Isles should provide an idea of the relative 'take-up' of Roman fashions from the late first century AD to the collapse of central government authority in the early fifth. Similarly, those areas where villas are absent should, in theory at least, be reflective of those areas where the population did not desire, acquire, or even aspire to, the cultural attributes of Rome.

VILLAS

The Roman villa is an easy enough type-site to identify archaeologically in Britain. Villas were high-status, Romanised houses and, as such, can clearly be distinguished from the more 'normal' rural buildings that preceded them. Villas possessed a broadly rectangular plan, comprising a range of rooms connected by a corridor or veranda. Walls, especially those in public areas, were often decorated, whilst the provision of solid floors allowed the opportunity to invest in mosaic pavements depicting scenes from classical mythology. Architectural details, such as ornate columns, glazed windows and tiled roofs, embellished the whole whilst major structural 'add-ons', such as the integrated bathing suite and underfloor heating system, were often brought in as and when finances allowed.

Villas can take a variety of different forms, as one would expect from a type of structure that appears to have developed organically, without direct imposition from the State; in Britain the basic identifiable types are the Cottage House, Corridor House (sometimes with wings) and Courtyard House. Cottage or 'Strip' Houses represent the first form of Romanised rural buildings, comprising little more than a linear cluster of four or five squared rooms covered by a single roof. Corridor Houses represent an advance in domestic planning, allowing increased privacy together with the possibility of being able to create room hierarchy, dividing public and private space as well as separating the house owner from his or her family, servants or employees. Corridor Houses often developed from more simple Cottage or Strip designs, whilst later developments sometimes included wings, at either end of the main corridor, constructed in order to accommodate a bathing suite or heated rooms. The third type of villa, the Courtyard House, represents the final evolutionary phase of Romanised rural building, with three or four ranges of domestic activity developing from a primary phase cottage or Corridor House.

As villas represented the grand architectural centrepiece to a great agricultural estate, most possessed very clear demarcation of space for two very different forms of social activity: private and public. Public activities would include forms of local jurisdiction, such as the settlement of legal or land disputes between family members, tenant farmers or their dependants, and the punishment of misdemeanours. Private activities would include the entertainment of friends, family, social equals and superior officials. Zones set aside for entertainment and social climbing are clear enough to identify within the ground plan of most Roman villas, for such rooms usually possess the most ornate and exquisite elements of interior décor.

97 Bignor villa, West Sussex. Painting by Samuel Lysons of the Four-Seasons mosaic shortly after its discovery in 1812. *Reproduced with kind permission of the Tupper Family*

Bignor in West Sussex and Chedworth in Gloucestershire represent two well-studied, developed villa sites where specific public and private zones can be identified.[109] At Bignor, the later fourth-century phase villa possessed a large room containing a hexagonal stone water basin, probably for a fountain. The mosaic that surrounded this water feature is a fine piece of craftsmanship depicting Ganymede, a prince of Troy, in the moment of being kidnapped by Jupiter (Zeus) appearing in the form of an eagle. Though Ganymede served as a cupbearer to the gods, the story seems to have been popular within certain circles of Greek and Roman society because it seemed to give legitimacy to the love between an adult male and a young boy.

Around the stone pool a myriad of poorly attired women holding tambourines danced in an endless cycle. These women were probably maenads, the followers of Bacchus, the Roman god of wine. At Chedworth the *triclinium* or dining room can be identified as one of the larger rooms in the west wing of the early fourth-century villa. The mosaic occupying the floor of this enclosed space is divided into two discrete areas: a complex geometric design upon which furniture was almost certainly arranged, and the figurative designs beyond, with the four seasons (indicating the passing of a year) and scenes of nymphs and satyrs dancing in a state of undress and advanced intoxication. The designs used at both Chedworth and Bignor make it

98 Was the owner of a villa British or Roman?
Courtesy of the Sussex Archaeological Society

clear that these rooms were, in every sense, designed for the pursuit of pleasure.

As a significant seat of localised power, villas required a formal space where landowners could fulfil their public duties. At Bignor, there is an apsidal-ended room situated at the north-western margins of the villa which could be entered independently from outside the complex. Such an arrangement means that the room possessed structural independence from the main domestic range. Any visitor could be swiftly ushered in and out of the hall without disturbing the household beyond. As an audience chamber, the existence of underfloor heating was imperative, considering that the space was probably in use all year round. The room was entered from the south-west, the floor mosaic clearly distinguishing the use of space from the

apse, where the owner or their delegated representative sat on or close to an image of Venus, goddess of love and fertility, and the space occupied by the petitioner, separated from the apse by a strip depicting gladiatorial combat; the ultimate statement in the dispensation of justice. At Chedworth, the aisled reception room or audience chamber, again heated by a hypocaust, appears to have been in the extreme north-eastern corner of the main domestic range.

Aisled villas represent a distinctive type of Romanised constructional design away from the more developed form of country estate. Aisled villa buildings comprise a large rectangular structure containing two parallel lines of posts, usually running the entire length of the building. These posts would originally have supported the roof, dividing the internal space of the structure into a central nave and two side aisles. One end of the building, or hall, is generally given over to more private, Romanised forms of accommodation. Aisled structures are seldom in complete isolation, generally being found close to villas of the Cottage or Corridor variety.

Aisled houses are not uncommon in Roman Britain and may reflect a form of building in which a family and its animals could be contained under one roof; a very UnRoman feature. In such a scheme, any potential change or modification to the original ground plan could indicate a gradual desire to become ever more 'Roman' due to an increase in disposable income, political necessity or simple peer pressure. Certainly the form taken by such aisled buildings seems to reflect a more agricultural origin than some of the more grand and luxurious Corridor and Courtyard villas. The basic division between large hall and smaller private rooms beyond is not actually dissimilar to the division we see between human and

99 Dispensing justice. Detail from the Venus and gladiators mosaic at Bignor villa, West Sussex. *Reproduced with kind permission of the Tupper Family*

animal living space recorded from within certain medieval longhouses, such as those noted on Dartmoor. If an aisled hall had not originally been designed to accommodate livestock, it is possible that it may have served broader communal purposes, the smaller rooms behind indicating a desire for privacy and separation from everyday domestic activity.

Alternatively, when found in close association with more usual Corridor or Courtyard villas, aisled buildings may have been specifically designed for administrative purposes (as an estate office) or as a place for semi-public assemblies and meetings. It could even be that those aisled buildings or halls provided with private internal space were intended to function as a residential building for a farm manager and their family. In such a model, the provision of a discrete set of rooms at one end of the hall or barn

(for meetings, animals, farm equipment or the storage of foodstuffs) could relate to the upgrading of office space or the subsequent improvement of domestic accommodation for those who saw to the day-to-day running of the estate.

Despite the large number of villa sites that have been excavated across Britain, we are no closer to being able to answer, with any certainty, the question: 'Who lived in the villas?' This is a shame, as it is the one question that will always demand a response. No known inscriptions (funerary or otherwise) outlining the background, life and career path of villa owners in Britain has survived or been positively identified, and those fragments of information that have been found serve only to tantalise and infuriate in equal measure. A qualification to the original question on villa ownership: 'Was it a Briton or Roman who lived here?' is,

100 Wadfield, Gloucestershire. A Roman villa (now covered by trees) at the centre of a vast agricultural estate

101 Agricultural tools displayed at Fishbourne Roman Palace, West Sussex. Although we know much about how villa owners spent their fortunes, we know comparatively little about how such income was originally generated. *Courtesy of the Sussex Archaeological Society*

however, easier to answer, for although the *ethnic* origins of the owner cannot be determined, we can confidently state that they were all *culturally* Roman. Ethnicity is almost impossible to establish within the archaeological record (unless one is fortunate to find a tombstone which spells out the birthplace of the deceased) and the owner of a Romanised house in Sussex could just as easily have originated from Egypt, Gaul, Spain, Italy or anywhere else in the Empire, having retired from the army or arriving in the hope of being able to make money in the new province, rather than having been born and raised in Britain. Roman society was fluid and we know, by analogy elsewhere, that provincials were keen to exploit the opportunities for business that arose within newly acquired Roman territories. Soldiers too, though recruited from overseas, may have found on retirement that it was easier (or indeed cheaper) to stay in the province that they had served and make a new life as a civilian farmer.

Whatever their origins and ethnicity, a villa owner, in building a Roman-style house for themselves complete with all the trappings of a classical lifestyle (including baths, painted plaster on the walls and mosaics on the floors), was clearly demonstrating on some level their interest in Roman culture and their desire to fit in and be seen to be successful. Their ancestry or tribal background, if they wanted to remember, honour or celebrate it, became combined with Roman attitudes, culture and beliefs. The villa owners worshipped Romanised gods, spoke (or made an attempt to understand) Latin, the universal language of Empire, traded and paid tax in Roman coins and gave Roman names to their offspring. Archaeologically speaking, such people were no longer identifiably 'British', 'Gallic', 'German', 'Spanish', 'African' or 'Italian'.

It is, perhaps, only natural to believe that villa owners must have been ethnically British; descendants of those that tilled the land throughout the Iron Age and who finally 'saw the light' and adapted to the new fashion order. It seems more plausible; more comforting somehow and in many cases it is no doubt true. It is also suitably far away from the standpoint of the earliest antiquarian investigators of villas in eighteenth-century England, who frequently expressed the view that villas were the homes of an incoming Roman elite, drawn primarily from Italian, southern Gallic, North African or Spanish society; these were the powerhouses of conquest; the homes of a non-native elite; the dwellings of the Roman master race. Such perspectives possess the uncomfortable whiff of colonialism and British imperialism about them and were, as a consequence, rejected by archaeologists during the more 'enlightened' times of the later twentieth century. In fact, as so often, the truth is probably a little more complex.

Buying and holding land was, for the Roman aristocratic classes of the late Republic and early Empire, one of the only respectable ways of earning a living. Investing in good agricultural land was acceptable; actually getting your hands dirty was not. Throughout the early years of the Empire, we hear references to estate holders attempting to increase profit margins by snapping up neighbouring estates, especially if a neighbour had fallen on hard times, died in a recent war, invested unwisely, possessed a disputed inheritance claim or supported the wrong candidate in a period of civil unrest. The most successful landowner, at least in the first and second centuries AD, was the emperor, thanks mostly to property that he had acquired directly through inheritance, claimed by right of conquest or obtained

102 Rockbourne, Hampshire. The foundations of a native roundhouse and primary phase cottage villa marked out with modern materials

through confiscation. Such lands, classed as imperial estates, could be found across the entire Empire and were, in the absence of the emperor himself (who could not be in all places at once), managed by delegated representatives (usually freedmen/women who owed their status to the emperor's goodwill). By the second century AD, as speculators, corrupt government officials and business entrepreneurs began to exploit the wealthy provinces, there was an increase in the number of private individuals owning vast estates. These were often known as *latifundia* and were usually run on behalf of the owner by tenants or freedmen using large amounts of slave labour.

We hear of one such owner of vast rural estates, Melania the younger, from a late Roman source, Palladius, Bishop of Helenopolis (in around AD 400), whose work, the *Lausiac History*, chronicles the lives of a variety of saints, monks, nuns and religious figures. Melania was a super-rich heiress who, at the age of 13, had been married to a cousin on her father's side. When both husband and wife converted to Christianity, Melania found the possession of immense wealth incompatible with spirituality and, in a huge act of charity, handed significant amounts of her inheritance to both the Church and the poor.

Having entrusted her silver and gold to a certain Paul, a monk of Dalmatia, she sent … 10,000 pieces of money to Egypt, 10,000 pieces to Antioch and its neighbourhood,

103 Whitehall villa, Northamptonshire, a third-century AD corridor villa, with ancillary building, set around an earlier roundhouse. *Courtesy of John Hodgson*

15,000 to Palestine, 10,000 to the churches in the islands and the places of exile, while she herself distributed to the churches in the West in the same way … And she freed 8000 slaves who wished freedom, for the rest did not wish it, but preferred to be slaves to her brother; and she allowed him to take them all for three pieces of money. But having sold her possessions in the Spains, Aquitania, Tarragonia, Britain and the Gauls, she reserved for herself only those in Sicily and Campania and Africa and appropriated their income for the support of monasteries.[110]

It is possible that at least some of the enlarged powerhouses of the province that we see today were not in the possession of an indig-

enous elite at all, but absentee millionaire landlords such as Melania the younger.

NON-VILLAS

It would be wrong to assume that everyone lived in a villa or Romanised house during the time that Britain was part of the Roman Empire, in fact far from it. As already noted, it is their archaeological visibility, and their unashamed cultural Roman-ness, that has meant they have been extensively studied and catalogued, whilst the more typical forms of rural settlement design tend to be overlooked. We suffer from the same elite-bias today perhaps, preserving the remains of 'the great, the good and the wealthy' (the

104 Chûn Castle, Cornwall. *Kite photograph courtesy of Hamish Fenton*

mansion, stately home and townhouse) at the expense of the typical and everyday abode (the terraced house, farm labourers cottage or urban slum).

For most people, being 'Roman' was probably well beyond their financial means and may well have conflicted with their feelings of identity and community. Villas tend to occur only in those areas of Britain where the soils are rich – rich enough to support the necessary levels of agricultural surplus production required to generate significant levels of wealth. One might also add that villas would only occur in those areas of Britain where the benefit of being 'Roman' was considered to be significant. Villa buildings, even the relatively moderate examples

of Cottage House or aisled building were, with regard to rural settlement forms across Roman Britain, by far and away the exception. They are also a comparatively late development in the rural settlement pattern of Britain, for although there are early Romanised buildings evident in some areas of the countryside from the late first century AD (such as Fishbourne in Sussex and Eccles in Kent), the proliferation in architectural embellishment, from native-style farm (or small cottage-style house) to villa, did not occur until the mid to late third and early fourth century.

Despite all the attention afforded them, villas represent less than two per cent of the known rural settlement pattern of Britain

105 Chysauster, Cornwall. Courtyard House. *Kite photograph courtesy of Hamish Fenton*

during the first to fourth centuries AD. The majority of the rural population of Roman Britain, it would appear, saw no real benefit in becoming Romano-British.

Examples of the limited effect that Roman culture had upon rural communities can be found within the native agricultural settlements of what is now England and Wales. Here the lifestyle, nature of food production and settlement type appear to change little from the Early Iron Age into the Roman era. Sometimes the 'Roman' period farm can be shown to occupy the same general plot as its prehistoric predecessor, although sometimes with a slight shift of design, outlook or nucleus. Good agricultural land, after all, would have remained profitable,

diminishing the desire for rural populations to move elsewhere. Fields were ploughed, animals tended, metal worked, pottery manufactured, food produced, babies born and houses built in the same, traditional manner. Occasionally Roman goods, such as the odd coin, brooch or cooking pot, might appear, possibly following a good day selling surpluses at the local market, but few people would have seen benefit in radically changing their lifestyle.

Across much of Wales, away from the twin implanted civic centres of Caerwent and Carmarthen in the south, and the small number of comparatively modest villas that grew up around them in the third and fourth centuries, the settlement pat-

106 Chysauster, Cornwall

107 Fogou, Carn Euny,
Cornwall

tern remained largely unaltered throughout the Roman period. A significant number of hillforts seem to have continued in use, with no obvious sign of dismantling or forcible resettlement. At Tre'r Ceiri, on the Lleyn peninsula in Gwynedd, a drystone wall enclosed a large number of circular and sub-circular hut platforms (in excess of 140 are known). Although not all the houses were contemporary, it is clear from the small range of imported pottery vessels that the main phase of occupation was between the mid second and the very early fifth century AD. Din Lligwy, on Anglesey, appears to have been the fortified residence of an individual family or small clan group, comprising four rectangular structures and two roundhouses surrounded by an impressive stone wall. It is not known whether all the units were contemporary, though dating evidence suggests creation in the mid to late fourth century AD.

In the north of England, the picture with regard to rural settlement is broadly similar, although here the Roman army represented a more considerable presence, the area between York and Newcastle/Carlisle representing the most densely militarised zone in the British Isles. As noted in Chapter 4, the combination of dispersed, decentralised society and upland terrain meant that

108 The unenclosed roundhouse 'Roman'-period settlement Cefn Cwmwd, Anglesey. *Courtesy of John Hodgson*

109 Clay-walled 'Roman'-period roundhouse at Melyn y Plas, Anglesey. *Courtesy of John Hodgson*

110 Enclosed upland settlement at Castle Hill, Lancashire. *Courtesy of John Hodgson*

111 Enclosed upland settlement at Warton Crag, Lancashire. *Courtesy of John Hodgson*

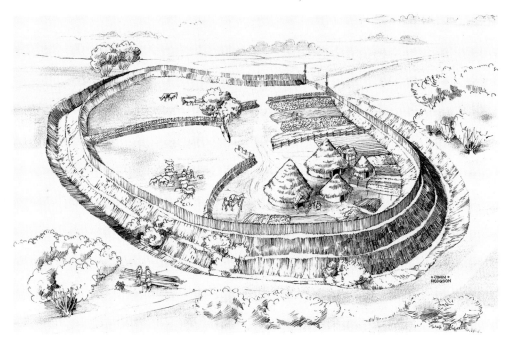

112 Enclosed 'Roman'-period settlement at Grovely Wood, Wilton, Wiltshire. *Courtesy of John Hodgson*

Rome found it difficult to govern northern England without significant numbers of troops. The presence of such a garrison, however, effectively retarded the development of a native elite, limiting the kind of indigenous political structures that central government found it convenient to delegate power to in the southern lowlands. Late Roman villas do appear here, concentrating in the East Riding, but in relatively low numbers when compared to the south and east of England.

Elsewhere, so-called in northern England, 'native' sites predominate, clusters of 1–3 roundhouses set within oval or roughly rectangular walled enclosures, on average less than 0.4ha in area, surrounded by field systems and paddocks. Houses are often placed around a central, somewhat sunken courtyard. The reasons for the courtyard being at a lower level may reflect the need for drainage from the houses or from the deliberate removal of earth in order to provide more

spoil for the construction of the enclosure banks. Alternatively, the effect may derive from the fact that the house platforms themselves contain more uncleared structural debris than the courtyard areas they surround. Despite the presence of field banks, it is clear that, given the relatively marginal nature of the land, many upland settlements relied predominantly upon the rearing of livestock rather than arable cultivation. The artefact assemblages recovered from such sites tend to support this view, with loom weights and spindle whorls (suggesting extensive weaving activity) clearly dominating the numbers of sickles and querns.

A variety of settlement forms are known in Cornwall and the west. Chysauster is often cited as the 'classic' Cornish form of native settlement; it is certainly the best preserved, and, in its present form, needs little in the way of imagination to picture the site in its heyday. At least nine roughly oval stone-walled houses are known, eight

113 A rural Romano–British longhouse excavated as part of the Durotriges Project at Bournemouth University in 2010

114 A rural longhouse of the 'Romano-British' period recreated at Upton Country Park, Poole, Dorset

arranged in pairs. Field systems, apparently contemporary, surround the settlement. The style of domestic build is referred to as a 'Courtyard House', each with an entrance facing in a broad north-east to east direction, away from the prevailing wind. A terraced/embanked area to the side of each entrance may originally have formed a small allotment or kitchen garden, providing additional foodstuffs growing under the watchful eye of the house owner. Each courtyard was probably open to the sky, a series of covered cells/rooms facing out into it. The largest cell, lying directly across from the entrance, may have served as the main residential unit for each Courtyard House; smaller rooms at one side of the entrance probably acted as storage facilities or areas for specific craft or production activities. All houses possessed good drainage facilities, possibly in order to sluice animal waste from the residential area, assuming of course that, as with a later medieval longhouse, livestock was kept with the family. The vast majority of artefactual material retrieved during the excavation of each house was derived from the largest cell/room. Pottery indicates activity in the first century BC with the main settlement phase being between the mid first to later second century AD. Chysauster may have been abandoned by around AD 300.

A feature that the majority of 'typical' Courtyard House settlements appear to possess is the *fogou*. The *fogou* is a subterranean passage or gallery (the name means 'cave' in Cornish) accessed directly from one of the houses. Interpretation of the *fogou* varies, a problem that is not helped by the general absence of artefacts that could help identify function. They have at times been viewed as food storage facilities, akin perhaps to the ice houses of seventeenth- and eighteenth-century stately homes, ritual passageways and bolt-holes, bunkers in which the residents could hide in times of attack. Given the obvious nature of the *fogou* at ground level, the storage facility combined, perhaps, with some religious element, may not be too far off the mark.

Stone-walled Courtyard-style houses such as Chysauster and Carn Euny are usually found in close proximity to a hill-fort. Some view the relationship between defended hillfort enclosure and more open settlement as essentially friendly, assuming of course that both were broadly contemporary, the hillfort acting as a place of refuge at times of severe stress. Others see the placement in rather more sinister terms, the houses perhaps being in some way subservient to the enclosure; Iron Age serfs within sight of their lord and master. There is no way that we can realistically resolve the issue, although the quantity of status objects retrieved from within Courtyard Houses seems to indicate that these were probably not the abode of hard-up farm labourers.

In southern England, within areas thought to be predominantly 'Roman' in outlook, the native rural settlement predominates. Along the eastern slopes of Thundersbarrow Hill, West Sussex, a settlement developed alongside a pronounced sunken droveway, outside the remains of a disused hilltop enclosure of the Early Iron Age. Artefact remains suggest a largely unbroken period of settlement activity here from the late first century BC to the mid fourth century AD

and, although there can be no definite proof, it is understandably tempting to think of the villagers as the descendants of those that had previously occupied the hilltop enclosure. A series of grain storage pits, corn-drying ovens/malting floors, possibly used in the production of beer, and other features were examined during the course of the excavation, although little is known about the structural nature of domestic buildings. Linear field banks spread all around and up to the disused enclosure and, whatever their origin, these seem to have been broadly maintained into the Roman period.

Settlements of comparable nature to Thundersbarrow, and displaying a similar range of finds (including both local and Romano-British fine ware pottery), have also been investigated across Hampshire, Dorset and Wiltshire, most famously at Chalton, Rotherley and Woodcuts. At Chalton, in Hampshire, a settlement akin to Thundersbarrow, comprising rectangular timber houses set within droveways and field systems, has been recorded, whilst at Rotherley the principal house appears to have been set within a circular enclosure. The main elements of the economy at such sites were, as far as could be ascertained, purely arable, native houses being closely associated with field systems, animal pens, threshing floors, corn dryers, granaries and storage pits, whilst carbonised seed, animal bone (mostly sheep), pottery 'cheese presses', loom weights and spindle whorls were all in evidence.

At Park Brow, in West Sussex, a range of domestic units displaying a certain degree of Roman influence have been traced along both sides of a sunken droveway and associated field systems. Excavations across an area of settlement spanning the Late Iron Age and Early Roman period revealed five rectangular timber buildings within an area of pits, associated postholes and boundary ditches. One of the five rectangular buildings was set in a small terraced platform, its walls constructed of timber with wattle and daub infill. Although not nearly approaching the wealth and prestige of a villa, the interior of the main house had been keyed with deep gouges in order to receive a layer of simple red-painted plaster. Finds suggested a roof of red tile whilst window glass and an iron door key suggest further elements of a more Roman lifestyle. Similar evidence has been found at Woodcuts, an otherwise non-Roman farmstead in Dorset, comprising corn driers, storage pits and a domestic structure provided with wall plaster at some point in the later second or early third century.

It is not sure whether the Park Brow and Woodcuts settlements represented small, closely associated kin groups or the successive development of individual, unrelated structures. One view, which has gained currency in recent years, is that such clusters of prehistoric buildings were perhaps the product of a single phase of family or kin-group occupancy, each structure performing a subtly different purpose. In such a model, an individual 'hut' would be the equivalent of a single room in a house or villa. A cluster of huts, as represented at Park Brow, would not therefore have functioned as a village or hamlet of different families or individuals, but as a 'household', possibly for no more than a single extended family.

A common feature at a number of 'native' rural settlements and, indeed, small Cottage-style and aisled villa sites across lowland Britain, is the so-called 'corn drier'. In basic form the corn drier comprises a Y- or T-shaped channel, usually cut into the ground and lined with stone, with a hearth or fire-pit at one end and evident signs of heat-discolouration and burning throughout. Well-preserved examples have shown that the channels acted as flues, conveying heat beneath the floor of an above-ground structure of stone or timber, upon which, it is likely, grain was spread in order to dry large amounts quickly. Experimental work, such as that conducted at sites like Butser Ancient Farm in Hampshire, has demonstrated that 'grain driers' may plausibly have also been used as malting floors – barley grain being encouraged to sprout in the warm and well-ventilated atmosphere of the building – in order to manufacture large amounts of beer; probably the most UnMediterranean of alcoholic drinks.

Unfortunately, rural settlement has, until fairly recently, received little consideration within the context of Romano-British studies, especially when compared with the more monumental villa estates. This is unfortunate for, although they are perhaps less visually impressive than a site with stone walls, mosaic and a bath house, they would appear to be closer to the norm as far as regards rural settlement of the period. However these so-called 'peasant' settlements are interpreted, it is clear that, even by the third century, contact with the Roman markets had, only at a comparatively low level, begun to affect (and infect) the attitudes of farming communities. There's little evidence that the occupants of such rural sites had any desire to be (or to be seen as) fully integrated members of Roman society, unlike the villa owners, even though they were willing, on occasion, to purchase certain objects and buy into a few minor aspects of Roman (or Romano-British) culture in order to facilitate and improve their own lifestyle.

6

BRITANNIA – REBEL EMPIRE

I T probably can't be emphasised enough the extent to which Britain's fate within the Empire was dictated by the timing of the occupation. There seems little doubt that eventually, if Rome had arrived earlier in Britain, Britain would have ended up being significantly less UnRoman, and perhaps even really Roman. However unenthusiastic about Rome the Britons were, if Rome had stayed permanently, they would presumably eventually have got used to the idea and been more completely assimilated.

By the time Rome invaded Britain in 43, northern Gaul had been under Roman rule for almost a century, and Roman Africa, plus parts of Spain and parts of southern Gaul, had already been under Roman rule for up to two centuries.

In addition, the mere date of the start of Romanisation was only the beginning of the story. The example of other provinces demonstrates that it could take a long, long time for a territory really to settle down under Roman control. There were still revolts in Gaul well into the first century AD. In 21, the revolt of Florus and Sacrovir affected almost every tribe, according to Tacitus, but particularly the Aedui, Sequani, Treveri, Andecavi and Turoni.[111] While in 68 Vindex, a Roman governor in Gaul, but with an aristocratic Aquitanian background, rose against Nero. In 70, a revolt of the Batavians and Frisians under one Claudius Civilis led to a wider rebellion against Rome in Gaul, featuring the tribes of the Treveri, Lingones and Nervii. With many of the rebels thinking that the civil wars and chaos of the era after Nero's death meant that the Roman Empire was coming to an end, the idea of creating a separate Gallic Empire (*Imperium Galliarum*) was even raised, but past tribal grudges prevented it and eventually ensured the collapse of the rebellion.[112]

In a society with significant levels of illiteracy, it may be worth taking into account the time span over which accurate, oral memories of complex historical events can survive among families. Research suggests that the period in question is up to two centuries.[113] A recent real example of this is a person who told how his father told him that his grandmother told him that when she was young, a person came to her house and shouted up the stairs about the capture of Napoleon, 'They've ta'en Boney'.[114] Obviously, in a time when lifespans were shorter, there would have been fewer people passing on oral memories of long ago, but there were still people who lived to very old ages (one Claudia Crysis from Lincoln, for instance, is recorded as having lived to the age of 90, while in Caerleon, Julius Valens lived to the age of 100, while his wife lived to the age of 75). Moreover, in a society before television, such things would have been talked about more frequently, and their

115 The walls of Silchester. Many cities and towns in Roman Britain were given their first, often earthwork, defences in the late second century

effect would also have been strengthened by longer-lasting and more formal means of conveying oral memories, such as epic oral poetry telling of the deeds of tribal heroes.

The idea that a territory could only even begin to settle down under Roman rule after strong memories of pre-Roman rule were extinct is an interesting one and, judging by the long periods taken by some territories to settle under Rome, it may have some validity. If it is applied to Britain then we might expect Britain to be settling down some time in the early third century. And, as a matter of fact, there is some sign of something similar to that occurring.

We have already seen how rebellions against Roman rule disrupted the Romanisation process in the first century

and throughout the second century the north remained volatile. Towards the end of the second century, this volatility may even have spread south. A unique feature of Roman Britain's archaeology is that there is a programme of building defences around towns and cities earlier here than almost anywhere else in the Empire. In Gaul, most towns and cities remained undefended until the Germanic incursions of the middle of the third century. However, here in Britain most major cities and quite a few smaller ones received defences towards the end of the second century. It has been suggested that these are prestige works, to demonstrate the affluence of the town and cities involved. Some details of the defences, such as the way those of Towcester cut through existing town blocks, suggest more strongly that these were created for some urgent defensive purpose. This interpretation is strengthened by the fact that, of the smaller towns defended, many are near *civitas* boundaries, suggesting a defensive scheme based around the *civitates*. Bearing in mind the probable surviving strength of tribal identities in Britain, such a move would be perfectly understandable. It's hard to know precisely what crisis could have sparked this rash of expensive defensive construction, but it may be connected to hints of a rebellion among the Brigantes early in the second half of the second century.[115]

Beyond this, though, there are few signs of tribes to the south of Hadrian's Wall rebelling in the third century. This is not to say that Britain was necessarily content with or enthusiastic about Roman rule, but that memories of pre-Roman Britain were fading and that discontent in Britain was liable to show itself in ways other than open tribal rebellion.

An indication of what was to come, in the third century, is first seen in events at the end of the second century AD, for increasingly rebelliousness inside Roman Britain seems to have been demonstrated not in conflict with the Roman army in Britain, but through, and in association with, the Roman army in Britain. This, as Zosimus helpfully points out in an account of later events, eventually came to incorporate some of the 'most aggressive and rebellious' soldiers of the Roman army.[116]

Already in AD 185 the army in Britain was mutinous and sent a deputation of 1500 to Rome to complain to the emperor Commodus about unpopular measures taken by one Perennis, praetorian prefect. Shortly afterwards, Pertinax, a strict disciplinarian, was sent to Britain to get a grip on the situation. There seems to have been some attempt by the army to set Pertinax up as a rival emperor to Commodus. However, he resisted this, only for a legion to rebel. He survived and took harsh measures against the mutineers only to be forced to resign in 187 because of complaints from the troops.

A few years' later the Roman army in Britain was again ready to rebel and make its first grab for power. On the last day of AD 192, the praetorian prefect arranged the killing of Commodus and set Pertinax up in his place. Pertinax, however, seems to have found it as hard to win popularity in Rome as he had in Britain and after a reign of 87 days the praetorian guard murdered him as well and auctioned off the imperial throne to the highest bidder. One Didius Julianus had the dubious distinction of winning this auction, but across the Empire three commanders, Clodius Albinus in Britain, Pescennius Niger in Syria and Septimius Severus in Pannonia, refused to accept the new emperor and prepared their own bids for power.

Septimius Severus was the first to make for Rome and took control there, after the praetorians murdered Didius Julianus. Severus then bought himself time to tackle Pescennius Niger by designating Clodius Albinus his junior partner and successor. After Severus defeated and killed Pescennius Niger, however, things seem to have gone downhill between Severus and Albinus, and in 196 Severus made a failed attempt to assassinate Albinus. Albinus' response was to invade Gaul with as large an army as he could gather. Dio Cassius indicates that his army was 150,000 strong when he met Severus' similarly sized army outside Lyons. The figure, if that's what the writer meant, must be a huge exaggeration but it may still indicate that Albinus had managed to gather a very large force, in which case his army may have included significant numbers of fresh British recruits in addition to those Britons already in the regular forces. Certainly Severus is shown by Herodian, a near-contemporary, as referring to Albinus' forces as 'island-bred' which may be more than just a general reference to the army's origins. This first great continental jaunt of the British army, however, was not to go well for them. After a long, hard-fought battle, Albinus' forces were defeated and he was killed.

This was the first major rebellion involving the Roman army in Britain but it was just the first of many that were to come over the next centuries and it's worth pausing for a moment to consider the position of the Roman army in Britain and what might have been causing this rebelliousness.

To start with, it has to be pointed out that the Roman forces stationed in Britain were by no means the only ones rebelling against central Roman authority in the third and fourth centuries. Such rebellions were endemic in the period across large parts of the Empire. Britain, however, for the longevity and impact of its rebellions on the main flow of Roman history, deserves a special mention.

Part of this is, of course, attributable to the way Rome's failure to conquer Ireland and Scotland necessitated the long-term stationing of large numbers of troops. In the third century, a significant part of the entire Roman army was stationed in Britain, with three legions and numerous auxiliary and support units.

Part of the British legions' long and distinguished career as rebels was also down to the sheer geography of the territory. The fact that Britain was an island made it easy for rebellions to grow. As long as any rebels could get the troops of the army in Britain on their side, then the Channel and the North Sea made it extremely hard for central authorities rapidly to reimpose control.

However, there may be even more to the rebelliousness of the legions in Britain and it may be connected with some of the core issues linked to Roman Britain's UnRoman nature.

We have already seen how the beginnings of the Roman army in Britain's career of rebelliousness coincided roughly with the ending of direct tribal rebellions in Roman-controlled Britain. There are a number of possible reasons for this.

There is no doubt an element of pure coincidence about it. Britain's period of settling down under Roman rule happened to coincide with a period when civil conflict was becoming endemic across the Empire and, inevitably perhaps, the legions in Britain were affected by this.

There may also be something of a cause and effect situation. It is possible that fewer campaigns north of Hadrian's Wall in the third century, led to boredom and discontent among the legions in Britain due to a lack of opportunities for action, rewards, booty and promotion. Having said that, it's very noticeable that as the security situation north of the wall and across the North Sea deteriorated through the fourth century, the army in Britain showed no sign at all of becoming less rebellious.

It may be that we need to consider another factor.

In the first century AD legionaries and auxiliaries were often recruited in one region of the Roman Empire and despatched to serve and fight in another. Gaul, Spain and Italy, for instance, were originally the most common sources of legionaries in Britain,[117] while the majority of auxiliary units sent to Britain had originally been raised in the areas of Germany, Gaul and the Danubian provinces.[118]

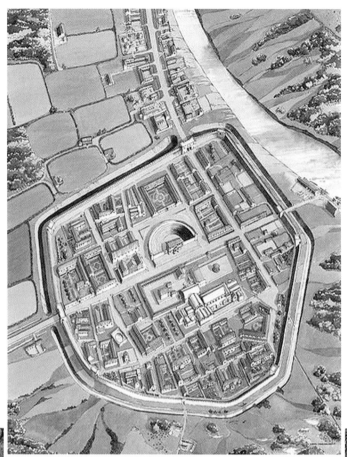

116 Reconstruction of Bath.
Courtesy of John Hodgson

117 The walls of Cirencester

118 Reconstruction of the gateway into *Durnovaria* (Dorchester, Dorset) in the Roman period. *Courtesy of John Hodgson*

Inevitably, though, particularly where units were stationed in the same location for decades and even longer, strong bonds did form with the local communities. Even if marriage was, at first, forbidden to ordinary serving soldiers, there was nothing to stop the soldiers finding themselves local long-term girlfriends and having children with them. In addition, many veterans on retirement from the army would settle and marry close to where they had served rather than returning to distant (both chronologically and geographically) homelands. Legionaries were normally recruited from citizens, and veterans from the auxiliary units were also made citizens on retirement and would have passed citizenship onto their children. In this way, there grew up communities tied both to the local population and to the army.

We know of two British women by name married to one definite foreigner and one possible foreigner with probable military connections. An already mentioned tombstone from South Shields, records Regina, the Catuvellaunian, married to Barates, a Palmyrene, who most probably was linked to the military in some way; while another tombstone from Templeborough records Verecunda Rufilia, a Dobunnic woman and wife of Excingus, who may have been a soldier in *Cohors III Gallorum* at the fort there.

In the second century, with the expansion of the Empire grinding to a halt, units increasingly recruited from the areas where they were stationed,[119] and this practice became even more widespread in the third century, after Septimius Severus allowed serving soldiers to marry and Caracalla made all inhabitants of the Roman Empire citizens, and therefore eligible for the legions. There was still, of course, some movement. Recruits from areas where no units were stationed would, for instance, have to serve elsewhere, as would the increasing number of recruits born outside the Empire. There are a number of recorded instances of captives from outside the Empire being sent to Britain to serve with the Roman army, which may be a sign that the manpower needs in Britain were too large to be filled from local recruitment alone. Equally, there was still some unit mobility, where units would be moved from their positions either for long-term strategic redeployment or short-term tactical needs. There is, for instance, evidence of a detachment from the Twentieth Legion at Chester being in Germany at Mainz, in around 255, and a tombstone at Caerleon mentions a soldier Tadius Exupertus killed on an unspecified 'German' expedition. It's interesting to note that Tadius' mother who was buried in the military settlement at Caerleon has the distinctly Celtic name Tadia Vallaunius, so she and he may well have been locals. Finally, in the fourth century, recruitment was made hereditary and obligatory.

In other words, in the second and even more so in the third and fourth centuries, the Roman army in Britain was increasingly becoming an army that had a significant proportion of its troops recruited from people born in Britain. Thus, a second-century Gloucester man is recorded enrolling in a unit stationed in Britain and in the late second century a man from the *civitas Brigantium* is recorded serving at Mumrills. It's very hard to be certain about specific percentages. Due to the size of the garrison in Britain, and due to British lack of enthusiasm for Rome, the process of the army becoming local may have progressed more slowly than in other parts of the Empire.[120]

However, as indicated previously, already by the time of Clodius Albinus, the historian Herodian has Severus referring to Albinus' forces as 'island-bred'[121] and depicts the conflict as a battle between Britons and Illyrians (Severus' men), and certainly by the third century, evidence from elsewhere in the Empire suggests that most legionaries recruited, where their origins can be determined, were local.[122] *Legio III Augusta*, for instance, stationed at Lambaesis in Algeria, originally recruited in Africa, then in Numidia, and in the end actually in Lambaesis.[123] The Roman army in Britain, therefore, must eventually, particularly in the later third and fourth centuries, have acquired a somewhat British flavour – not British in a narrow sense, since the military areas would still have been far more cosmopolitan than most of Roman Britain, but British nonetheless. For whatever reasons, as significant numbers of Britons were increasingly being absorbed into the Roman army in Britain, that army seems decreasingly likely to be found fighting Britons in Britain, and increasingly likely to be found in conflict with Romans in mainland Europe. Local priorities would have taken over from imperial ones in a similar way to that recorded for some legions in Gaul in the fourth century. When Constantius ordered Gallic legions to be sent to the east of the Empire, they refused to go, because they didn't want to leave Gaul. They preferred to rebel, attempting to raise Julian to be emperor, and even though Julian declined their offer he had to reassure them that they would not be asked to serve beyond the Alps.[124]

After early moves at the end of the second century, the army in Britain really started on its career of rebellion in the middle of the third century. As a result of the activities of Clodius Albinus, Septimius Severus, or his son Caracalla, had divided Britain into two separate provinces, with the aim of making rebellions in the country less likely. It is not a measure that seems to have had much impact.

If, as oral memory faded, many ordinary Britons were in some, perhaps reluctant, sense beginning to accept the presence of Rome 200 years after the invasion, what they were accepting was not the Rome of its glory days in the first and early second centuries AD. This was not the Rome that territories conquered earlier had come to embrace, a world superpower, confident and constantly expanding with an imperial ethos that emphasised Rome's natural right to rule and civilise the world. The Rome of the mid third century was a much less attractive proposition for anybody thinking of buying metaphorical shares in it. The last emperor of the Severan line, Severus Alexander, had been killed in 235. From then on, for most of the rest of the third century Rome was ruled by a succession of generals, who mostly murdered their way to the throne and were fairly shortly afterwards despatched by another general making the same journey. And there were more problems in store in addition to civil war. Beyond the Rhine/Danube frontiers, barbarian peoples were on the move and in the East the ailing Parthian Empire, long Rome's eastern neighbour, had been replaced by an aggressive, self-confident new force, the Sassanid Empire. In 251, the emperor Trajan Decius was killed by an army of Goths, the first Roman emperor ever to fall in battle against a foreign enemy. It is hard to overestimate the impact this news would have had on the inhabitants of the Empire. The Empire had lost battles against 'barbarians' before, but to lose the emperor himself in such a defeat was unprecedented. Then, less than 10 years later, it happened again. This time Valerian, having left his son and co-emperor

119 Statue of Septimius Severus. © *Trustees of the British Museum*

Gallienus in the West, was captured by Sassanids, and though it is not certain when he actually died, he was lost to the Empire from that point onwards. With things spiralling out of control, and with the Empire in need of loyalty from every one of its inhabitants, the British army did exactly what one would have expected, and rebelled, joining

120 Tile with the stamp of the Fourteenth Legion, which probably played a key role in fighting Boudicca

in an act of mass secession that took Britain and another large chunk of western Europe out of the central Empire for 13 years.

Looking back on the history of the Roman Empire we tend to see a broad, sweeping narrative that ends in Britain in around 410 and in the western Empire as a whole in 476. Our minds are pre-conditioned, when we look at any point prior to those dates, to see it as a fixed point on that immutable course. Logically, we know that contemporaries experiencing the events would not have seen the situation in the same way, and would have had no idea how long Roman power could last. A Briton in the mid third century might have assumed it would last forever, or they might have thought it would end in a few months, and frankly, when we look at the history of the period, the latter option at times must have seemed a lot more plausible.

In AD 260, a general called Postumus rebelled against Gallienus, killed his son Saloninus who had been made co-emperor with Gallienus after the capture of Valerian, and formed a separate empire alongside the Roman Empire. This separate empire is usually today known as the Gallic Empire, the '*Imperium Galliarum*'. It is the name that the Gallic rebels of 70 had used for their idea of a separate empire created at a time when they had thought the Roman Empire was coming to an end.

Postumus established his capital at Cologne and his rule was recognised in Britain, Spain and almost all of Gaul. He seems to have campaigned against Germanic invaders and he took the title of *Germanicus Maximus* presumably to indicate a victory against Germanic tribes. In AD 265 Gallienus attempted to crush the Gallic Empire on two occasions but failed on both. In 268, Postumus had the opportunity to invade Italy when Aureolus, one of Gallienus' commanders and stationed in Milan, rebelled in support of Postumus. Postumus could have used the incident to mount an invasion, but did not, and Aureolus finally surrendered to Gallienus' successor. In 269, Laelianus rose in rebellion against Postumus at Mainz. Postumus took Mainz and Laelianus was probably killed, but so was Postumus by his own troops when he refused to let them sack Mainz.

The troops then raised one Marius, allegedly a former blacksmith, to the throne of the Gallic Empire briefly, before he too was killed, and Victorinus, who had been tribune of the praetorians for the Gallic Empire and a co-consul with Postumus, was made emperor in his place. Victorinus does not seem to have been recognised in Spain, but was still recognised in Britain and much of Gaul and kept the capital of the Gallic Empire at Cologne.[125] His position was, however, threatened by a revolt at Autun which declared for the central emperor, Gallienus' successor, Claudius II Gothicus. After a siege, Victorinus managed to recapture and partly destroy Autun in the summer of AD 270. However, by early 271 Victorinus was himself dead, killed by one of his own officers, allegedly unhappy about an attempt by Victorinus to seduce the officer's wife.

Two coins of a certain Domitianus have been found which seem to date to around this period and he may have been a short-lived claimant to the throne of the Gallic Empire in the confusion after Victorinus' death. One of these incredibly rare coins comes from Britain, from Chalgrove near Oxford, while the other was found in the Loire region of France. This could imply Domitianus' activities were concentrated somewhere in Britain and/or north-western France, so in an intriguing sense Domitianus might be considered Britain's lost emperor. Ultimately, however, it was Tetricus, the governor of *Aquitania*, who was to become the last emperor of the Gallic Empire. Tetricus again was recognised in Britain and much of Gaul, but

121 Tombstone of Flavinus, a standard bearer in the Ala Petriana. *Courtesy of Hexham Abbey*

not in Spain. He campaigned successfully against Germanic raiders, made Trier his capital instead of Cologne, and managed to extend the borders of the Gallic Empire a little by retaking ground from the central Empire in south-eastern *Aquitania* and western *Narbonensis*. However, a new central emperor, Aurelian, successfully reimposed his authority in the east, though his prior abandonment of *Dacia* (roughly equating with modern-day Romania south of the Carpathian Mountains), the only European province conquered later than Britain, must

122 Roman legionaries and auxiliaries in action with the emperor, as shown on Trajan's Column in Rome

have been a huge shock to inhabitants of the Empire and in many ways served to underline the fragility of the Empire's hold on its less Romanised provinces. When Aurelian finally turned his attentions to the Gallic Empire, the decisive battle came near Châlons sur Marne in 274 and after bitter fighting Tetricus' forces were defeated. Tetricus, however, was spared by Aurelian and lived quietly in Italy to an advanced age.

As indicated, the Empire of Postumus and his successors is usually called the Gallic Empire, but in fact the name is seriously misleading, particularly as regards Britain, since it has tended to minimise Britain's key role in the Empire. A better name for the Empire would be the Channel Empire. Postumus himself seems to have control-led most of Spain, Gaul, Britain and the Rhineland. However, his successors lost

Spain and southern Gaul, and it is fairly clear that the heart of the insurgency was Britain, northern Gaul and the Rhineland, territo-ries on either side of the Channel.

There are two main views of the Gallic Empire, with a range of more nuanced views between the two extremes.

At one end of the spectrum, there are those who regard the Gallic Empire as little more than a rebel part of the Roman Empire. They point to the fact that concern for the neglected Rhineland defences may have played a key part in Postumus' initial decision to rebel, and in the support given him by the population of the territories he controlled. They highlight the point that coinage of the Gallic emperors lies, in many ways, in the mainstream of Roman imperial coinage, using the same iconography and many of the same messages.[126] They point

123 Depiction on the Column of Marcus Aurelius in Rome showing late second-century Roman troops in action against an unRomanised culture

out that Postumus in some ways emphasises his connections to Rome by doing things in Roman ways within his empire. For instance, the Gallic Empire had consuls like Rome, and a praetorian guard like Rome. They underline the fact that the secession from Rome was not permanent and that, at the end of it, the Gallic Empire rejoined the main empire apparently fairly smoothly with few reprisals.[127]

At the other end of the spectrum are those who regard the Gallic Empire as a secession that represented a genuine regional desire for freedom and separation from the Roman Empire. They point out that the biography of Gallienus in the *Historia Augusta*, charting the rise of the Gallic Empire, refers to the Gauls as a people, selecting Postumus as emperor.[128] They state that none of the Gallic emperors ever made

any attempt to invade Italy or take over the whole Empire, as would have been the normal course of a provincial rebel in the third century. They point to the appearance of local deities, Hercules Magusanus and Hercules Deusoniensis, on the coins of Postumus, alongside the usual classical deities. It is mildly interesting to note that in a description of Tetricus in a procession he is portrayed wearing a red cloak, a yellow tunic and specifically Gallic trousers![129]

As so often, the truth probably lies between the two extremes. It would, without doubt, be wrong to see Postumus and his successors as Gallic or Celtic freedom fighters with a modern view of Celtic or Gallic nationalism. There is no doubt that many, perhaps all, of the key figures had risen through the Roman system and were in many ways a part of it. Equally, it seems

124 Carving from Adamclisi showing a heavily armed Roman soldier attacking locals

126 Tombstone from South Shields recording Regina, a Catuvellaunian woman married to Barates, a Palmyrene. *Courtesy of Arbeia Museum*

127 Tombstone from Caerleon of Tadius Exupertus and his mother Tadia Vallaunius. *Courtesy of Caerleon Museum*

128 View of the *vicus*, the settlement outside Housesteads fort

likely that Postumus' initial military priority was indeed defending Gaul and the Channel area from barbarian incursions from the East rather than defending it from Rome.

However, there does seem to be somewhat more to the Gallic Empire than it being simply a rebel section of the Empire.

While the later Gallic emperors may have been too weak militarily and politically to try to seize Italy and control of the rest of the Empire, Postumus seems to have made a deliberate decision not to do so. When Aureolus seized control of Milan and declared for Postumus, it would have been a perfect opportunity for Postumus to invade Italy. Instead he stayed in Gaul. Even the presence of such Roman institutions as consuls and praetorian guards within the Gallic Empire in some ways emphasises the difference between it and more normal rebellions.

While ordinary rebels aspired to capture Rome and take control of the central system of consuls and praetorian guards, by setting up his own versions Postumus specifically emphasised the separate nature of the Gallic Empire.

Perhaps the strongest evidence that something specific, regional and UnRoman is going on is the geography of the Empire itself, particularly as regards Gaul. There was a significant cultural split in Gaul between the Romanised south and the much less Romanised centre and north, known in the early period by the Romans as *Gallia Comata*, or long-haired Gaul, from the custom of the locals of wearing their hair long in the Celtic style. Postumus seems to have controlled both southern and northern Gaul, but under Victorinus, inscriptions referring to the central emperor Claudius

Gothicus appear in the south of Gaul. In other words, support for the Gallic Empire was strongest in the least Romanised parts of Gaul, in the same areas that had provided the strongest support for the original *Imperium Galliarum* in the first century AD.

Economic factors may have helped this regionalism. There is plenty of evidence under the Empire of regional trade networks developing that linked Britain with other key areas of the Gallic Empire. An inscription from London, for instance, records one Tiberius Celerianus, involved in shipping in some form, and a citizen of the Bellovaci, in modern-day Belgium. There's a trader from *Gallia Lugdunensis*, Lucius Viducius Placidus, mentioned in an early third-century inscription from York. While at Domburg in Holland, there's a merchant specialising in the pottery trade with Britain, called Marcus Secundinius Silvanus, mentioned on an altar.[130]

Interestingly, at almost exactly the same time that the Gallic emperors were tearing a chunk off one end of the Roman Empire to create a separate regional domain, at the other end of the Empire, in another area of only partial Romanisation, someone else was doing pretty much the same. In the chaos after the defeat and capture of Valerian, Odaenathus, the king of the wealthy semi-Romanised city of Palmyra, took control of the East. At first, he seems to have done this with the agreement of Gallienus, who was just content to have somebody defending the Empire's eastern border against the Sassanids. However, eventually, under Odaenathus' widow, the formidable Zenobia, and their son Vabalathus, the so-called Palmyrene Empire came to dominate large parts of Rome's eastern territories, from Egypt in the south to Antioch in the north. As with the Gallic Empire, there is controversy over the extent to which the Palmyrene Empire was a move

129 Third-century tombstone of a standard bearer. *Courtesy of Chesters Museum*

for regional autonomy or a more conventional rebellion. Vabalathus did, for instance, issue coins bearing his head as well as that of the central emperor Aurelian. However, as we shall see later with another British rebel, having the central emperor on your coins does not necessarily mean you recognise their authority and the forces of Palmyra did violently occupy Egypt capturing the Roman prefect of Egypt in the process, and when Aurelian moved against them, in the period before their defeat at his hands, Vabalathus and Zenobia issued coins in their own names, with no reference to Aurelian.

It may be that we should not see the Gallic emperors as specifically anti-Roman. Perhaps we should instead see a situation

130 Milestone of Tetricus. *Courtesy of Rockbourne Roman Villa, Hampshire County Council*

where they were, like many of the people in the heartland of the rebellion, indifferent to Rome. If Rome served their purposes, they would use it; if it did not, they were happy to abandon it.

It seems likely that all the Gallic emperors were locals. Postumus is described as of humble birth, and it has been suggested from the appearance of deities local to the Rhineland on some of his coins that he may have been Batavian. Victorinus' mother seems to have been a Gallic aristocrat. And one of Tetricus' names is Esuvuius which is very Celtic. Their priorities and loyalties it would seem were local too, as were those of the inhabitants of the key Channel Empire areas of Britain, northern Gaul and the Rhineland.

Our evidence for what was happening in Britain under the Gallic emperors is fairly

thin. This is not entirely surprising since the surviving evidence for the Gallic Empire as a whole is not extensive and as always Britain would have seemed a far-off and distant land to Roman historians.

What we can say is that the extensive number of milestones found here that refer to the Gallic emperors seem to suggest solid support for the secession.[131] There is also evidence of some activity in military circles. A certain amount of work was done on restoring military bases. For instance, at Lancaster a unit known as the *Ala Sebosiana* (boasting the new epithet *Postumianae* out of loyalty to Postumus) restored, under the direction of Flavius Ammausius, prefect of cavalry, the bath house and a basilica exercise hall, and it is possible that work was done on some of the Saxon Shore Forts during the period of the Gallic Empire.[132] Some of the Gallic Empire activity in Britain may be linked to the island playing an important financial role in the Gallic Empire. Postumus had access to the Spanish mines for at least the vast majority of his reign but his successors did not. In that situation, the British silver mines could well have acquired major importance.[133]

It is also possible that one controversial aspect of late third-century archaeology in Britain may be linked to a reassertion of local priorities over those of Rome.

The third century in Britain sees a collapse in the number of public buildings being erected in cities within Britain.[134] By contrast, work on villas seems to dip comparatively slightly in the early to mid third century and then increase hugely in the later third century, and the number of rooms occupied in villas seems to increase fairly steadily through the third century.[135] In addition, comparative data from a number of major pottery industries suggests, after a slight dip in the early third century, a strong recovery in the second half of the third century.[136] Some of this economic resurgence may be linked to a decline in imports but clearly a lot of people were making pots and making money in Britain in the later third century.

If it were not for the different trend in villas and the pottery industries, this fall in public buildings might simply be put down to broad factors such as reduced imperial expenditure and troops in Britain, plus a difficult economic situation connected with civil conflict and external invasion of the Empire in the second half of the third century. Certainly some of the problems in Gaul's towns in the second half of the third century seem likely to be down to the twin problems of invasion by raiders from across the Rhine and fighting between the Gallic Empire and central Empire.

However, Britain was not invaded by 'barbarians' in the second half of the third century. There is no recorded fighting between local forces of the Gallic Empire and the central Empire here, and there is no particular evidence of extensive reprisals after the fall of the Gallic Empire. Tetricus, the last Gallic emperor, for instance, was, as we have seen, allowed to retire in peace and other former high officials of the Gallic Empire seem to have been allowed to continue in their careers in the central Empire,[137] which hardly suggests brutal purges of the supporters of the Gallic Empire.

It may, therefore, be worth considering whether the decline of public building works and a rise in money spent on villas suggests something rather different in Britain. The habit of constructing Roman public buildings had, after all, in the early Empire been a sign of local aristocrats aspiring on some level to be part of the Roman world. Could it be, therefore, that by choosing to spend their money on themselves rather than on the trappings of Roman civic life, the aris-

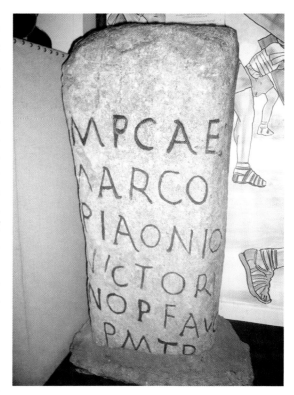

131 Milestone of Victorinus. *Courtesy of Peterborough Museum*

tocrats were demonstrating that even their brief love affair with the Roman way of running Britain was beginning to fade? It's certainly one possible factor to consider.

As much as anything, though, the evidence that the Gallic Empire was not a freak phenomenon but represented something significant about the Channel region in the third century, is that pretty much the same thing was shortly to happen again, with the rise of another breakaway empire, with Britain part of it yet again.

The years immediately after the end of the Gallic Empire saw, perhaps inevitably, more examples of revolts or unrest connected with Britain. Probus (276-82) suppressed a rebellion by a governor in Britain and is said to have sent Burgundian and Vandal prisoners to Britain to help put down further rebel-

132 Coin of Carausius '*et Fratres sui*'. © *Trustees of the British Museum*

lions, a probable sign that he knew he could not trust the army here. Around AD 281, a commander called Bonosus rebelled against Probus. His father was British and his mother Gallic and he took Cologne as his base, so he might have been attempting to recreate the Gallic Empire. If so, the attempt was a failure and he hanged himself when defeated by Probus. Shortly after, the emperor Carinus (283-285) took the title *Britannicus Maximus*, implying some kind of military triumph in Britain. If this was a successful attempt to suppress British rebelliousness, it was not successful for very long.

A few years later, in 286 or 287, Britain left the control of the central Empire again. Its leader Carausius had risen to prominence commanding ships against Frankish and Saxon pirates threatening the coast of northern Gaul. It is hard to know the precise motivations behind Carausius' rebellion. There is mention in the sources of Carausius allowing raiders through to their targets, just so he could relieve them of their booty on

their return journeys. However, since all the sources are written from a hostile viewpoint it's hard to know whether there is any truth in these allegations. Certainly, the state created by Carausius had strong echoes of the Gallic Empire.

He himself was a local, born in Menapia, and coinage evidence linked with hints in the sources suggest that, at the beginning of the rebellion, Carausius controlled substantial territory in northern Gaul (and perhaps Germany as well) in addition to controlling Britain. He even seems to have had a mint operating at Rouen.[138] It is also worth noting that again Carausius was a man who had made his name dealing with local security issues of concern to locals, and again he could, therefore, have been expected to take local defence seriously. The usage he makes of coinage too is familiar from the period of the Gallic Empire. Again, the coinage follows many traditional Roman themes, but he managed to issue an, in many ways, more impressive coinage than the central Empire,

133 Coin of Allectus. © *Trustees of the British Museum*

134 Medallion of Constantius. © *Trustees of the British Museum*

135 Reconstruction of the fort at Caistor-on-Sea, Norfolk. *Courtesy of Sue White*

136 In the distance, the late Roman walls of Portchester Castle, Hampshire, showing its closeness to the sea

137 The Roman fort at Pevensey, East Sussex

including the return of some solid silver coinage. His coinage also attempts to suggest a return to a golden age, rather explicitly in one case, with a medallion and coins carrying the acronym RSR which seems to stand for a line from Vergil, '*Redeunt Saturnia Regna*', which means 'The Saturnian [or Golden] Age Returns'.[139] Among the list of coin types are some which are designed specifically to appeal to his British citizens, including '*genius Britanni-*', and two rare issues, one a type showing Carausius as '*Restitutor Brita(anniae)*' and another showing Britain as his bride.

We can make mention of two other interesting categories of Carausian coins. One is a group of coins issued to commemorate the units loyal to him. Among the coins commemorating assorted legions is one commemorating the praetorian guard, proving that Carausius too had his own version of this.

A second category is those issued by Carausius in the name of the central emperors. Mostly these consist of individual coins issued in the name of Diocletian or Maximian, but a very rare type actually shows Carausius alongside the two other emperors with the inscription '*Carausius et fratres sui*', 'Carausius and his brothers'. These can be seen in two different ways, either as a rebel regime showing a desperation to be recognised by central authority, or as a self-confident regime cheekily asserting its equality with the central Empire. Such issues seem, however, to have ceased when Allectus took over from Carausius.

If the message of Carausius' coins was supposed to propitiate the central emperors in some way, it does not seem to have had the desired effect.

There is evidence of some kind of failed expedition against Carausius by Maximian in about AD 289, but this seems to have been followed in 293 by the recapture by Constantius, Maximian's Caesar, of Boulogne. Perhaps not surprisingly, this loss seems to have weakened the rebel regime, and shortly after the fall of Boulogne Carausius was assassinated by his chief finance officer Allectus, who then assumed power.

What followed was a pause of three years, during which Constantius gathered an invasion fleet and Allectus no doubt strengthened his defences. Construction of the Saxon Shore Forts at Portchester and Pevensey, for instance, probably started under either Carausius or Allectus, further extending an existing coastal defensive system.[140] Finally there was perhaps the Romans' last successful invasion of Britain. While Constantius was delayed by weather conditions, his praetorian prefect, Asclepiodotus, managed to dodge Allectus' navy in fog and land somewhere on the south coast, possibly somewhere near Portchester Castle. In the battle and pursuit that followed Allectus was killed, leaving the forces of the central Empire to take London and end the rebellion. It's interest-

ing to note here that Allectus' forces seem to have contained a large Frankish element. This is perhaps the first time we have evidence of large-scale Germanic forces being used in a civil war in Britain, but it was not to be the last.

The rebellion of Carausius and Allectus was the last attempt by Britain to form part of a separate empire. At the end of the Roman period, as we shall examine in Chapter 8, Britain did finally remove itself from the Empire. For the next century, instead, Britain was intermittently involved in attempts to take it over, with the first attempt (and a successful one at that), as we shall see in the next chapter, being ironically led by the son of the man who ended the separate empire of Carausius and Allectus.

However, Carausius was probably not forgotten.

It is a rare name, yet it is found recorded on a post-Roman sixth-century Christian tombstone from Penmachno.[141] Could it be that stories of Carausius as a British hero were still being told in the sixth century, just as stories of a fourth-century British rebel Magnus Maximus were?

It is even arguable that between them the Gallic Empire and this first 'British Empire' helped change the fundamentals of power within the Roman Empire. The emperor Diocletian seemed to understand the growing demands of regionalism within the Empire and he had already, before the fall of the Carausian state, split control of the Empire into a western and eastern division, with a team of two running each. Trier, for instance, became a seat of imperial power, as it had been under the Gallic Empire.

7

BRITAIN CONQUERING ROME

THE fourth century may have opened with another attempt to enforce Roman control on at least some of the Britons living north of Hadrian's Wall. Constantius is described as campaigning against the Picts shortly after he was raised from Caesar to Augustus in AD 305. It is uncertain what the aims of this campaign were, whether expansion or just punishment of tribes that had been causing trouble for the inhabitants of the Roman-controlled part of northern Britain. However, if conquest was part of Constantius' scheme then there is a very curious parallel with events almost a hundred years previously. Then the death of Septimius Severus at York put a decisive end to attempts to subjugate the Britons north of the wall. This time, it was Constantius who died at York.

And just as in AD 211, the death of Septimius allowed his son Caracalla to hurry south to pursue his imperial dream, so the death of Constantius, on 25 July AD 306, allowed his son Constantine to pursue his imperial dream and produced the first fourth-century example of the British army conquering Rome.

Under the Tetrarchic system (whereby the emperor passed power to an adopted successor, a Caesar, rather than to a son or other blood relative), Constantius should have been succeeded as emperor by the then Caesar, another Severus. Instead his father's troops proclaimed the young Constantine emperor. For a year he accepted the lesser title of Caesar to try to placate other members of the Tetrarchy. However, in AD 307 Severus was driven from power by another ex-emperor's son, in this case Maxentius son of Maximian, and Constantine took the title of Augustus.

Constantine himself had, unlike the Gallic emperors and Carausius, no personal links to the Channel area. He had been born in modern-day Serbia and his father was of local descent, while his mother Helena may have come from the eastern Mediterranean. However, there is some evidence of fairly close links between Constantine and Britain. He seems to have taken British troops to the continent to establish his capital at Trier, and coin evidence suggests that he may have visited Britain a number of times between AD 307 and 314. His adoption of the title *Britannicus Maximus* is likely to indicate some kind of military victory in Britain somewhere around the year AD 315.[142] However, Constantine was an ambitious man, and by the year AD 312, after a period of intense competition for power among a complex cast of characters, Constantine was on the move south to confront Maxentius in Italy. At the Battle of the Milvian Bridge outside Rome on 28 October AD 312, Constantine became the first person to use a rebellion in Britain to seize Rome. He was not to be the last.

138 Statue of Constantine outside York Minster

By the year 324, after further conflict, Constantine had consolidated his rule across the entire Empire and his reign brought an era of peace and stability. In Britain the first half of the fourth century seems to have been one of comparative affluence. There is not much sign of a return to the days of construction of monuments in cities. Those days seem to have been gone forever. However, the period does see significant expenditure on a number of large and imposing villas in the British countryside. From the very early to mid fourth century, for instance, the villa at Bignor was vastly expanded and some large and complex mosaics laid.

Constantine's reign also, of course, sees the arrival of Christianity as a new State religion for the Empire. Christianity had been gaining followers across the Empire in the third century. However, it is worth pointing out that none of the numerous alternative claimants to imperial power, whom Constantine beat on his path to becoming lone emperor, were Christians. Playing 'what if' with history is always a dangerous game, but it is conceivable that if the army in Britain had not been happy to rebel against the established Tetrarchic order in 306, then the Roman Empire might never have become Christian, and if the Empire had not become Christian, then the spread of Christianity would have been considerably hampered.

It's hard to know how much influence Christianity had in Britain in the early fourth century. There were clearly some Christians here. A conference was held at Arles in AD 314 to sort out a church dispute, and it was attended by three British bishops, Eborius (which may be a name or just a derivation from the Latin name of York, *Eboracum*) of York, Restitutus of London, and Adelphius, plus a priest and a deacon. The development at some stage in the late Roman period of the shrine of the martyr St Alban outside *Verulamium* may imply the existence of a Christian community there in this period, and it is possible that the Water Newton treasure, with many of its pieces bearing the Chi-Rho symbol, may date to roughly this period. Some time around 320-340 a probable church was built in the Butt Road cemetery at Colchester.[143]

However, Christianity may well not have been as widespread in Britain as it was across the Channel to the south at the same time. There had, for instance, been a significant Christian community in Lyons since at least the late second century, with writings by its bishop, St Irenaeus, still surviving. By the 320s, construction had begun on a large cathedral at Trier, and there is significant evidence of early shrines developing around burials of significant Christian figures from the third and fourth centuries – at Bonn, for instance, an altar table, perhaps connected with the martyrs Cassius and Florentius, may date as early as 260.[144] By the middle of the fourth century in Gaul, such major ecclesiastical figures as St Hilary of Poitiers and St Martin of Tours were beginning their careers.

Constantine died in 337. The result was more competition for power among family members. At first, Britain fell within the territories of Constantine II, one of Constantine's sons. However, in 340 Constantine II invaded Italy in an attempt to seize control there from Constans, another one of Constantine's sons. Instead he was defeated and killed at Aquileia and Britain fell into the hands of Constans. There may have been some trouble in Britain under Constans because he seems to have visited Britain at the beginning of 343.[145] This would have been mid-winter and it seems likely that Constans would only have made such a journey for urgent reasons. It's impossible to know precisely what these reasons were but a hint by the historian Ammianus Marcellinus suggests that the emergency may have been in some way connected with a group called the *Areani*, or *Arcani*, who were basically spies operating north of the wall.

Constans did not have a bright future. In AD 350, a palace coup at Autun saw Magnentius elevated to the throne while Constans himself was captured in flight and killed. Magnentius' rebellion in some ways mirrored those of earlier separatist emperors in the Channel area. However, Magnentius did at least briefly control a much wider territory including Italy. Briefly, though, is the word. By 353 he was dead, defeated by Constantius II, another son of Constantine, in Gaul and Constantius' man, Paul 'Catena', was spreading terror and death among the supporters of Magnentius in Britain.

Whatever peace settled on Britain after this did not last long. By 360, Constantius II had put Britain under control of his cousin Julian who was then forced by trouble on the northern frontier to send his *Magister Equitum*, Flavius Lupicinus, on an emergency mission to Britain with some of his best troops.

Seven years later, Britain was again a focus of imperial concern due to a mysterious event that became known as 'The Barbarian Conspiracy'. It is hard to know exactly what happened in this incident but it may be key to understanding the last few decades of the Roman period in Britain.

Our only information about the event comes from the works of one historian Ammianus Marcellinus. Basically what seems to have happened is that while Franks and Saxons raided the shores of Gaul, Picts, Scots and Attacotti attacked Britain. Some have thought there was actual collusion between the different groups of raiders but

139 Colossal head of Constantine in Rome

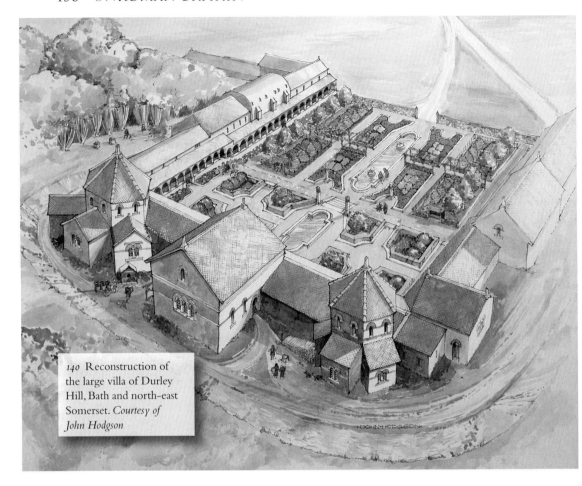

140 Reconstruction of the large villa of Durley Hill, Bath and north-east Somerset. *Courtesy of John Hodgson*

it is perhaps more likely that the raids just happened to coincide.

Whatever the background, the attacks seem to have had a fairly major impact in Britain, with a senior officer, Nectaridus, Count of the Maritime Zone, being killed and Fullofaudes, a *Dux*, being captured. A senior general, Count Theodosius, had to be sent over with four of the leading units of the field army, *Batavi*, *Heruli*, *Jovii* and *Victores*, to restore order.

There are a number of hints in the historical account that also suggest that something rather more significant than a few border raids occurred in Britain at this time. There seems to be some question of the *Areani* colluding with the attackers and it may not

just have been the *Areani* who were causing trouble. A significant number of the soldiers in Britain at this point just seem to have abandoned their posts. When Theodosius arrived in the country, he had to try to lure deserters back to the army so he could sort out the chaos. Another sign of internal trouble is the description of a rebellion in Britain by a Pannonian called Valentinus which seems to occur some time after the start of the main trouble.

The geography of the event too is mysterious. The mention of Picts, Scots and Attacotti would suggest trouble in the north and west of Britain. Yet when Theodosius arrived in Britain he encountered raiders with their booty near London. Either these raiders were adventurous Picts or Scots or Attacotti; or they were Franks or Saxons who decided to abandon raids on Gaul and try Britain; or they were either Roman deserters or Britons who decided to exploit the situation for a spot of tribal raiding of their own.

In terms of archaeology it is hard to tie down any precise link to the 'Barbarian Conspiracy'. There is little evidence of destruction that could be linked specifically to the event and only to the event, just as there is little evidence of reconstruction that could be specifically linked only to the alleged efforts of Theodosius to restore security after he brought Britain back under the control of Rome. Furthermore, where there is evidence of destruction or reconstruction, it's hard to tie it so tightly chronologically. However, there is, for instance, increasing evidence of people from north of Hadrian's Wall and possibly from Ireland present at some stage in strategic parts of southern Britain in the late Roman period, in the form of items such as the so-called 'door-knob spear butts',[146] perhaps in the period around 367, and nothing contradicts the basic idea that something rather major happened here in 367.

The best evidence that something major did happen at about the time of the 'Barbarian Conspiracy' is the archaeological evidence of developments in Britain in the years after.

The most noticeable thing is that the affluence seen in Britain in the earlier part of the fourth century seems to decline fairly markedly after the 'Barbarian Conspiracy'. If we, for instance, try to get some sense of what happened in the countryside and look at the number of rooms in villas occupied, then we see that the highest number of villa rooms occupied during the entire Roman period is during the first half of the fourth century. After 350, and certainly after 375, that figure drops massively and there is

141 Arch of Constantine showing detail of the Battle of the Milvian Bridge, as Maxentius' troops flounder in the Tiber

142 British Christianity.
Probable fourth-century church
at Butt Road, Colchester

evidence for a significant number of villas being abandoned well before the traditional end of Roman Britain.[147] In the towns too, there are signs of decline in the last decades of the fourth century. A survey has shown a decline in public activity there.[148] Similarly, if we want to get some idea of the health of the manufacturing sector we can look at figures for the introduction of new forms of pottery. Again this is at a peak in the early fourth century but after about 375 very few new forms are being introduced.[149] All in all, it seems reasonable to see 367-9 as some kind of turning point in the fortunes of Roman Britain.

This sense of major changes being under way is supported by another intriguing development in Britain some time after about 360. British-made buckles and other belt fittings start appearing across the Romanised parts of Britain in both military and non-military areas. We are used to all sectors of societies wearing buckles and belts, so to the average modern person this is unlikely to appear strange. However, traditionally only soldiers in Roman society had worn belts and buckles, and had done so in order to signify their status and to act as a way of carrying a knife, dagger or sword. It is probable that some officials, in a partly militarised civil service, also took to wearing elements of military kit, like belts, in the fourth century, but it has to be said that most published finds of similar buckles and other belt fittings in mainland Europe, so far, have come from either military contexts or military zones, like the border regions.[150]

Roman military equipment is by no means unknown on civilian sites in Roman Britain prior to this. Roman soldiers could be stationed in or travelling through civilian areas for a wide number of reasons, and the presence of significant numbers of third- and fourth-century military and official brooches in *civitas* capitals in Britain may suggest the presence there of military garrisons. However, this phenomenon seems to be different. The chronological intensity is different in the sense that, considering the short time period we are looking at (about four decades), the numbers of buckles and other belt fittings being found is proportionately much higher. And the geographical patterns are different as well. While the brooches are clearly clustered around main towns, the distribution of these buckles and other belt fittings is much less focused. Broadly speaking the picture is much more of a general distribution across town and countryside. There are some concentrations, but these are not always linked to towns.

It seems hard to escape the conclusion that these buckles and other belt fittings were mainly being manufactured and worn by British civilians; the vital question then is, 'Why?' The late Roman period did see an increasing use of jewellery and some of these buckles and belt fittings were highly decorated (though overall they tend to be smaller and less highly decorated than many contemporary buckles and other belt fittings used by the Roman army in main-

land Europe), so it is conceivable that there might be a fashion motivation for the production of at least some of these buckles and other belt fittings. However, to Britons of the late Roman period buckles and belts were not just a new style, but a completely new item of clothing. There is, so far, little clear evidence that belts and buckles were widespread among the civilian population in the Empire as a whole (outside incoming Germanic groups) and there is little clear evidence of such a fashion surviving beyond the end of the Roman period in non-Anglo-Saxon parts of Britain.[151] By contrast, some of the probable soldiers buried at Lankhills were buried wearing British-made buckles and other belt fittings, and a similar phenomenon, at about the same time, in Spain is associated with burials, sometimes incorporating spears, in which the locally made buckles and other belt fittings were clearly used to carry military-style daggers.[152] It's also very noticeable that the distribution of this material, though essentially civilian, has significant military overtones. Buckles and other belt fittings that are not British-made and have probable military connections in mainland Europe (chip-carved material and triangular plate buckles) show similarities in distribution (if in lesser numbers) to the British-made material. Furthermore, some of the British material is found, in addition to Lankhills, at the fort of Richborough and at the nearby workshop site at Ickham. Generally, it's also worth asking, with many indications that in the late fourth century Roman Britain was in trouble and economic activity in a number of areas was in decline, why the production of military-style buckles and other belt fittings should be one of the few growth areas. In the last quarter of the fourth century, when Roman Britain was under threat in a way it had not been before, when no new villas were built

143 Richborough, where Theodosius landed to restore Roman rule after the so-called 'Barbarian Conspiracy'

from scratch and there were no major extensions or refurbishments of existing ones,[153] would people in villas suddenly start spending money instead on military-style buckles and other belt fittings when they'd never even worn belts and buckles before? And why would there still be British-made buckles and other belt fittings (the Quoit Brooch Style type) being manufactured at a time in the fifth century when almost everything else distinctive of Romano-British culture had gone out of production? While fashion may have played a part, something more than fashion on its own seems likely here.

It is conceivable that some of the wearers of these buckles and other belt fittings were civilian officials of the type described above. However, Britain seems to have quantities of buckles and belt fittings that are more characteristic of militarised zones of the Empire than civilian ones.

Attempts have been made to draw a distinction between wider chip-carved buckles and belt fittings being more military and the narrower forms being somewhat less military, but this is probably to some extent based on modern conceptions that military belts should be wide. Third-century Roman belts were, for instance, generally quite narrow, like some of the narrower fourth-century examples, and buckles of similar size to the narrower type are also found in some early Germanic and Anglo-Saxon warrior graves, where their function was clearly as knife belts or sword belts.[154] In any event we also know that, in at least some instances, smaller buckles were actually fitted on much wider belts with a much narrower piece of the belt passing through the buckle. In general, there is too much of an overlap in terms of distributions and contexts between broader and narrower buckles to make any such hard and fast distinctions seem particularly valid.

It's a controversial conclusion, partly because of its huge implications, but it seems most plausible, with the current information available, to suggest that while no doubt some buckles and other belt fittings were worn for an assortment of non-military reasons, most of the buckles retained a primarily military or paramilitary function, and that therefore many of these buckles and belt fittings could indicate the presence of armed civilians.[155] It is possible this should be seen as a late Roman successor to the situation in pre-Roman Britain and precursor of the situation in Anglo-Saxon England, where wearing a belt and a knife on it was commonplace, but it is perhaps more likely from parallels elsewhere that it should be seen as a more organised phenomenon.

It was one of the cornerstones of social order in the Empire that civilians were not generally allowed to carry weapons. However, under exceptional circumstances arming civilians did happen. For instance, an Athenian militia led by the historian Dexippus was used against raiding Goths in Greece in the late third century. There is some evidence of private militias being formed in the northern parts of the Empire in mainland Europe in the chaos of the later third century.[156] In the late fourth century at Adrianople we know of a citizen militia under the command of the chief magistrate.[157] In Spain in the early fifth century supporters of Honorius raised a civilian militia to counter Gerontius' attempt to take control there. In the chaos surrounding the end of Roman Gaul in the later

fifth century, Sidonius Apollinaris records his friend Ecdicius raising, equipping at his own expense, and leading a troop of cavalrymen.[158] There are also hints in Gildas that, at the end of the Roman period, the Romans helped arm Britons (he says the Romans gave the Britons patterns for weapons). It is also reasonable to argue that Honorius' famous instruction to the citizens of Britain in 410 to look after their own defence (whether it really applies to Britain or to Bruttium in Italy as some have suggested) is an implicit instruction to raise militias for defence or perhaps an implicit recognition of their prior existence. Equally, Zosimus, in his description of the Britons finally freeing themselves from Rome, indicates that the Britons took up arms on their own behalf to fight 'barbarian' attacks, which suggests an already existing degree of military knowledge and self-confidence, as indeed does the rebellion against Rome itself. In another sign of weapons usage spreading wider in society, in the late Roman period, we also see the rise of the *bucellarii*. These were private armies raised by wealthy people, for much the same reason as the civilian militias were probably being raised, in order to provide an element of security and power that the State no longer could, in a world where casual violence was becoming more and more a feature of everyday life. A law of AD 476, for instance, made it illegal to keep gangs of armed slaves, *bucellarii* or Isaurians, but the practice continued. We should probably see the late fourth and particularly the fifth centuries as periods where distinctions between armed soldier and armed civilian became much less significant than in previous, more stable times, just as distinctions between armed Roman and armed 'barbarian' serving a Roman leader were also disappearing fast. In his great victory over the Huns at the Catalaunian Fields in 451,

144 The originally Roman wall of London. Whatever the so-called 'Barbarian Conspiracy' actually was, the turmoil created seems to have reached as far south as London

Aetius' forces included not only 'barbarian' forces, such as Saxons, Franks, Sarmatians and Burgundians, but also citizens of the Empire, Armoricans and 'other Celtic … tribes'.[159] Should we call these soldiers or armed civilians? By that stage, the distinction, in what was left of the western Roman Empire, was probably becoming, in many senses, fairly meaningless.

Certainly, it could be argued that the events of the 'Barbarian Conspiracy' represented exceptional circumstances. The Roman army in Britain had shown itself incapable of defending Britons against the threats they faced, and in that situation, it would seem entirely reasonable that Britons should arm themselves or be armed to protect themselves, and prevent a recurrence of the events of AD 367. It's not something that we, in our cosy, stable, well-organised modern western society are used to, but that's what generally happens in societies where police and armed forces are perceived to have failed. In the years between 367 and 410 Britain was under threat from external raiders from a number of different directions and went through two periods of rebellion against Rome, with no doubt some accompanying civil conflict in Britain and perhaps reprisals after the fall of Magnus Maximus.

With all that going on we should probably not be asking, 'why would people arm
themselves?' but much more 'why wouldn't
they?'

Finds of fourth- and fifth-century weaponry and other military items such as shield
fittings are not particularly common in
Britain, even on occupied military sites
such as forts in the Hadrian's Wall area,[160]
so we should not expect significant levels
of weapons finds from civilian militias. But
arrowheads, spearheads, knives similar to
some of those in the Lankhills burials and
military-style burials in mainland Europe,[161]
and even military weighted darts and the
occasional sword guard, have been found
on civilian sites in Britain that have also
produced buckles and/or other belt fittings
from the late Roman period. For instance,
only six spearheads were found in the
excavation of the large late Roman fort at
Portchester, yet four[162] were found in the
excavation of the fourth- and fifth-century
settlement at West Overton in Wiltshire
(close to the line of Wansdyke) plus belt
fittings.[163] Late Roman belt fittings, two
arrowheads from the fifth century, a knife
similar to some of the Lankhills knives and
another undated arrowhead or spearhead
were found at the Barnsley Park site in
Gloucestershire. From the Shakenoak Farm
villa in Oxfordshire come a variety of late
Roman belt fittings and three late fourth-
century spearheads. From the villa at Castle
Copse, Great Bedwyn in Wiltshire, where
buckles have been found, comes an undated
spearhead, a knife similar to some of those
at Lankhills and a late fourth-century
antler sword guard. Weighted military darts,
plumbatae, have been found at Caerwent,
Cirencester, Nettleton and Kenchester
which have all produced late Roman belt
fittings as well.[164] Some of these weapons,
of course, could have potential civilian
uses such as hunting, or could be dual use
civilian/military, but it is interesting confirmation nonetheless that weapons were
available to British civilians, perhaps in significant quantities, at this time. It might also
be worth, in this context, drawing attention
to a number of curious weapons deposits
from the late Roman period from civilian
contexts. At Silchester a sword and a spearhead were found deposited in a pit and a
well among civilian metal items. At the late
Roman temple at Jordan Hill in Dorset,
two swords and two spearheads were found
carefully buried in a pit along with such
items as a steelyard, a bucket handle, a crook
and other iron items.[165] At Caversham, the
remains of a destroyed Christian lead font
were found in a well along with fourth-
century pottery, a spearhead, a scythe and
two iron-bound wooden buckets.[166] All

145 A so-called 'door-knob spear butt'. Cassius
Dio describes the Caledonians and Maeatae as
having 'bronze apples' on the end of their spear
shafts and these mysterious items may be what he is
describing. They certainly seem to originate from
north of Hadrian's Wall or from Ireland and their
presence in England may be linked either to raiders
from those areas or to former raiders serving with
Roman forces

146 Buckles and other belt fittings of the late Roman period

these deposits may have ritual significance, and may continue pre-Roman traditions of weapon deposits in Britain, but they also may demonstrate something of a civilian concern with weaponry in the late Roman period.

The late fourth century and early fifth century (particularly after the defeat of the Roman army at Adrianople in 378, which destroyed a significant part of the main Roman forces and led to a situation where even men who had cut their thumbs off to avoid army service were being pressed into service)[167] saw a massive increase in the use by Roman leaders of armed men from outside the official Roman army. Mostly this consisted of the use of various different groups of Germanic warriors. If you were armed and prepared to fight for them, even if you'd previously been fighting against them, Roman leaders would probably want to recruit you. There seems no particular reason why Rome would have rejected British militias as an available source of manpower. Something similar may have happened in Spain. As

already noted, there is literary evidence of landowners in northern Spain arming their workers at the end of the fourth century, and military belt sets carrying knives do start appearing in graves in northern Spain in the later fourth century. It has also been argued that some of the burials with weapons in northern frontier areas of the Empire on the European mainland should also be seen as those of armed local civilians.[168] With a similar mix of weapons and with a similar mix of buckles and other belt fittings found in these burials, as on some British civilian sites, it may be that we should see a broader pattern of civilians being armed or arming themselves in a number of the more remote and more threatened areas of the Empire. Manpower issues may, however, have been particularly critical in Britain in the late fourth century. It's a controversial subject but it seems hard not to conclude that, in the last decades of Roman rule, at least, some units of the conventional Roman army were being taken to fight in continental conflicts, never to return. Gildas indicates that Magnus

Maximus took soldiers from Britain to the continent who never returned. There is also a suggestion from the poet Claudian that Stilicho withdrew a legion from Britain, and the *Notitia Dignitatum*, the late Roman army list (though it may be incomplete for Britain), lists only two legions in Britain, rather than the previous three, and suggests that one of the remaining legions may have been a fraction of its former size. If the garrison was being dramatically downsized, at a time when external threats to Britain were increasing, there would be even more reason for Rome to welcome the existence of British militias.

There is a hint in Gildas that Britons may have been helping man Hadrian's Wall and some of the Saxon Shore Forts towards the end of the Roman period (Gildas describes the Romans building the wall and the forts to be manned by Britons), and there is some archaeological evidence to support this idea. The excavator of the Saxon Shore Fort of Portchester Castle uncovered what he termed ordered occupation for the period 354-364 and what he termed 'disordered' occupation for the period 364-400+.[169] On Hadrian's Wall there are some intriguing inscriptions, possibly of fourth-century date, recording work on the wall by squads of Britons from a number of *civitates*, by Dumnonii, by Durotriges and perhaps by a group of Catuvellauni as well. It is possible that these were work gangs, but most work on the wall was carried out (and recorded in almost identical inscriptions) by soldiers serving on the wall. So these inscriptions could record British militiamen serving on the wall.

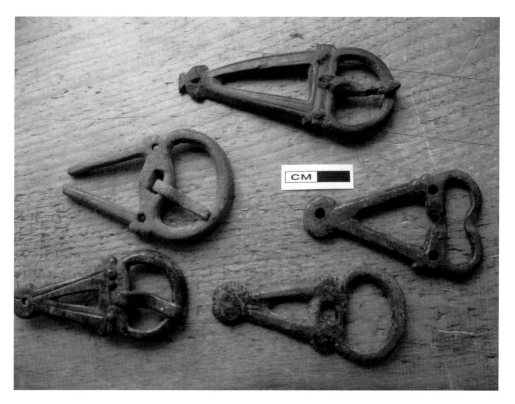

147 A type of plain, utilitarian buckle, maybe manufactured in State arms factories and widely found both in Britain and in military zones on the continent

148 The temple at Jordan Hill, Weymouth, site of a mysterious deposition of weapons in the late Roman period

All of this brings us to one particularly interesting aspect of these buckles and belt fittings, something which could potentially tell us something significant not just about possible British militiamen in the late Roman period, but also perhaps something about UnRoman Britain itself.

Most of the buckles and other belt fittings from this period found in the country seem, as indicated earlier, to have been made here, because they are slightly different in design to those made in mainland Europe. This, in itself, is quite interesting but what's more significant is that there seems to be some evidence of differences in design between some of the buckles and belt fittings that appear in different tribal regions of Britain,[170] just as we noted earlier design differences between fourth-century mosaics.[171] Bearing in mind how UnRomanised Britain was, it would hardly be surprising if it was the *civitates*/tribes themselves who were organising their own tribal militias but here (and perhaps with the *civitas* inscriptions from Hadrian's Wall) we may have specific evidence of that. In other words, just as Rome found a land divided up between tribal armies, in the dying days of Rome in Britain, something similar may have been beginning to re-emerge. There are interesting parallels in other remote and relatively UnRomanised parts of the Empire. In Mauretania, in the mid fourth century, a local tribal king, Flavius Nubel, is recorded on an inscription as a *praepositus* in the Roman army and seems to have fought invaders on behalf of Rome or, at least, on behalf of his local power base. He was then killed by his brother Firmus in a tribal revolt against Rome in 373, while another brother, Gildo, rose to be military governor of Africa, before also rebelling against Rome in 397. Finally, in the fifth century power in the area returned to the tribes.[172] In Armorica there are signs of tribalisation in the post-Roman period[173] and we have already noted armed Armoricans in action. In northern Spain tribal politics also seems to re-emerge at the end of the Empire. Different styles of belt fitting appear in areas belonging to different tribes here, the Vaccaei and the Carpetani. The Basques would also reassert their independence.

As we shall see in the next chapter this factor could be significant in understanding how and why Roman Britain ended. However, for the moment, it's enough to note that even after over 300 years of occupation, Britons still seem to have been organising themselves along tribal lines and to note that, while they probably weren't fighting each other at this stage, at least some British civilians do seem to have been all set to rebel against the emperor in Rome (or Ravenna) alongside the Roman army in Britain.

We've already seen how, in the third century, the death of Trajan Decius and the capture of Valerian preceded a period of intense fragmentation and rebellion. The death of the emperor Valens plus a large part of his army at the hands of the Goths, in the Battle of Adrianople in 378, may have had something of a similar effect.

In 383 a rebellion in Britain thrust a senior Roman commander, Magnus Maximus, forward in a bid for imperial power. We are only 27 years from the end of Roman Britain at this point and it's a good point at which to assess just where Britain ranked in Rome's rebelliousness stakes. We are now 340 years since the invasion. Could Britain still really be that rebellious? The simple answer seems to be probably yes.

There were, of course, rebellions in other parts of the Empire in the fourth century, but there does seem to be a strong tradition that Britain, even at this stage, had a particular reputation for being difficult and rebellious.

If we are looking at the British army in particular, Zosimus helpfully makes the point that the troops in Britain were the 'most aggressive and rebellious'.[174] If we are looking at Britain as a whole then Saint Jerome, writing in 415, sums up Britain with the sweeping phrase that it is 'fertile in tyrants'.[175] Tyrants didn't mean then quite what it does now. A tyrant was a ruler elevated to power without legitimacy, a usurper. So Magnus Maximus would have been to Jerome a 'tyrant', so Jerome is basically saying that Britain is an island 'fertile in rebels'. And Gildas, the earliest British historian, writing less than a century and a half after the end of the Roman period in Britain, seems pretty clear about the attitude of many Britons to Rome when he notes:

> This island, stubborn to the core, from the time people first lived here, rebels ungratefully sometimes against God, sometimes against its own citizens, and often against foreign kings and their subjects.[176]

In addition, of course, as we will consider in the next chapter, Britain has the unique distinction of actually walking out of the

149 A weighted military dart, a *plumbata*

Empire altogether and forever in 410, something no other western Roman territory achieved.

Magnus Maximus was sent to Britain perhaps as *Dux Britanniarum* in 380. He started his career in Britain by fighting a successful campaign against the Picts and Scots, but rapidly seems to have been persuaded by the rebellious troops in Britain to make a bid for imperial power.

His bid was successful for a while. After crossing to Gaul, he defeated the western emperor Gratian outside Paris, established his court at Trier (like Constantine before him) and took control of Britain, Gaul, Spain and Africa. He seems to have managed to come to some kind of, at least temporary, terms with the eastern emperor Theodosius I and Gratian's successor in the west, Valentinian II, who was left in control of Italy. At some point, though, Magnus Maximus decided he would invade Italy. This he successfully did. However, Valentinian II fled east to Theodosius I and the two emperors advanced together against Magnus Maximus, who was captured and executed at Aquileia. Apart from being yet another example of the rebelliousness of the Roman army in Britain, Magnus Maximus' effort to grab and hold imperial power is also interesting for what it says about the situation in Britain at the time. For Magnus Maximus may have had British militiamen, perhaps in significant numbers, in his forces. When he is described amassing forces to invade Italy, he is said, by Sozomen, writing in the first half of the fifth century, to have recruited 'a large army from British men, neighbouring Gauls, Celts and other nations'.[177] In addition, a distinctively British buckle plate has been found at Aquileia, the scene of his final defeat. Finally, and most intriguingly, his memory lived on in medieval Welsh tradition. He appears as Macsen Wledig, Prince Macsen, and beside obviously mythical components there are also elements which may include fragments of historical truth, including the suggestion that a number of Britons captured Rome for him, which could potentially represent the presence of Britons in his army.

After the death of Magnus Maximus Britain was back under central Roman control for about five years until 392, when Valentinian II was either killed or committed suicide and his Frankish *Magister Militum* Arbogast made Eugenius, a former teacher emperor. Britain duly went along with the rebellion, as it always did, and it was not until 394, after the defeat of Arbogast and Eugenius at the battle of the Frigidus, that Britain was back under central imperial control. This time it was under the control of the young emperor Honorius, the last official central Roman emperor to control Britain.

150 Stone from Hadrian's Wall, commemorating the presence on the wall of a squad from the *civitas* of the Durotriges. The Durotrigans were probably doing work on the wall, but may have been serving as militiamen there as well, just as Roman soldiers both worked on the wall and served there. *Courtesy of Chesters Museum*

Little is known of events in Britain over the next 12 years, Britain's last under central imperial control. Stilicho seems to have campaigned against the Picts here in 400, but by 402 there is mention of troop withdrawals from Britain, and by 406, Britain was in rebellion yet again. The last four years of Roman Britain were, like so many years before, to be passed outside central imperial control.

What seems likely from the start of the rebellion of 406 is that Britons were this time playing a leading role. They may have been present in significant numbers in the forces of Magnus Maximus, but he himself was Spanish. In the rebellion of 406 there were Britons represented at all levels.

The start of the rebellion is a complex affair that sees two other men briefly elevated to imperial status before the rebels finally settled on Constantine III who was to lead them into Europe. One of these two predecessors, another Gratian, was himself British. We don't know the origins of the other predecessor Marcus and Constantine III himself. However, Constantine III's main general, one Gerontius, also seems to have been British and since Constantine himself was said to be a low-ranking soldier before his elevation to the throne, it may be that Gerontius and Constantine III's other generals, a number of whom were Germanic and therefore thought, at the time, ineligible for the throne, may have been initially the real powers behind it.[178] Just as other generals did in this period, they may have made emperors and disposed of them until they found one they were relatively happy with.

In 407 Constantine crossed to Gaul and, after Gerontius and his fellow general

151 Hadrian's Wall, near Housesteads

152 Portchester Castle. Scene of what the excavator termed 'disordered' occupation for the period 364–400. This may represent the presence of armed civilians

153 Gold coin of Magnus Maximus. © *Trustees of the British Museum*

154 The walls of Tarragona. The British general, Gerontius, in control of Spain set up his own puppet emperor Maximus at Tarragona

155 The Roman walls of Arles. The end of the road for Constantine III's dream of conquering Rome from Britain

156 Ivory carving probably showing the late Roman commander, Stilicho

Edobichus had seen off a challenge from Stilicho's general Sarus, Constantine established his court at Arles in southern France. He secured the Rhine frontier which had been overrun by a large group of Vandals, Suevi and Alans who had managed to cross the frozen Rhine on the last day of 406. Constantine, however, does not seem to have attempted to evict the invaders who slowly made their way across Gaul towards Spain looting as they went.

Pursuing the dream of imperial power, Gerontius set off for Spain to destroy the forces raised by landowners loyal to Honorius from their workers, which he eventually managed to do. Meanwhile in Italy, Honorius had other problems, in addition to Constantine and Gerontius, on his mind when internal intrigues left him without his generals Stilicho and Sarus and facing Alaric's marauding army. In a tight spot, Honorius recognised Constantine as fellow-emperor and the two became joint consuls.

However, Constantine's success was not to last. Shortly afterwards, perhaps feeling that Constantine had become too independent, Gerontius broke with him and elevated a man called Maximus, either a member of his family or staff, to the throne in Spain. The general then tried to use some of the Vandals, Suevi and Alans against Constantine and launched an invasion of Gaul. The Briton killed Constans, the son of Constantine, at Valence and then besieged Constantine in Arles. Almost certainly among the forces of Gerontius were a number of British militia-men. British buckles and belt fittings have been found in northern and north-eastern Spain where Gerontius' forces would have been based. And one example has also been found in southern France between the Spanish border and Arles.[179]

Gerontius at this point was one of the most powerful Britons there had ever been, perhaps the most powerful. He may even have held Britain at this point as well. Britain seems to have rebelled against Constantine at about the same time as Gerontius broke with him, so there may be some kind of link.

Gerontius' success was, however, not to last either. While Constantine III had Edobichus trying to raise an army to fight Gerontius and relieve Arles, Constantius, a general loyal to Honorius, forced Gerontius to retreat towards Spain. Mutinous troops subsequently surrounded Gerontius and he committed suicide after a dramatic siege.

Constantius now took over besieging Constantine III in Arles and, after Edobichus' army was ambushed by Constantius, Arles fell and Constantine was captured and subsequently killed. Honorius would eventually regain control of Gaul, but would never regain control of Britain.

Ultimately, the rebellion of Constantine III and Gerontius represents the point where the rebelliousness of British civilians became fully fused with the rebelliousness of the Roman army in Britain and the Britons in it. It is the point at which Britons had effectively taken back control of Britain from Rome, and perhaps in some sense the end of Roman Britain was now inevitable.

8

LEAVING THE EMPIRE

The barbarians from beyond the Rhine, attacked without hindrance and prompted those living in Britain and some of the Celtic peoples to leave Roman control and live their own lives, free of Roman laws. The Britons took up weapons, and facing the danger for themselves, liberated their cities from the barbarian threat.[180]

Zosimus

… the army of the Visigoths … marched into Gaul, and Constantine, having been defeated in battle by Honorius, died along with his sons. However, the Romans were never able to regain control of Britain, and from that time on, it remained under the control of tyrants.[181]

Procopius

A T some stage, between AD 409 and 411, Britain passed out of the control of Rome forever. The actual date of the end of Roman Britain is controversial. The rebellion mentioned by Zosimus seems to have taken place in 409. Zosimus states in a subsequent chapter that, sometime around early summer 410, the emperor Honorius wrote to the cities of Britain telling them to look after their own defences. If this is not, as some think, a mistaken interpretation of an imperial communication to the cities of Bruttium, in southern Italy, then this is presumably Honorius accepting a fait accompli

of British independence, and 410 has long marked the traditional end of Roman Britain. Alternatively, there are those who would prefer to see the death of Constantine III in 411 as also marking the death of Roman Britain itself. They point to the fact that Procopius indicates that after this the Romans were never able to reconquer Britain and that from there on it was ruled by 'tyrants', warlords. Whatever the case, the years between these events and the emergence of Anglo-Saxon kingdoms in England mark some of the most controversial, most unclear and yet, ultimately, most important in British history.

We have seen, through the course of this book, the ways in which Britain did not Romanise during its centuries under Roman control. In this chapter we will look at how even the parts of Britain that had been most Romanised became comprehensively de-Romanised in the years after the end of the Roman period, before considering in the final chapter how and why in the centuries after Rome, large parts of Britain became, by contrast, thoroughly Anglo-Saxonised.

The overriding feature of early fifth-century archaeology in Britain is the sudden disappearance of most elements associated with Roman culture. The lack of new coinage makes dating the progress of this disappearance difficult to date entirely accurately, but within the space of perhaps 20-35 years after AD 410, give or take a little

157 Looking from the walls of
Roman *Verulamium* across to
where the medieval town of St
Albans would grow around the
shrine of the British martyr St
Alban in the Abbey

158 The amphitheatre at
Cirencester. There seems to have
been some attempt to fortify it at
the end of the Roman period

POST-ROMAN TOMBSTONE (5-6th century A.D.) OF BRIGOMAGLOS
THE FORMULA 'HIC) IACIT' (here lies) MAY BE CHRISTIAN

159 The Brigomaglos inscription from Vindolanda.
Courtesy of Chesters Museum

(and depending on area), the construction of Roman-style buildings, the manufacture of Roman-style artefacts, such as ceramics, on a large scale, the occupation of towns on a significant scale, the occupation of villas and Roman-style rural buildings on a large scale, probably even the widespread use of coinage, all had disappeared. There is some low-level continuity and no doubt people were recycling old Roman-period items and living in dilapidated buildings from the Roman period for decades, but something fundamental had changed.

In towns, new signs of occupation, such as there are, in the years after 410, seem to be mainly in the form of small numbers of low-tech buildings, small wooden huts that may be associated with either the last stages of British occupation or the first stages of Anglo-Saxon occupation. There is evidence for something like this at both *Verulamium* and Canterbury, for instance.[182] At Cirencester the amphitheatre seems to have been fortified. The most extensive example of urban continuity is probably Wroxeter in

the west, where there is evidence of substantial timber buildings being constructed on the site of the baths basilica, probably in the sixth century.[183]

In the countryside, most villa usage comes to an end shortly after 410. There is an argument for continued fifth-century activity at some sites, but again, it is comparatively low-tech and nothing like, for instance, the early fourth-century activity on a lot of villa sites. At Whitley Grange, in Cornovian territory in the west, the baths were last used some time between 410 and 510 and at some stage after that, four simple buildings and two storage buildings were constructed among the villa's ruins. These were probably occupied in the fifth century and maybe into the sixth.[184]

With non-villa rural sites the picture is a little more confused, partly because many of these sites had so few datable Roman items even during earlier centuries. Continuity on these sites as a group may be stronger than on villa sites, but there seems to be a significant degree of discontinuity as well, particularly in the more Romanised areas.[185]

One area that does seem to show significant continuity is the Hadrian's Wall area, with signs of continued activity at a number of sites, including the post-Roman inscription commemorating one Brigomaglos from Vindolanda, and the famous instance of a timber hall built over a granary at Birdoswald. However, the Hadrian's Wall area, being a military region under unified military command, is in many ways unique and, therefore, it should not be surprising that its archaeology from this period is also unusual.

Both manufacturing and trade seem to decline dramatically after 410. There is little evidence of goods being moved around Britain and the large-scale industries of the Roman period come to an end. Where there is evidence of continued manufacture of goods it is on a much smaller and much more local scale. Thus, there is evidence that suggests the Black Burnished Ware industry based around Poole, which at its height exported pottery across Britain as far north as Hadrian's Wall, may have limped on through much of the fifth century, but mainly only selling its wares within Durotrigan territory.[186]

Certainly all these aspects of the Roman lifestyle seem to have disappeared well before the arrival of Anglo-Saxons in significant numbers in the middle of the fifth century, because there is little or no evidence of an Anglo-Saxon presence overlapping with the continuing creation of new elements of the Roman lifestyle. And this is not simply a matter of invaders rejecting the existing culture in the country they have invaded. As will be discussed later in this chapter, so-called Anglo-Saxon culture already contained large doses of Roman culture before the first Anglo-Saxon settlers set foot in Britain and there is plenty of evidence of culturally Anglo-Saxon people using culturally Roman artefacts in Britain. It is just that, when they do so, these seem to have been old artefacts, either items passed down through families or chance finds.

To consider the de-Romanisation of Britain, first let's state some basics. Looking back at the end of Roman Britain with the benefit of hindsight, there can seem a certain inevitability about it. Roman control disappears, the argument goes, so Roman culture disappears too. But that's far too simple an equation. Roman culture didn't disappear in this country during the years Carausius and Allectus ruled an independent Britain. Instead, quasi-Roman rule continued outside the control of Rome. Similarly, as Roman control collapsed in Gaul, in the late fifth century, Roman culture didn't disappear entirely there either. In the south of Gaul particularly, Roman culture continued to flourish under the Visigoths and subsequently the Franks, with writers such as Sidonius Apollinaris and Avitus of Vienne demonstrating the survival of a flourishing Gallo-Roman culture under new Germanic masters. In the north of Gaul and west of current-day Germany there are many more signs of sites abandoned at the end of the Roman period and it is hard to find evidence for continuity in some of the towns in the most northern areas. As we have seen, this area had similarities to Britain during the Roman period, and there are similarities in the post-Roman period as well. However, there is still significantly more evidence for continuity than in Britain. Trier, for instance, still manages to provide one of the largest collections of post-Roman inscriptions in Gaul, occupation continues at Paris, though in reduced form, and a significant number of towns continue to have a function as centres of power for the new Germanic rulers (such as Cologne, Tournai, Namur, Tongres and Soissons) and/or centres of religious authority for the Catholic Church. The example of Bishop Remigius based in Reims (capital of the Remi tribe) is perhaps the most famous. There was plenty of economic disruption from the warfare that intermittently swept across the area but, for instance, manufacture of Rhenish glass seems to have continued and wheel-turned pottery in the tradition of Argonne Ware also continued and ceramics could still be traded over substantial distances, even in the sixth century.[187] There is no inevitability that the end of Roman political control in Britain had to mean the total end of Roman-style culture.

Obviously a key element in the sudden disappearance of Roman culture in Britain has to be the weakness of it in Roman Britain in the first place. As we have documented in previous chapters, Rome was later Romanised and less Romanised than almost any other part of the western Roman Empire. Almost half of so-called 'Roman' Britain shows distinctly limited signs of being culturally Roman throughout the period, so the lack of Roman culture there in the post-Roman period is hardly a surprise. But even in the parts of central and eastern Britain where Roman culture had taken a hold, there seems to have remained perhaps an ambiguity about Rome, among all classes, that persisted right to the end of the Roman period.

By contrast with Gaul, where the Gallic aristocracy became a key component of late Roman imperial administration and political life, the British aristocracy seem, with the exceptions of Gratian and Gerontius (assuming they were aristocrats), to have remained insular and uninterested in joining the imperial power structures right to the end. This lack of bonding with mainland Europe seems to have been reciprocated, with one Gallic poet expressing extreme reservations about even the most Romanised parts of British society. Ausonius, as we have already seen, quips about a British poet named Bonus (incidentally, as indicated earlier, the only evidence we have for anyone in Roman Britain writing poetry, by contrast with the large number of surviving poems written by Romanised Gauls) that it is a contradiction in terms for a Briton to be called Bonus, 'Good'.

Further evidence of British resistance to Roman culture, even among the aristocracy, compared to Gaul may come from the much thinner evidence for Roman-period Christianity in Britain. Constantine had made Christianity the official imperial religion and it rapidly became the dominant religious force in Gaul. As we have already seen, there is plentiful evidence in Gaul of an extensive network of bishops and churches in the late Roman and in the immediate post-Roman periods.[188] And Gallic aristocrats who might once have concentrated on making their way through the civil political and administrative system, now increasingly entered the Church, the new spiritual administrative structure, as well – people like Sidonius Apollinaris, who was Bishop of Auvergne in the late fifth century, or Ruricius, Bishop of Limoges at the end of the fifth century.

By contrast, as we have already seen, in Britain evidence of Roman-period Christianity is a little more sparse. There is a reference to the attendance of British bishops at a number of ecclesiastical councils. The case of the Council of Arles in 314 has already been mentioned, and there were, for instance, also British bishops at the Council of *Ariminium* in 359/60. The *Life of St Germanus* mentions the shrine of the British martyr St Alban at *Verulamium*, a Christian site and martyr also mentioned in Gildas, our earliest British source for the history of Roman and post-Roman Britain. Archaeologically there is evidence of a few structures that are claimed to be small churches (one of the best examples, already mentioned, being that at Butt Road outside the Roman walls of Colchester) or in one case, at Richborough, a font, and there are also a number of elaborate octagonal pools attached to villas that have been claimed to be baptisteries, plus there are mosaics featuring Christian symbols (including the portrait on a mosaic from Hinton St Mary that shows a youthful male head with a Chi-Rho symbol behind it, widely assumed to be a portrait of Christ, though it may instead be a portrait of a Christian emperor) and, of course, there is the famous room at Lullingstone villa decorated with a wall painting of praying Christian figures. In addition, there are a number of cases of

probably Christian cemeteries from the late Roman period, however, it is not safe to assume that all burials aligned east-west with no grave goods are necessarily Christian.[189] Much of the evidence for Roman-period Christianity in this country comes from artefacts. There are a number of small lead tanks that have been found that are probably baptismal in purpose and a range of other artefacts that carry Christian symbols. The most well-known of these is the spectacular Water Newton treasure (which consists mainly of silver vessels and plaques, many of them carrying the Chi-Rho symbol). There is some evidence of abandonment, and even destruction, of pagan temples, particularly in towns and military areas, as the fourth century proceeds, that could be linked to the spread of Christianity.[190]

Interestingly, a significant proportion of the contemporary literary references to Christianity in Britain in the Roman and immediately post-Roman period almost all concern heresy. Obviously, Britain was far from alone in this period in being affected by theological disputes but it's interesting nonetheless. A theologian called Pelagius, who originated from the British Isles, brought down the wrath of contemporary Catholics, and an accusation from Jerome of being a porridge-eating idiot, for rejecting ideas of salvation by grace and supporting the idea of man much more as a free agent able to choose right or wrong and earn salvation by doing right. It's hard to know to what extent Pelagius' religious views may or may not have been affected by his origins in the British Isles, since he spent much of his career in Rome. However, it is interesting to note that St Germanus came to Britain to counteract the spread of Pelagianism here, and also worth bearing in mind Gildas' comments about Arianism in Britain or, as he puts it, 'the Arian treason, fatal as a serpent, and vomiting its poison from beyond the sea, caused deadly dissension between brothers inhabiting the same house'.[191] A fifth-century clergyman of British origin, Faustus of Riez, who was active in the south of Gaul, though himself opposing Pelagianism, expressed in his work views that have since come to be known as Semi-Pelagian, and that were condemned as heretical after his death. There have also been suggestions of some British Christians of the period mixing Gnostic ideas into their beliefs and showing some of those ideas in the mosaics they commissioned as, for instance, at Frampton.[192] It is not necessarily a convincing picture of an island at the beginning of the first century enthusiastically joining in the imperial religion of officially approved Christianity.

This possible sense of Britain being out of step with mainstream imperial culture at the end of the Roman period is perhaps supported by evidence of paganism remaining strong, later than in Gaul and most other mainland parts of the Roman Empire. A number of pagan temples seem to continue in use in Britain until the end of the fourth century and maybe even beyond.[193] This is despite the fact that paganism had long been subject to imperial disapproval and sacrifices and temples were banned altogether by Theodosius in 391. The *Life of St Germanus* records him conducting a mass baptism of locals during his visit to Britain, which may suggest a substantial number of Britons still being pagan in 429. As late as 450-550 an enamelled penannular brooch was deposited, probably ritually, in the springhead at Bath.[194] Gildas, writing in the early sixth

century, makes no mention of pagans still existing in his day and, since his goal is to castigate sin, he presumably would have done so if they had existed. However, in a little noticed passage, he does mention rotting idols, indicating that they still existed in his lifetime and had not all been removed or destroyed by Christians. One of the many mysteries of this period archaeologically in Britain is the fate of a number of the lead, probably baptismal, tanks. A number have clear Christian symbols on them, so they seem definitely linked to Christianity, yet some have been found apparently deliberately defaced or destroyed. One was found, for instance, folded up at the bottom of a well.[195] There is no single clear explanation for these finds. It has been suggested that they could be linked to factional strife between different Christian sects. Alternatively, it has been suggested that there might be a pagan connection. The positioning of the tank in the bottom of the well is in some ways reminiscent of pagan British practices of burying deposits or placing them in water.

Ultimately, the Britons, even after hundreds of years of occupation, simply don't seem to have seen themselves as particularly Roman. Gildas, when looking back on the occupation from a distance of 100 or 120 years or so, draws a fairly clear distinction between Britons and Romans throughout his account of the Roman and post-Roman period. In his view the Romans came, occupied and then left. It could be argued that Gildas' view of Britishness is affected by his attempt to identify a British identity in opposition to the Anglo-Saxon invaders of his day, but it is interesting nonetheless.

In the last chapter we reviewed the evidence for a reassertion of tribal identities in military terms in the fourth century. We should not be at all surprised if at the end of the Roman period the inhabitants of

Britain saw themselves not as Romans but still primarily as Dobunni, Catuvellauni, Iceni or a member of one of the other tribes. Even in Romanised Gaul there is plenty of evidence to suggest that in the fourth and fifth centuries tribal identities still persisted. In a panegyric delivered to the emperor Constantine, an orator thanking the emperor for tax breaks, in a setting where he might have been expected to stress his Roman identity, instead talks about the pride and heritage of his tribe, the Aedui, and how they had been allies of the Romans for hundreds of years. It is a salutary reminder for any who think that the sheer scale of the Roman Empire would have swamped such loyalties that it, in fact, was not always the case. One might guess, in some sense, that the opposite is often true, that the very scale of the Roman Empire led people, in some circumstances, to hang on even more tightly to local identities built on a more human scale, and, in an age before television and air travel, concerns would naturally have tended to be much more local. Even the Romano-Gallic poet Ausonius, who is so scornful of Britain, mentions his own descent from Aeduan nobility, while the writer Sidonius Apollinaris, in a poem about the Moselle river, lists the names of a number of peoples who lived along its banks and he also makes reference elsewhere to his own people, the Arverni. It's also fascinating to note, as discussed in Chapter 3, that at the very end of the Roman period in Gaul, tribal capitals often lost the Roman elements of their names, but retained the tribal element, and in *Aquitania*, in the post-Roman period the individual *civitates* became key in terms of raising armies. There is also evidence in Gaul that some of the Catholic Church's administration was based on the old *civitas* boundaries and identities. Thus, for instance, it seems probable that the boundaries of the medieval diocese of Arras are closely based on the boundaries of the tribal *civitas* of the (Gallic) Atrebates.[196] If this was all the case in Romanised Gaul, then it would have been so much more the case in lightly Romanised Britain. The different styles of mosaic found in different British tribal areas, and the pottery industries located on tribal borders to take advantage of more than one market, suggest a significant part of British economic life may still have been organised on tribal lines. A fascinating find of lead ingots from the seas off France, some of them carrying the names of the *civitates* of the Brigantes and the Iceni, and which may well date from near the end of the Roman period in Britain, may support this view.[197] The evidence of different belt fittings in different tribal areas suggests something similar about defence. In religious terms, it's interesting to note the presence of a number of late pagan cults in pre-Roman hillforts, probably powerful symbols of a tribal past, as at Uley, Maiden Castle and Lydney.

However, the most obvious evidence of British lack of enthusiasm for Rome at the end of the period is the unique way in which Britain ultimately just walked out of the Empire. Rome had abandoned provinces before, *Dacia*, for instance, in the third century. However, the British provinces abandoning Rome altogether is a stunning and landmark event in the history of the Roman Empire.

The mechanics of what exactly happened are unclear, but it can only be interpreted as an active rejection of Rome, perfectly in keeping with Roman Britain's long history of being UnRoman.

The relevant passage in Zosimus seems to indicate clearly that the Britons thought they could do a better job of defending themselves than the Roman Empire. This would sit very well, with a probably growing

161 The brick font at Richborough

162 The fifth- or sixth-century baptistery at Riez in southern France. Faustus, of British origin, was Bishop of Riez until his death in the last years of the fifth century

sense of military self-confidence, probably represented by the rise of tribal militias. However, there may be other specific factors at work as well. The rebellion of 409 seems to coincide roughly with the split between Constantine III and his British general Gerontius. If Gerontius was a senior figure in British society he may well have taken the opportunity to incite Britain to split with Constantine III at the same time that he did.

Alternatively, maybe it was also a question of too much tax. The tax burden in the late Roman Empire was heavy, particularly on influential members of society, like the aristocracy, but also on the poor. There are a number of reports of people in the late Roman Empire who considered that paying imperial taxes could be worse than being ruled by 'barbarians'. Salvian, for instance, writes, 'The enemy is more lenient to them than the tax collectors'[198] and, 'There is only one reason that I can think of that the poor and deprived taxpayers do not flee en masse to the barbarians. The only reason they do not do it, is that they couldn't carry with them the few possessions they have, their households and their families'.[199]

One of the few things British taxpayers of the late Roman period might hope to get in return for their taxes was defence from foreign attack. If even that was not forthcoming, then there could easily have been a taxpayers' revolt. It is worth remembering that, when the Byzantines sought to re-impose imperial rule on Vandal-held North Africa in the sixth century, some of the main opposition they faced was from African peasants unenthusiastic about re-entering the imperial tax system.[200]

However, a lack of enthusiasm for Rome and its culture, both spiritually and materially, is not sufficient on its own to explain the dramatic and sudden de-Romanisation of Britain. No doubt the value placed on

Roman culture in Britain slumped even further in the period after the end of Roman control, but the dramatic and comparatively rapid cessation of almost all Roman-style culture, with the enormous effects that that must have had on the lives of those Britons in the more Romanised areas, can't simply be explained by a mass, concerted, voluntary rejection of Roman culture. There must be more to it than that. So what did cause the cultural end of Roman Britain?

Traditionally, of course, the end of Roman Britain was put down to rampaging Saxons torching villas, demolishing Roman city walls and generally putting paid to Roman culture in an orgy of destruction, looting and killing. Certainly there is evidence of raiding into Roman Britain in the late fourth century. However, as discussed in the last chapter, much of this seems to have been down to Picts, Scots and Attacotti attacking from Ireland and Scotland. The hoards of late Roman silver found at Coleraine in Northern Ireland and at Traprain Law in Scotland may represent the loot from such raids, though it has also been suggested that they could be payments for mercenary services. Equally, the signal stations erected along the Yorkshire coast in the late fourth century and the probably late Roman fort of Caer Gybi on Anglesey all seem more likely to be aimed at defence against incursions from Scotland and Ireland, rather than from the Anglo-Saxon homelands in mainland Europe. The passage in Zosimus that recounts the great British rebellion does seem to be talking about Saxon raids against Britain and elsewhere, and there are other mentions of such raids at this time. However, while these could certainly have made life in some coastal areas very unpleasant and intermittently disrupted life inland, there is nothing to indicate they could have been on such a

163 The fifth-century church of Santa Sabina in Rome, a superb example of late Roman church-building in mainland Europe

scale so as to change completely the lives of up to three million or so Roman Britons. The Saxons, after all, were not the biggest of tribes (though people from other tribes no doubt also joined in the 'Saxon' raids) and not all Saxon raiders came to Britain. There were Saxons headed to Gaul, and Saxons headed south into mainland Europe as well. More to the point, in order to reach Britain, the raiders had to row their small boats hundreds of miles and what evidence there is strongly suggests small groups of raiders rather than huge fleets under unified command.[201] Much of the reason for the idea that the Saxons destroyed Roman Britain can be put down to the same Gildas we have already mentioned. He has several lurid passages of rampaging Saxons, and makes reference to Saxon attacks on cities.

So all the settlements were brought down by constant shocks from battering rams, and all the inhabitants along with bishops, priests and people were mown down, with swords flashing and flames crackling. A terrible sight, in the middle of the streets lay high towers, thrown to the ground, the stones of tall walls, sacred altars, and human body parts, covered with bright, clotted blood, looking like they had been mangled in a press, and with no hope of burial, except in ruined houses, or in the hungry bellies of wild animals and birds.[202]

If Saxons did indeed go on such a rampage right across Britain, a question we shall return to later, they almost certainly did it long after the main collapse of Roman culture in Britain. The earliest significant settlement of Saxons seems to have taken place around

420-425, but only really accelerated in the second half of the fifth century and in the first half of the sixth.[203] As pointed out previously in this chapter, there is basically no archaeological evidence that suggests early Saxon settlers encountered a fully functioning Roman-style culture on their arrival in Britain, and there is no archaeological evidence of Saxons being instrumental in the destruction or abandonment of sites at the end of the Roman period.

It is also worth pointing out for the record that Roman culture does not just suddenly disappear in the early fifth century in those areas of eastern England most vulnerable to Saxon raiding. It grinds pretty much to a halt in the Romanised parts of central and western Britain as well. Contrast this with Gaul, which spent much of the fifth century being fought over by assorted Germanic peoples which had arrived by land in large unified groups, and even had its own Saxon sea-raids and settlement in addition. Here, a few elements from the Roman-period culture continued even in parts of the less Romanised and more battered north, while in the more Romanised and less battered south, Roman-style culture positively flourished.

Violence in the late Roman Empire, however, was not confined solely to state institutions and 'barbarians' from outside. A shadowy group called the *bacaudae* or *bagaudae* were also intermittently spreading panic and chaos across parts of Western Europe in the final centuries of the Empire. They're first heard of in Gaul in the late third century and then they re-emerge, mainly in Gaul, but also in Spain, in the fifth century. It used to be thought that the appearance of the *bacaudae* represented straightforward peasant uprisings against their wealthy overlords. This tends to be how they are represented in the texts which were written mainly by people who originated in the wealthier classes. However, reading between the lines a slightly more mixed picture emerges. Some of the *bacaudae*, like Eudoxius who was a doctor, were definitely not peasants, and local aristocrats may also have been involved.[204] In addition, their activities seem to cluster in some of the least Romanised, and most 'Celtic', parts of the western Empire on the European mainland, like northern Spain, Armorica, and Alpine areas. This raises the question of whether, like tribal militias in Britain, the *bacaudae* may in some sense represent a re-assertion of local identities. A description of the *bacaudae* in the late third century almost sounds like the forming of one of the tribal militias discussed earlier:

> … inexperienced farmers looked for military kit; the plowman imitating the infantryman, the shepherd the cavalryman.[205]

In the end, however, we may be wrong in trying to tie down one individual identity to the *bacaudae*. Times of extreme crisis such as the last centuries of the Roman Empire often see desperate people driven to brigandage and different members of the same group may have a variety of different motivations. It certainly seems likely that such groups did operate in Britain at the end of the Roman period, and on into the post-Roman period. Zosimus, for instance, in his description of the British revolt against Rome, links activity in Britain to activity in Armorica, a known area of *bacaudae* activity, which may indicate similar activity over here. However, there is no specific evidence of them in operation on a large enough scale, right across the Romanised part of Britain, to cause the total failure of Roman culture. On the contrary, what literary evidence there is of post-Roman political organisation in Britain, such as the descriptions of kings and judges in Gildas, and the mention of two people holding high local rank in the *Life of St Germanus*, consistently portrays hierarchical structures. The great villa estates are abandoned at the end of Roman Britain, but then so are most Roman-style sites of any kind, and, on the evidence of their activities on the continent, it seems unlikely that these groups on their own could have caused the wholesale collapse of Roman culture in Britain.

So far we have been looking at looting as a cause of the end of Roman Britain, but could violence be the end result, rather than the primary cause?

A certain amount of emphasis has been placed in recent years on the implications for the British financial system of the removal of Roman control. For a start, basically no new coinage enters Britain after the very earliest years of the fifth century. This is presumably caused partly by the collapse of trade with the continent but also, and probably more significantly, by the end of official supplies of coinage. After this, at some stage in any case, without the authority of the Roman State to back it, the Roman base metal coinage would presumably have ceased to have any value. In addition, the Roman government of Britain played a significant role in the economy of Roman Britain by gathering taxes and spending money on the military and State apparatus. There may still have been up to 30,000 Roman soldiers in Britain in the late fourth century, who with all their dependants would have formed a key element of the late Roman British economy. By 410, these soldiers had either left the country or were needing new employers from within Britain itself.

Again, there can be little doubt that such changes can only have had a negative effect on the British economy. Just imagine if the coins in your pocket were suddenly worth-less and you had to rely more on barter to get the goods you wanted and needed. However, again it seems unlikely that this on its own can have been sufficient to cause the sudden and almost entire collapse of Roman culture in Britain. For a start, not all coins suddenly became worthless. Whatever the official value of Roman silver and gold coinage, ultimately its value was based on the value of the gold and silver they contained. The 'barbarian' tribes, for instance, who happily accepted payments in gold and silver Roman coins in the fifth century may not have been too interested in the coins' official value, but were interested in the gold and silver itself (like the 5000 pounds of gold and 30,000 pounds of silver allotted to Alaric by the senate in one payment).[206] On this basis, therefore, Britons too could presumably (unless other factors prevented them) have continued trading using their gold and silver, valuing it by sheer weight if necessary. And indeed one of the major features of the archaeology of this period is the finding of clipped *siliquae*, silver coins.

The clipping involves removing the outer portion of a silver coin. Strictly forbidden under the Empire, its widespread appearance in Britain is evidence of the collapse of imperial authority, but it is also, since there is no indication of it being used to make new coins, evidence of silver being valued purely for its metal. In addition to this, barter had probably always played a much greater role in Roman Britain than it does today. Plus there is the fact that the end of Roman Britain was not exactly the first time Britain had been cut off from central Roman control. As we have already seen, Britain spent regular periods beyond central control in both the third and fourth centuries. In all these cases there must have been a certain amount of disruption of government finances and coinage supplies, yet in none of these cases did Roman culture

164 Hinton St Mary, Dorset. Head of either Christ or a Christian emperor with the Chi-Rho, the first two letters of Christ's name in Greek, from a fourth-century mosaic. © *Trustees of the British Museum*

collapse. Then again, it's always been questionable to what extent Britain made a net profit or gain from the Roman occupation. True, some government money came in, but also some taxes, both in coinage and in goods, left the country. With the end of Roman control these outgoings would have ceased. As mentioned earlier, when Justinian tried to reconquer Africa from the Vandals he faced the most opposition not from the Vandals themselves but from African peasants who didn't want Roman taxes back.[207] Finally, and again it's crucial to bear this in mind, Gaul went through similar changes at the end of the Roman period, but they did not have the same devastating effect.

Could a killer plague be the answer? Certainly large numbers of people were killed by plagues in the ancient world. We know, in some detail, from the later experience of the Black Death in Britain, how a particularly savage plague could have catastrophic consequences and we do have some evidence of plague in Britain in the sixth century. The ruler Maelgwn, king of Gywnedd, is said to have been killed by 'a great mortality' in 547. However, we have no particular evidence of a plague that could have affected Britain at the right time in the early fifth century. Hydatius, writing in the fifth century, mentions a plague in about 443 which according to him, 'spread across

165 Christian lead tank of the late Roman period found at Ashton. *Courtesy of Peterborough Museum*

almost the whole world'. However, this has to be an exaggeration on some level, since we have no evidence of a global plague at this time and, in any case, a plague in the 440s is significantly too late to have brought about the end of Roman Britain. What's more, even with particularly destructive plagues, there seems little evidence that they, on their own, could destroy a whole society's way of life.

We're worried today about global warming but could the climate have had a major role in the end of Roman Britain? Some people think so. There's no evidence that hotter temperatures might have damaged Roman Britain but, on the contrary, there is some evidence that colder temperatures might have. After roughly three and a half centuries of weather being warmer than average, drier and less stormy, Britain's

weather seems to have deteriorated slowly from about AD 250 onwards, getting cooler and wetter in the later fourth century, with a marked decline starting around 400.[208] This has been linked to evidence of abandonment of some marginal lands. It is certainly true that in a still largely agricultural society, a long-term downturn in the temperature could have a significant cumulative effect, but it is hard to see that its effect could have been as fast and dramatic as a search for the cause of the collapse of Roman culture in Britain demands. Moreover, the evidence for the environment in post-Roman Britain is patchy, controversial and difficult to read. While some high-altitude sites do show abandonment, others do not,[209] and while there is evidence of abandonment of marginal lands in the Upper Thames Valley, overall pollen evidence and the evidence of

166 Detail of the late Roman Christian lead tank from Icklingham, Suffolk. © *Trustees of the British Museum*

survival of field systems from Roman into post-Roman times do not tend to suggest a vast lowering in agricultural output.[210] Gildas does mention a famine, and it is possible that cooler temperatures could have contributed to this, but as we shall discuss below, there may well be other reasons for a famine as well. Finally, and we come back to it, once again, whatever may have been happening to the north European climate from 410 onwards, it did not totally eradicate the Roman cultural order in Gaul either before the end of Roman political control in the late fifth century or after that.

Many of these factors considered above, in combination with the basically UnRoman nature of Britain, and the relative weakness here of the Church that did so much to maintain Roman culture elsewhere, may have been part of the apparent weakening of the economy in Roman Britain towards the end of the fourth century and may well have contributed to the sudden collapse of Roman culture here in the early fifth century. However, neither alone or in combination do any of these seem sufficient to explain the sequence of events seen so clearly in the archaeological record. What we are looking for is some cause that is comparatively fast and vast and something that does not apply to the other nearby parts of the western Roman Empire in mainland Europe.

The answer may lie, as does so much else connected with Britain's history during and after the Roman occupation, in the UnRoman nature of Roman Britain.

The use of the phrase Roman Britain doesn't just disguise the UnRoman nature of Britain in the period. By the use of the

167 The late Roman temple built on the Durotrigan hillfort at Maiden Castle, looking towards the Roman-period capital of the Durotriges at Dorchester

word Britain it also imposes a false unity that just wasn't there. Britain wasn't even a single unified Roman province at the end of the Roman period, and the Britons almost certainly weren't a single unified people. Gildas with his Roman education and his desire to distinguish Britons from Anglo-Saxons may refer to Britons as a group, but, as we have considered previously, it is likely that the Britons primarily saw their identity in terms of their tribe. Just as we today may have several levels to our identity, so the Britons at the end of the Roman period may have had a British level to their identity, but in a time of crisis their primary loyalty would have been to their tribe.

Perhaps the strongest evidence that this may have been the case comes from a comparison of the situation in former Roman territories in Western Europe and coastal North Africa in about 520, with the situation in Britain. As others have noted, what is immediately striking is that while former Roman Western Europe and Africa is dominated by the large-scale kingdoms of the Visigoths, the Franks, the Ostrogoths, the Burgundian and the Vandals, Britain by contrast is split into a bunch of very small kingdoms all squeezed onto a small island.[211] What is even more interesting is that if you look closely at these kingdoms and compare them with maps of the tribal areas of pre-Roman and Roman Britain, you can convincingly derive most, perhaps almost all, the kingdoms of the sixth century in formerly Roman Britain, both the British and the Anglo-Saxon kingdoms, in some sense from the original tribal areas. Some boundaries have shifted slightly and a few tribal

168 Horse and Rider brooches, with possible pagan ritual significance, which remain in use until the very late Roman period in Britain

169 Clipped *siliquae*. The outer rims of the coins have been clipped off to produce spare metal but leave coins that still basically look like coins

areas have split in two, but usually along dividing lines that were already evident in the culture and history of the area in the pre-Roman and Roman period.[212] In other words, at some stage between AD 410 and the sixth century, Britain probably fragments back into the tribal areas that were there when the Romans arrived in the first place. It is yet another way that Roman Britain was UnRoman.

It is impossible to be certain when post-Roman Britain fragmented but it's most probable that it happened very soon after 410 and may even have started happening before.

There is very little evidence to suggest political organisation above the *civitas* level in the post-Roman period. A vague reference in Gildas to a post-Roman ruler consulting a council has been taken to refer to some kind of council of Britons running the country as a whole. However, even if the reference is accurate, there is no reason that the council in question could not just be a local tribal council. Equally, it has been suggested that the pattern of early Anglo-Saxon immigration, in terms of which parts were settled by which groups, may reflect provincial boundaries from the end of the Roman period.[213] This is an interesting argument, and there could conceivably be something in it. It is, however, hard to be sure, because we are so unclear as to where some of the late Roman provincial boundaries actually were and because there are other equally, or more convincing, reasons to explain the patterns in question, as we shall see below.

By contrast, Zosimus in his account of the rebellion refers just to Britons, rather than

170 Dark skies over Richborough. A deterioration in the climate of fifth-century Britain could have been one factor in the end of Roman culture on the island

any unifying force or figures, taking up arms on behalf of their cities and, in his account, Honorius' message to the Britons (assuming it is to the Britons rather than Bruttium), telling them to look after their own defences, is also addressed to the cities of Britain. Pretty much anything archaeological that might show a persisting British unity after 410 almost instantly disappears. It is most notable, of course, and something that has received too little attention, that nobody arises in Britain to issue new coinage. Coins had always been one of the most obvious ways of visually expressing political power in the Roman world, which is why issuing coins was always among the first acts of any usurper. After 410 no new Postumus or Carausius starts issuing coins. What is more, the fragile evidence of trade and commerce in fifth-century Britain tends to suggest that what trade survived probably became largely confined within the territories of individual small-scale political entities. The

few coins of Constantine III that made it to Britain are mostly confined within the territory of the Catuvellauni/Trinovantes, unlike the coins of the previous short-lived emperor Eugenius which are spread across the country. The days when raw materials and manufactured goods were traded over long distances across Britain seem to have rapidly disappeared. We have already noted how the Black Burnished Ware industry based around Poole, which once had sent its wares across large parts of Roman Britain, seems in the fifth century to be purely producing pottery for local consumption, and there are other examples of very late wares which seem to have very local distributions, like Surrey Buff Ware, for instance.

One of the most interesting features of post-Roman archaeology in Britain is the evidence of large-scale linear earthworks slicing up the countryside. These consist of a ditch and a bank behind the ditch. We should not see these as permanently manned fortifications, but nonetheless they must originally have been a considerable statement of territorial division. They would have not been impossible for a determined person to cross, but equally they would have been a considerable obstacle and anybody crossing them would not have done so unawares. We should perhaps see them as the equivalent of a high and heavy-duty barbed-wire fence. Dating such earthworks can be difficult, but some of them are known to be late Roman or post-Roman, like Wansdyke in Somerset/Wiltshire and Bokerley Dyke in Dorset, for instance. What is particularly interesting about some of these, though, is their links to pre-existing territorial divisions. Bokerley Dyke seems likely to follow a pre-Roman boundary line,[214] while Wansdyke links into the positioning of pre-Roman hillforts and there is also the possibility of it incorporating pre-existing linear structures.[215] The linear earthworks near Cambridge are built close to and along the same alignment as the probably pre-Roman Mile Ditch, while Grim's Dyke north of London is a development of a pre-Roman ditch. West Norfolk is another area where there are a number of linear earthworks, some of which may be pre-Roman in origin and some of which may be post-Roman, at least in their final form.[216] This suggests very much that in post-Roman Britain, already existing local divisions were re-emerging strongly. And this may not just have been occurring in post-Roman Britain, but it may have started to occur in late Roman Britain too.

The range of possible dates for the first phase of construction of Fleam Dyke on the Iceni/Catuvellauni border (AD 330–510) could conceivably place it in the late Roman period,[217] and the archaeology of Bokerley Dyke on the Durotriges/Belgae border is complicated but, again, it could conceivably indicate work on the ditch already by the late Roman period. The most spectacular of the post-Roman linear earthworks is the complex collectively known as Wansdyke. Wansdyke is known to be post-Roman but there is little evidence so far from the earthwork itself to date it very closely. However, what is interesting is that the earthwork not only lies roughly along the probable border between Dobunni and Belgae, but it also lies roughly along a line of villas affected by fires, which can be dated either definitely or possibly to the late Roman period. It's tempting to speculate that the earthwork and the fires are connected and are both indications of conflict along this tribal border.[218]

The potential reasons behind such a tribal fragmentation are not hard to find. If Britons did not see their primary identity as British and still saw their primary identity in terms of their tribe, then the departure of Rome was almost bound to see extensive friction and conflict between the once again independent tribes. It's a scenario that's been seen elsewhere in the world when the departure or expulsion of an imperial force leaves a sudden power vacuum. Even if separate peoples had briefly united under the imperial power, that unity is rapidly lost as the newly independent peoples compete to define their new borders. Old grudges re-emerge and new ones are added, as the new political entities fight for control of towns and resources in areas where populations have become mixed under imperial rule. And with existing tribal militias quite possibly already in place before Rome's final departure from Britain, the tribes would have been in a position to start jostling each other over borders in the chaotic last decades of Roman rule in Britain, during which Britain was regularly beyond central imperial control.[219] It is not a scenario that probably just applies to Britain at the end of the Roman period. There is evidence of

171 Wansdyke, Wiltshire

an, in many ways, similar process of tribaliza-tion in the late Roman period in a number of other areas of the Empire, including Mauretania, northern Spain and Brittany.[220] What these areas all have in common, among other things, is that they are rela-tively remote, relatively UnRomanised; in each instance there is evidence of the locals developing an independent military capabil-ity of their own, of taking up arms in the last decades of Roman control, and in each instance the area either did not go directly from Roman control to control by new Germanic rulers or did so (in the case of northern Spain) only partly.

It's hard to know how much direct damage such border disputes could have done to Britain, but one should not perhaps underestimate it. The *civitas* of the Belgae

was apparently created by the Romans contravening existing tribal boundaries, contrary to their usual practice in Britain, taking away a chunk of Dobunnic terri-tory and putting it under Atrebatic control. The location of Wansdyke, and the villa fires and other unusual features of the area such as what seems to be the appearance of a garrison of Pannonians at Winchester, capital of the *civitas* of the Belgae,[221] the unusual late fortifications of the small town of Mildenhall, linear earthwork defences north and west of Silchester, a difference in the types and quantity of buckles and belt fittings found north of Wansdyke and south of Wansdyke, make it tempting to see this territorial dispute reigniting, literally, towards the end of the Roman period.[222] Such a scenario could also be supported

172 Bokerley Dyke, Dorset

173 Fleam Dyke, Cambridgeshire

174 Milestone erected by the *civitas* of the Belgae. *Courtesy of Winchester City Museum*

175 Mosaic from Lullingstone villa, Kent. Lullingstone was destroyed by fire at the end of the Roman period. *Otto Fein Collection*

by a perhaps exceptional number of unretrieved hoards found in the area for which it is geographically hard to account by reference to foreign raiders. If such a central area of Roman Britain did descend into chaos, it would have had ramifications far beyond the territory of the *civitas* of the Belgae.

There would also probably have been chronic political instability within the individual tribes and *civitates* as different figures fought for control of the newly independent states. No doubt members of the traditional tribal aristocracies would have played key roles in the new power structures, but judging by the evidence of pre-Roman power struggles in Britain and Gaul, suddenly having to establish an accepted tribal leadership could well have been a messy business. Gildas indicates as much when he writes:

> Kings were anointed, not according to
> God's ordinance, but such as showed them
> selves more cruel than the rest; and soon
> after, they were put to death by those who
> had elected them, without any inquiry into
> their merits, but because others still more
> cruel were chosen to succeed them.[223]

However, what's particularly interesting about this scenario is that it could finally explain the difference between the situations in post-Roman Britain and many other former parts of the western Roman Empire in their post-Roman periods, because it seems very likely that it is the rapid fragmentation of Britain that is most responsible for the rapid de-Romanisation of Britain.[224] In Gaul, even though regional identities were still important at the end of the Roman period, there was no fragmentation, because the Church and higher levels of Romanisation provided a stronger element of unity and because new large-scale Germanic kingdoms took over from Rome. Whatever ethnic tensions there were in post-Roman Gaul, they would have primarily been between the Gallo-Romans and their new Germanic overlords, rather than between different tribes of Gallo-Romans. As a result, even though post-Roman Gaul was affected by many of the same problems that would have affected post-Roman Britain, such as raiding, climate change and collapse of coinage, nevertheless the basics of Roman and Christian administration and culture survived across most of it.

In Britain, by contrast, fragmentation would rapidly have destroyed an economy and a culture which relied to a surprising degree on long-distance trade. Imagine a scenario today where county boundaries suddenly became impassable. Supplies of raw materials would not be able to get to manufacturers and manufactured goods would not be able to get to customers. Obviously Roman Britain did not have quite such a complex economy as modern Britain, but pottery could be distributed over wide areas across the country from the large pottery industries that had emerged by the end of the period, food such as grain could be transported over long distances,[225] and even heavy raw materials such as stone could travel a long way before use. From Durotrigan territory, for instance, Purbeck marble travelled as far as London, St Albans and Chester.[226] Beyond the damage to the economy, fragmentation would also have involved an element of physical damage caused by inter-tribal fighting, and it would have made impossible any unified response to the other problems affecting Britons in the post-Roman period, instantly making them worse.

9

FROM UNROMAN BRITAIN TO ANGLO-SAXON ENGLAND

IN the last chapter we constructed a potential model of how Britain could have de-Romanised so quickly after the end of Roman political control. However, when looking at the mysteries that surround the End of Roman Britain, this is only one half of the coin. The counterpart to the de-Romanisation mystery is the question of how, and why, a part of Britain that had failed in a number of ways fully to embrace Roman culture throughout an occupation that lasted over 360 years could within a few hundred years of Rome's departure have turned into a thoroughly Anglo-Saxon England. We may be a little closer now to knowing how Roman Britain died, but how was England born?

For a start we need some geographical definitions. Primarily, we will be discussing in this chapter the parts of central and eastern England that had formed the core of the Anglo-Saxon kingdoms by around 600: the kingdoms of Kent, the East Angles, the South Saxons, the West Saxons, Mercia, Deira and Bernicia. However, before we turn to these areas that are so key to understanding the birth of England, it's worth taking a brief look at what's happening on the rest of the island, where even if there is not such huge cultural transformation there are still interesting cultural developments.

To the west and north of these areas lay large parts of Britain that, at that stage, were only indirectly affected by Anglo-Saxon culture. Much of this area had, as we have seen, also been comparatively little affected by Roman culture during the Roman period, and it seems reasonable to assume that there was a large degree of cultural and political continuity in this area from pre-Roman to Roman to post-Roman times. As mentioned in the previous chapter, it seems possible to trace the development of many of the Roman-period tribes into many of the post-Roman kingdoms that we know existed in this area.[227] The reoccupation of hillforts in the post-Roman period, at a number of places in this area, also gives a strong sense of tribal continuity. The same should also probably be said about what seems to be the development of an Irish cultural and political identity in some areas of modern-day Wales and Scotland that border the Irish Sea, particularly in Dalriada in the north and in Dyfed.[228] It's certainly possible, and indeed likely, that contacts across the Irish Sea increased after the departure of Rome, with perhaps some immigrants settling here at that time, either with or without the cooperation of the locals. However, in recent years there has been a tendency to see this as a reaffirmation of traditional links across the Irish Sea rather than seeing it as a totally new development. Some of the tribal names in Ireland could conceivably suggest links with tribes on the British

176 The hillfort at South Cadbury, Somerset, reoccupied in the post-Roman period

side of the Irish Channel, and finds of probably British material, from the early Roman period, on the small island of Lambay, also suggest longstanding links across the sea.

This period also sees the emergence of a British identity in Brittany. There has been a tendency to equate the arrival of Britons in Brittany with a passage in Gildas which mentions Britons fleeing overseas to avoid the Saxons. However, there is little evidence to suggest the Breton identity was created by refugees from eastern England. On the contrary, the evidence of links between Britain and Brittany in the post-Roman period, such as it can be found in the lives of saints and place name connections, rather implies connections with western Britain and again these may be seen as a reassertion, in some sense, of longstanding traditional links.[229]

Ironically, perhaps, one of the most significant post-Roman developments in the western area of Britain is that this region seems to become in some ways comparatively more Roman, particularly in the late fifth and the sixth centuries, than it was under Rome. Latin inscriptions from the Roman period, apart from those of a military background, are rare in this area, but in the post-Roman period significant numbers of Latin inscriptions are found on stones commemorating the dead. Similarly, while, under Rome, Roman-style artefacts were much less common in this region than in the Romanised parts of Britain, in the post-Roman period, the situation is reversed. While pottery and goods likely to have come directly, or nearly directly, from the Mediterranean (as opposed to being passed from trader to trader across Europe) are rare in the rest of Britain, there is increasing evidence of contact between the Mediterranean and western Britain, particularly in the shape of sherds of Mediterranean pottery.[230] There are even suggestions of significant Latin influence on the development of the phonology of Cornish in this period.[231]

However, while in some ways these contacts seem to echo aspects of Romanisation,

177 Post-Roman inscription. The Drustan stone,
Cornwall, mentioning one Cunomorus

to bolster their own prestige, it's perfectly likely that British aristocrats in the West did the same. In doing so, of course, they would also have been echoing the actions of their ancestors in pre-Roman times who did exactly the same thing. Now that Rome was at a safe distance, and initial post-410 disillusionment with Rome was fading, they could afford to play with its symbols and enjoy them, without the connotations they would have had earlier. How far this post-Roman cultural cooperation may have been reflected in political cooperation is not known but it is interesting to note that in the late fifth century a British king known as Riothamus is recorded to have crossed the sea to Gaul with an army, at the request of the emperor Anthemius.[232] The expedition was an attempt to prevent the Visigoths taking control of Gaul, but ended unsuccessfully when Riothamus was defeated by their king Euric.

A central part of western Britain's renewed interest in Roman culture in the post-Roman period is Christianity. Many of the post-Roman Latin inscriptions commemorating the dead are explicitly Christian and the post-Roman period does see Christianity beginning to flourish throughout the area, as shown in Gildas' descriptions of the post-Roman kingdoms and by the large number of saints said to have been active in this area in the period. Obviously this spread had a spiritual and religious aspect, but again we should not ignore the wish of local aristocrats to be seen to be involved with the religion of the Empire and also a religion that would help them define themselves against the pagan Anglo-Saxons. Close cooperation between local secular leaders and local Church leaders in the administration of a single unified faith could also have potentially offered those local secular leaders an element of

and have been argued to represent some kind of survival of interest in being Roman, at least among aristocrats, they should probably be seen in a rather different light. It seems inherently unlikely that people in these parts would suddenly develop an interest in actually being Roman, half a century or more after a long and unenthusiastically embraced occupation had come to an end, and just as Roman power was finally collapsing across the rest of the West. However, the eastern Roman Empire was still the dominant military and political force in Europe, and just as Germanic kings there adopted certain selected elements of Byzantine culture

control over their subjects that a multiplicity of decentralised pagan cults simply could not.

What happened in the west in the post-Roman period is fascinating. However, ultimately, the manner of England's creation was to a great extent to be determined by the process of Anglo-Saxon settlement and developing Anglo-Saxon cultural and political control in the centre and east of Britain.

First, let's look at what's widely agreed about the process on the basis of what the archaeology and assorted ancient texts say about it.

The first Anglo-Saxon immigrants arriving in any numbers seem to have settled in central and eastern England sometime around AD 425-450, with subsequent settlement expanding across much of eastern and south-eastern England in the second half of the fifth and particularly in the early part of the sixth century. Both British and Anglo-Saxon sources agree that the first Anglo-Saxons arrived as mercenaries at the invitation of a British leader and that they subsequently rebelled against him. Anglo-Saxon kingdoms began to emerge in the east and south-east of Britain in the late fifth century and were well-established by the late sixth century. In the late fifth century and into the sixth century some broad differences begin to appear between the artefacts in the parts of Britain defined by the historian Bede as Anglian, and the parts of Britain that he defines as Saxon. The distinction is not at all clear-cut, with the distribution of some categories of artefacts fitting the template better than others, but it may represent some very broad distinctions in the emerging culture of Anglo-Saxon England. During the period 425-600, while Anglo-Saxon artefacts gradually become more common in the east and south-east of Britain, there are, with the occasional notable excep-

tion, few clear signs of British culture in these areas and, by the time in the seventh and eighth centuries that written evidence about life in these areas becomes more available and more trustworthy, few signs of any people with a recognisably British identity.

That's the broadly accepted picture but, obviously, it leaves so many questions unanswered that historians have long tried to fill in more of the detail of how England came to be Anglo-Saxonised.

Traditionally, of course, the prime role in the Anglo-Saxonisation of England was put down to rampaging Saxons. The argument was that, in addition to destroying Roman Britain, the rampaging Saxons also wiped out the Britons and their culture in eastern and south-eastern Britain and replaced it with a new Anglo-Saxon culture brought by large numbers of immigrants pouring across the North Sea. This view was based on the clear distinctions between English and Welsh/Scottish identities in recent centuries and by passages in the few available texts. We have already seen some of Gildas' vivid portrayals of rampaging Anglo-Saxons and it's worth quoting him here again because he has been so influential in establishing the traditional view of the end of Roman Britain.

> So vengeance's fire, justly sparked by earlier crimes, burned from coast to coast, fanned by the hands of our enemies in the east. It did not stop, until, after ravaging neighbouring towns and territories, it came to the far side of this island and dipped its wild and crimson tongue in the western sea.[233]

The *Anglo-Saxon Chronicle* seems to back Gildas up, with brief, but apparently clear, statements that Anglo-Saxons came to this island and regularly slaughtered Britons.[234]

178 The pre-Roman defences at Poundbury on the outskirts of Dorchester, Dorset. Poundbury is also the site of significant post-Roman activity

Bede was thought to be the final proof, from the Anglo-Saxon side, of the traditional scenario, when he stated the origins of the people of each of the Anglo-Saxon kingdoms. He gives an origin from across the North Sea for each of the peoples with no mention of any British contribution.[235] When all these references were added to an emerging archaeological picture that showed few signs of Roman or British culture in the east and south-east in the fifth and sixth centuries, and plenty of evidence of Anglo-Saxon culture, it seemed to be a clear-cut case of Anglo-Saxonisation through genocide and mass ethnic cleansing.

This basic narrative was believed by many for much of the nineteenth and twentieth centuries and still has a lot of supporters particularly among the general public. It seems to be a simple and dramatic explanation that fits the main facts, and in many ways it does fit some of the more obvious facts. It is really only when we start looking at the detail, that the traditional picture begins to fall apart and something more complex, more intriguing and, incidentally, much more in line with the history of UnRoman Britain as we have charted it, begins to take its place.

For a start, it seems extremely likely that Gildas, ultimately the key text in all this, the one that really conjures up vivid mental pictures of genocide, is exaggerating wildly. Prior to his widely read account of rampaging Anglo-Saxons, Gildas has a not-so-widely-read brief history of Britain up to that point, in which he describes rampaging Romans killing and enslaving in Britain after Boudicca's revolt, rampaging Roman pagans slaughtering Christians in large numbers, and rampaging Picts also doing vast amounts of killing and destruction. The Picts in particular Gildas describes as doing almost as much as damage as the Saxons. Now nobody is suggesting that raids by the Picts wiped out a big proportion of Britons. Gildas' motivation for such exaggeration probably derives from a combination of the fact that he's writing a fiery diatribe (and most writers of fiery diatribes are prone to huge exaggeration) plus the fact that Gildas is dedicated to the Christian faith and must have been as unhappy about the Saxons bringing a wave of paganism to the country as he was about Roman persecution of Christians. Churchmen down the ages have understandably been very distressed by pagan raiders burning and raiding churches, and Gildas in his diatribe specifically makes a point of highlighting bishops and priests fleeing the Saxons.

Then again, as we examined in the last chapter, the disappearance of Roman culture in the east, centre and south-east of England can not really be put down just to the Anglo-Saxons. No doubt their raids did damage to the Roman lifestyle in this country, but it disappears before the Anglo-Saxons settle in any numbers, and not just in the parts most vulnerable to raiding and the parts that see early Anglo-Saxon settlements, but in all the other parts of Britain where it existed as well.

Equally, while there is comparatively little obvious archaeological evidence of British activity in the south and south-east in the fifth and sixth centuries, there is not that much more in the west. Apart from the signs of imported Mediterranean culture mentioned above, the evidence for British activity in the west is thin and not made any more obvious by the Christian practice of burying people without grave goods. We know there must have been Britons living in the west in the fifth and sixth centuries in significant numbers, but they are hard to see. Their culture must have been one with low archaeological visibility. The best guess is that it consisted of old Roman-period items, some simple handmade pottery hard to distinguish from pre-Roman and early Anglo-Saxon pottery, simple homes hard to distinguish from those of earlier and later periods, burials without grave goods often hard to distinguish from those of other periods, a lot of use of perishable materials such as bone, wood and leather for artefacts, and even the use of materials such as wickerwork for huts. In that context, their apparent absence from the archaeological record in the east and south-east as well, then appears in a very different light, particularly since some of the few recognisable British products of the period 410-700 – penannular brooches and hanging bowls and hanging bowl decorative elements – have actually been found in significant quantities in central and eastern England.[236]

A further archaeological anomaly in terms of the traditional picture is that some of the areas listed by Bede as Anglo-Saxon in origin actually show comparatively few signs of Anglo-Saxon culture. This is particularly true of Bernicia in the north, but the further west you go, the less Anglo-Saxon Mercia, as well, looks archaeologically. Even in the south, there is, as had long been recognised, a large area to the north and east of London that shows no signs of early Anglo-Saxon settlement.

A closer look at the patterns of early Anglo-Saxon settlement also raises serious questions about the scenario of mass hordes

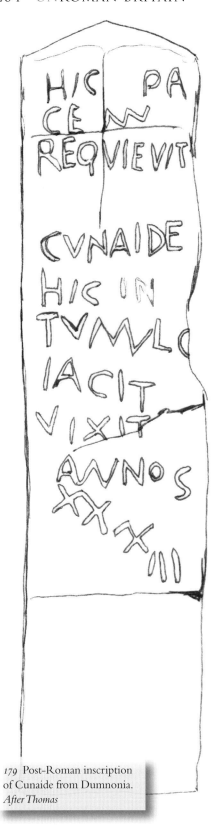

HIS PA
CE N
REQVIEVIT

CVNAIDE
HIC IN
TVMVLO
IACIT
VIXIT
ANNOS
XXXIII

179 Post-Roman inscription
of Cunaide from Dumnonia.
After Thomas

of Anglo-Saxons sweeping away all Britons and British culture in their path. We have already touched upon the way early Anglo-Saxon kingdoms seem to be built, in terms of their boundaries, on the old British tribal territories. In addition, a lot of the geography of the early Anglo-Saxon settlement seems to be dictated by British strategic need and by the positioning of existing Roman-period settlements, with early Anglo-Saxon settlements often appearing in border areas, suitable for mercenaries, and with many Anglo-Saxon settlements appearing very close to existing Roman-period settlements.[237]

Then again, there are small hints even in the surviving sources that the disappearance of the British from south and south-east England may not have been as comprehensive as once assumed. Even Gildas, for instance, is prepared to admit that Britons still lived in the Anglo-Saxon areas, even if he thought they'd be better off dead, and some of the early supposedly Anglo-Saxon kings actually have British names, like Cerdic, and Cædwalla of Wessex, or Cædbæd of Lindsey.

Above all, it's the logistics of and motivation for the supposed genocide and mass ethnic cleansing that do not seem very feasible. At its height, Roman Britain had a population of maybe three million.[238] There probably was some depopulation in the late Roman period and there was certainly some in the post-Roman period (with population levels ending up perhaps as low as half of what they had been).[239] However, as discussed in the last chapter, there seems overall only limited evidence of abandonment of land between the end of Roman Britain and the arrival of the Anglo-Saxons, so there must have been still considerable numbers of Britons around when the first Anglo-Saxons arrived, and most of the evidence for early

Anglo-Saxon settlement suggests the arrival of relatively small groups in relatively small numbers, not a human tidal wave that could have swept away so many Britons.

As to an inclination to genocide and mass ethnic cleansing, the evidence from mainland Europe suggests this is unlikely. Like many early medieval rulers, Germanic invaders were certainly capable of individual acts of great cruelty, but mass genocide and widespread ethnic cleansing wasn't something that seems to have particularly interested them.

Taken all together, such evidence makes it hard any longer to accept the traditional story of how Anglo-Saxon England was born. Having said that, finding a new agreed narrative has proved extremely difficult. However, a common tendency to separate studies of the Roman period from studies of the early medieval period has certainly hampered the search. We can't know how the Britons are likely to have interacted with the early Anglo-Saxons and their culture unless we know how they interacted with Roman culture, and the people who brought it to this island, and unless we understand developments in Britain immediately prior to the Anglo-Saxon arrival. With a better understanding of all that, we can perhaps have a much better chance of making sense of the apparent anomalies in the evidence about the birth of Anglo-Saxon England.

The motivations behind the Anglo-Saxon arrival seem to be, almost inevitably, a mixture of push and pull. As we have already seen, there is evidence of raiders operating from the continental North Sea coastline from at least the third century onwards. There is some evidence of coastal flooding there that may have hampered farming and prompted such raiding and, of course, any cooling of the climate after 410 would have had more impact in areas that were already marginal for agriculture.[240]

However, there is also the fact that easy loot has always been attractive and even Britain in the period after the collapse of Roman culture no doubt provided opportunities for getting comparatively rich quick. What's more, just as in mainland Europe, the frequent reaction of Roman leaders to Germanic invaders was to recruit them rather than attack them so, in Britain, it seems clear that British leaders too reacted to Saxon raids by looking for recruits for their own wars. In this way, Anglo-Saxon invaders of Britain would have had two opportunities of getting rich – raiding and mercenary work. They were probably happy to take either but for small groups, mercenary work was probably less risky, probably paid better in the long term and probably offered better opportunities for settlement and acquisition of territory.

We have already noted that both sides agree that the first Anglo-Saxons were invited to settle in Britain as mercenaries by a British ruler. Gildas simply refers to the ruler in question as '*superbus tyrannus*' which may be a pun on the British name given him in the *Anglo-Saxon Chronicle* and a later British source, the *Historia Brittonum* – 'Vortigern'. Gildas only specifies that this action occurred 'on the east side of the island'. The Anglo-Saxon sources, and a later British source, specify Kent. Archaeologically there seems to be some confirmation of the idea of individual British rulers settling Anglo-Saxon immigrants on their borders with their by now probably hostile British neighbours. Many of the earliest Anglo-Saxon settlements, as already mentioned, are near such borders.[241]

It's also worth pointing out here that, while we tend to assume from our modern European perspective that basically all land has a function and a value, in fifth-century Britain this wouldn't necessarily have been the case.

180 Tintagel, Cornwall

There may already have been some spare land at the end of the Roman period and, after the depopulation of the post-Roman period, there would have been more spare land available by the middle of the fifth century, perhaps particularly in vulnerable border areas where fighting may have forced abandonment of farming. In that context, settling Anglo-Saxons, prepared to serve as mercenaries, might have made economic and military sense, and could have been done without too much friction with the local population.

As noted above, there were several ethnic groups among the Anglo-Saxon immigrants, including particularly the Angles, the Saxons and the Jutes, and it has been suggested that the eventual grouping of culturally Angle settlements mainly in one area, and the grouping of culturally Saxon settlements mainly in another, might indicate the survival of provincial structures and strategies in Britain in the post-Roman period. This is certainly possible, but it is equally possible that what we are seeing here is the survival of tribal strategies. If one tribe took to recruiting Germanic mercenaries from one ethnic background, then any hostile neighbours might logically take to recruiting from a different one. Thus the earliest settlement around the borders of the territory of the Catuvellauni/Trinovantes seem to have been mainly Saxon. By contrast, in the territory of their neighbours to the north and east, the Corieltauvi and the Iceni, there is mainly settlement by Angles. There may have been conflict at times between the Corieltauvi and the Iceni but, in terms of their pre-Roman culture anyway, generally they seem to have had more in common with each other than they did with the Catuvellauni to the south. So, if the Catuvellauni were employing Saxons, then employing Angles might have seemed a good idea to the Corieltauvi and the Iceni.

None of this, of course, excludes the possibility that some Saxons did arrive here and settle areas by means of violence against the local population. We noted earlier that Gaul, as well as Britain, was raided by Saxons and there is mention of a small group of Saxon raiders who seem to have briefly settled on islands in, or off, Gaul before being attacked and destroyed by Gallo-Romans and Franks.[242] If such raiding parties did attack post-Roman kingdoms in Britain, the fragmented nature of Britain would probably have meant that any kingdom attacked would have had to fight the attackers alone, leaving it much more vulnerable. However, even if the Anglo-Saxons arrived uninvited that does not necessarily mean all Britons continued to resist their presence. It was standard procedure in the late Roman period, where ejecting 'barbarian' invaders would have been too difficult, to accept their presence in return for military services. The Visigothic, Burgundian and Frankish kingdoms all, for instance, emerged in this way. In terms of the Saxons specifically, we have already noted their presence in the army of the Roman general Aetius at the Battle of the Catalaunian Plains in 451, alongside contingents of, among others, Burgundians and Franks. There is little evidence of the Franks inviting Saxons to settle but we do, for instance, find a group of Saxons settled in Normandy and known as the *Saxones Baiocassini* − either because of their links with the local *civitas*/tribe, the Baiocassi, or the local town Bayeux (the name of which derives from the *civitas*/tribe) − who were used by the Frankish king Chilperic against the Bretons, and subsequently used by a Frankish queen Fredegund to fight alongside Bretons in a civil war against other Franks. Unless these Saxons were, in some way, the same as the Batavian and Suevian troops listed in the *Notitia Dignitatum* as settled at Bayeux and Coutances by the Romans in the late Roman period, this may be a case of Franks allowing Saxons to keep land they had taken, as long as they did military service.[243]

Perhaps the strongest evidence, though, that early Anglo-Saxon settlement in Britain should primarily be seen in a British political and strategic context, is the apparent fact, noted earlier, that the Anglo-Saxons, when they created their own kingdoms, seem to have built them on the basis of the British tribal states, rather than allowing geography, chance and their own priorities to dictate their initial borders. Unless early Anglo-Saxon settlement was mainly within a British context, it's hard to see why they would have done that.

The emphasis in the sources on Kent is interesting because it is here that we have perhaps the clearest evidence for a hybrid British-Germanic culture developing in the early decades of Anglo-Saxon-Jutish immigration. Quoit Brooch Style metalwork is, as so much with the fifth century in Britain, a controversial phenomenon. Apart from the Quoit Brooches themselves, most items made in this style are buckles and other belt fittings, and Quoit Brooch Style may in origin be the version for the Cantii of the tribal/regional styles of buckle and belt fitting that emerged at the end of the Roman period. There are many features of the style which are clearly derived from metalwork of the Roman period in Britain, though there is much in it that is also clearly derived from a late Roman metalwork style found more usually in mainland Europe. However, the Quoit Brooch Style of metalwork does not disappear with the end of Roman Britain. This is probably to be attributed to Kent's proximity to mainland Europe, where Roman culture survived, and indeed some pieces of Quoit Brooch Style metalwork have been found in northern France. What's more, around the time that the historical sources suggest Anglo-Saxons settled in Kent, that is around the mid fifth century, Quoit Brooch Style seems to become more distinctly Germanic in taste.[244]

When the tribal territory of the Cantii became the Anglo-Saxon kingdom of Kent (with basically the same name and with some possible evidence of continuity at Canterbury, the burgh or town of Cantii/Kent, its capital from Roman to Anglo-Saxon times) around the middle of the fifth century, it was the first time that a part of Britain came under Anglo-Saxon control. However, it was just the first in a series of replacements of British political entities by Anglo-Saxon ones. By the end of the fifth century, archaeology and the historical sources suggest that the kingdom of the South Saxons had emerged in place of the *civitas* of the Regni. To the west, by the early sixth century, the kingdom of the West Saxons was taking over from the *civitas* of the Atrebates and the Atrebatic half of the *civitas* of the Belgae. To the east, the kingdom of the East Angles emerged in place of the *civitas* of the Iceni and the kingdom of the East Saxons took over from the Trinovantes. The territory of the Corieltauvi seems to have been split along the lines of ancient tribal division to form two Anglo-Saxon kingdoms, that of Mercia and Lindsey. To the north of that, the *civitas* of the Parisi became the kingdom of Deira, and to the north of that, the tribal territory of the Votadini again seems to have split along an ancient cultural divide to create the Anglo-Saxon

kingdom of Bernicia and a separate British kingdom. In the centre of Britain, the territory of the Catuvellauni was also split along an old regional and cultural divide. The northern part, which had closer links with Corieltauvian territory, became a large part of Middle Anglia and in the late sixth century part of Mercia, while the core of Catuvellaunian territory became the territory of the Middle Saxons and was allied to the East Saxons, just as the Catuvellauni had been allied to the Trinovantes.[245]

The spread of Anglo-Saxon political control was matched by the spread of Anglo-Saxon cultural control, though it is impossible because of the weakness of the historical sources to know to what extent political control may have preceded cultural control or vice versa. Mainly the sources, if any trust can be put in them, seem to suggest the establishment of Anglo-Saxon political control some decades after the appearance in a territory of a significant Anglo-Saxon cultural element. This sequence could well be evidence of the process of British leaders employing Anglo-Saxon mercenaries, with at some stage a culturally Anglo-Saxon leadership taking over. On the other hand, it could simply reflect inaccuracies in the historical sources. It's impossible to be entirely sure.

When Anglo-Saxons did take over, it may have been a violent process involving the displacement of significant numbers of culturally British inhabitants, or it may not. Gildas' description of fleeing Britons could refer to such an event or it could perhaps refer more to events closer to Gildas' own time and the expansion of Anglo-Saxon kingdoms into new territory. An interesting document, the *Life of St Severinus*, is sometimes quoted by those who suggest significant numbers of British refugees fleeing west. It is true that, according to this document, in the late fifth century a number of towns on the Danube frontier were evacuated, under pressure from invaders from across the river. This, though, seems to have been a comparatively small-scale evacuation under direct threat from large, organised bodies of 'barbarians' arriving across land at the imperial border, and actually what is in some ways more notable about the *Life* than the ultimate evacuation of the towns is the way St Severinus, prior to that, is able to become friendly with a number of Germanic warlords and secure their willing cooperation in rescuing people and freeing captives. Severinus is said to be held in esteem by king Flaccitheus of the Rugii[246] and by Flaccitheus' son Feva, king of the Rugii.[247] Gibuldus, king of the Alemanni, releases captives to St Severinus.[248] Even the eventual evacuation is organised in the end by the new Germanic overlord of Italy, Odoacer.

We have already noted how some members of the Empire preferred Germanic rule to Roman rule, and generally there seems to have been a reluctance of locals, across the Empire, to die for an emperor, while fighting Germanic invaders. In any areas where those doing the taking over were Anglo-Saxons who had not been working with the British, there is likely to have been more violence. However, where the Anglo-Saxons doing the taking over had been mercenaries for the Britons for some time, then takeovers may not have been that violent and may have included the participation of ethnic British, as suggested by British names and names that suggest British ancestry that appear in a number of supposedly Anglo-Saxon royal houses including Mercia, Lindsey, Sussex, and Wessex.

Anglo-Saxon immigration started slowly but probably went on for a long time, perhaps over a period of 100 years. It is hard to know exactly how this process developed, but again we should probably imagine small

groups rather than mass waves of Angles and Saxons, Jutes and others. There is no evidence that the Anglo-Saxons possessed large ships or ships with sails at this point so, like the raiders, immigrants would probably have had to row themselves hundreds of miles down the North Sea coast and across the Channel in small boats. The *Anglo-Saxon Chronicle* records settlers arriving in groups of two or three boats, and even though the *Chronicle* is by no means eyewitness history, this may be fairly accurate. Not all the people entering the country at this period were from the traditional Anglo-Saxon continental homelands. Small groups from elsewhere were also involved. There were definitely Frisians in Britain, and certainly Frankish influence in the sixth century, particularly in Kent. And among the later arrivals there were probably

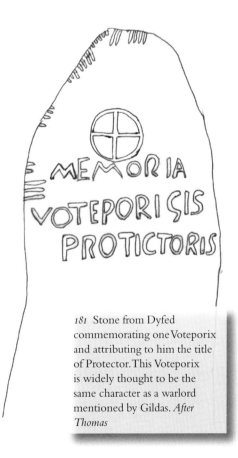

181 Stone from Dyfed commemorating one Voteporix and attributing to him the title of Protector. This Voteporix is widely thought to be the same character as a warlord mentioned by Gildas. *After Thomas*

182 The *Hugin*, sailed from Denmark to Britain to commemorate the 1500th anniversary of the traditional date of the arrival of Hengest and Horsa in Britain. Thanet, Kent

groups from Scandinavia, further north than the main continental Angle and Saxon territories, as suggested by the appearance of such Scandinavian fashions as wrist clasps. We should imagine the fifth and sixth centuries in Europe perhaps a bit like the period after the Second World War, with lots of small groups on the move in all sorts of directions. Not all of them were even coming to Britain. Some were leaving. Procopius writing in the sixth century describes Britons, Frisians and Angles all leaving Britain for the territory of the Franks.[249]

Efforts have been made in a number of ways to estimate the final scale of the Anglo-Saxon immigration. Efforts based on the archaeology suggest perhaps a maximum, spread over roughly a period of 100 years,

of about 100,000 immigrants.[250] Efforts based on new technologies such as DNA research and tooth enamel analysis have been inconclusive. With the genetic evidence it has been hard to tell the difference between people from northern Europe settling in England in prehistoric times, post-Roman times and Viking times. Some estimates based on genetic research have put the Anglo-Saxon immigrants at less than 10 per cent of the population.[251] Molar enamel has on a number of occasions indicated that people found in supposedly Anglo-Saxon contexts actually grew up in parts of Britain that were at that stage still culturally British. Thus, an 'Anglo-Saxon' skeleton from Bamburgh seems to have actually been of someone born in western Scotland.[252]

Efforts based on looking at skeletons seem to suggest a high degree of continuity in some locations between the Roman and Anglo-Saxon periods,[253] and it is worth noting that Tacitus suggests that some of the physical characteristics that came to be seen as separating the populations of England, Wales and Scotland in the medieval period, were already present in the Roman period.

… the red hair and big limbs of the Caledonians indicate a German origin. The dark complexion and curly hair of the Silures, together with their position opposite Spain, suggest that a long time ago, Iberian colonisers settled that country. Those Britons who live closest to Gaul, look like the Gauls.[254]

Whatever the situation, increasingly in the fifth century and certainly by the early sixth century, large parts of southern, central and eastern Britain were culturally Anglo-Saxon, which brings us to one of the key questions of British and English history – if the Britons in the area of early Anglo-Saxon settlement were not wiped out or forced out en masse by the Anglo-Saxons, what did happen to them in those years and why are there so few obvious signs of them?

As mentioned earlier, it's quite possible, and indeed likely, that many Britons in the areas of early Anglo-Saxon settlement, like those outside it, simply led lives that, in archaeological terms, were of low visibility. Some cemeteries have been found that seem to be those of Britons of the post-Roman

183 The Saxon Shore Fort of Pevensey, East Sussex, scene, according to the *Anglo-Saxon Chronicle*, of Britons killed en masse by Saxon invaders

184 Penannular brooch from the post-Roman period, of a type found in western Britain, but also in eastern England

period, and it's quite possible that some Roman-period sites continued to be occupied later than has sometimes been thought. There are tantalising hints of survival even in cities. At *Verulamium* some evidence has been found of simple wooden structures being constructed in the fifth and sixth centuries, which are probably British.[255] The *Anglo-Saxon Chronicle* describes Britons fleeing to London in 456. In Metz, historical evidence indicates occupation in the fifth century, but there is little archaeological evidence of it.[256] The spread of British penannular brooches and hanging bowls and their decorative elements across the area may also, among other things, be an indication of surviving Britons and British tastes and it is assumed that many of the numerous Anglo-Saxon places that incorporate the word walh/wala indicate places connected with people still recognisably British by culture. However, generally, we can only assume that if there were large numbers of Britons in eastern and south-eastern England, then a significant proportion of them must have gradually adopted many features of Anglo-Saxon culture, just as many of their ancestors had eventually adopted many features of Roman culture.

There has been a tendency to assume that the arrival of the Anglo-Saxons represented a huge clash of cultures. Though people now tend to have slightly more sophisticated views of the early Anglo-Saxon period than that, there is still a certain basic reluctance to accept that the Britons could have actively wanted to adopt Anglo-Saxon culture.

However, as we have already seen, the real picture of life for the average Briton was very different to that. Even during the Roman period, many Britons lived in simple buildings with few of the trappings of the luxury Romanised lifestyle of the rich. And certainly by the time the Anglo-Saxons arrived in Britain, life must have been very basic indeed. Roman culture had almost entirely collapsed and Britons were making do with patched-up Roman-period items or items made out of substances such as bone or wood which have rarely survived. In such circumstances, Anglo-Saxon culture could have been attractive to the Britons of central, eastern and south-eastern England in three major ways.

Firstly, for those Britons who had actually led a Romanised lifestyle, Anglo-Saxon ways would often have been much more practical than trying to maintain some kind of continuity of their previous lifestyle. Unlike the Roman lifestyle, which depended on a complex economic network to maintain it, the Anglo-Saxon lifestyle was low-tech and easy to operate in difficult times. You could make your own pottery and build your own house, rather than relying on specialised craftspeople to do it for you. A villa might look impressive, but it would be much easier to keep an Anglo-Saxon hut warm in winter.

Secondly, Anglo-Saxon culture had strong elements of similarity to traditional British culture. The kind of warrior society the Anglo-Saxons brought with them was the kind of society that Britons had had before the arrival of the Romans, and though it may have been in the background during the Roman period, memories of it may have remained strong through oral epics of the sort that still survive recording warrior societies in Ireland, and perhaps through other means such as a strong tradition of hunting. Certainly, the kind of society portrayed in a post-Roman British poem like *Y Gododdin*, or the Irish *Story of Mac Dathó's Pig*, with their emphasis on such aspects of

185 A type of buckle in a late Roman tradition but found in Britain in association with early Anglo-Saxon settlement

186 Germanic troops serving in the Roman army shown on the base of the column of Theodosius in Istanbul

life as feasting and combat, is very similar to that portrayed in a poem like *Beowulf*. British paganism of the pre-Roman period and, to a certain extent, the Roman period too, with its emphasis on cults attached to landscape features like water and groves, also had a number of parallels in what we know of Anglo-Saxon paganism. The love of ostentatious displays of jewellery was another shared aspect of traditional British and Anglo-Saxon culture. And some key material items of early Anglo-Saxon culture, like simple huts for housing and simple handmade pottery with geometric decorations, were not too far distant from what traditional British society had been used to. Some forms of burial, like the secondary use of prehistoric ritual monuments, were also shared links between Anglo-Saxon and British culture.[257]

Thirdly, while Britons were less Romanised than most people think, the Anglo-Saxons, the Saxons in particular, were actually much *more* Romanised than most people think, and with levels of Romanisation in Britain dropping fast in the period after the end of Rome, levels of Romanisation between the indigenous Britons and the incoming Anglo-Saxons may not have been that different. Almost all early Anglo-Saxon metalwork in Britain is actually, in a sense, late Roman metalwork. Much of it is made with a technique called chip-carving which was adopted from fourth-century Roman military metalwork. And key items like the cruciform brooch are derived from late Roman crossbow brooches. Most tellingly of all perhaps is that the Anglo-Saxon language, even before the arrival of the Anglo-Saxons in Britain, had absorbed large numbers of Latin words. Many of these loan words are for items of a Roman lifestyle, such as *vinum*/wine, *moneta*/mint, suggesting a fair degree of familiarity with Roman culture.[258] It's even worth pointing out that the Anglo-Saxons organised their week, and possibly in some sense their pantheon, along Roman lines. The Anglo-Saxon, and hence English, days of the week are simply translations of the Roman days of the week in which an Anglo-Saxon god or goddess with similar attributes has been substituted for the relevant Roman god or goddess. Thus Tiw, the Anglo-Saxon god of war, was substituted for Mars to make Tuesday and Freya, the Anglo-Saxon goddess of love and marriage, was substituted for Venus to make Friday. With Saturday, the Anglo-Saxons presumably couldn't decide on a substitute, so they just kept the Roman god Saturn in the day's name. It's impossible to be sure precisely how the Anglo-Saxons developed all their experience of Roman

187 The defences of Caistor by Norwich, Norfolk, the Roman-period capital of the Iceni. There is evidence of early Anglo-Saxon settlement very close to it

culture. No doubt partly this was done via trading networks, but some of it too was probably done through Saxons serving as Roman mercenaries. The Romans used mercenaries from almost every Germanic group in Western Europe at some stage, so it would be a bit of a surprise if there had been no Saxons fighting for Rome at some point. Late Roman military equipment has been found ritually deposited in Danish bogs, and certainly, when the Anglo-Saxons finally arrived in Britain, a percentage of their warriors seem to have arrived wearing what are basically fifth-century Roman military belts.[259]

There is thus no particular reason why many Britons would not have adopted Anglo-Saxon culture, and in fact there are specific reasons to believe that that is exactly what at least a number of them did do, because within so-called 'Anglo-Saxon' culture in Britain are possible traces of British culture that may suggest how Britons subtly changed Anglo-Saxon culture as they adopted it. The effects may not be as dramatic as with the hybrid Romano-British culture that developed in Britain after the Roman invasion, but we have to remember that while the Romans invaded a land that had a strong, vibrant existing culture, the Anglo-Saxons

188 Fifth-century Quoit Brooch. *After Suzuki*

arrived in a country with an economy and a culture both at a very low ebb. It's worth noting that as soon as distinctively local cultural products, such as hanging bowls and penannular brooches, became available again, many inhabitants of the Anglo-Saxon region, whether they were ethnically British, Anglo-Saxon or a mixture, seem to have adopted them with enthusiasm.

Let's look in turn at some of the different key aspects of early Anglo-Saxon culture and see how Britons may have affected their development in Britain.

One of the most obvious signs of early Anglo-Saxon culture in Britain is Anglo-Saxon copper alloy metalwork, particularly consisting of brooches, but also including a number of other items of personal adornment as well. The different categories have been extensively catalogued and analysed, all under the heading 'Anglo-Saxon', but what's interesting here is that there are substantial differences between the body of 'Anglo-Saxon' metalwork found in Britain and that found in the continental

homelands of the Angles and Saxons. Some of the most obvious items, like cruciform brooches and square-headed brooches, show clear similarities on both sides of the North Sea. However, some items from Britain show very different styles and different ways of using the item. So-called wrist clasps, for instance, are worn by both sexes in Scandinavia, but only by women in Britain, and while some of the styles of British wrist-clasp have clear links to Scandinavia, a good number are of different styles, some with similarities (whether by chance or some stylistic survival) to late Roman metalwork.[260] What's more, there are types of brooch found in Britain which either have no links to types found on the other side of the North Sea or no obvious ones. Into this category fall the very common (in Britain) flat annular brooches and disc brooches.[261] It's impossible to know what accounts for these major differences, but certainly influence from indigenous Britons is one distinct possibility. The annular brooches, for instance, may have been influenced by post-Roman Quoit Brooches or by a taste for post-Roman penannular brooches found, as already mentioned, quite widely across supposedly Anglo-Saxon areas. Equally, the disc brooches could have links to similar Roman-period metalwork, or perhaps to British equivalents made in perishable substances such as bone. Some spearheads found in Anglo-Saxon graves are very similar to those found in the continental homelands of the Anglo-Saxons, but again, there are a number of significant categories that seem to have few continental antecedents and perhaps seem to have rather more in common with British antecedents.[262] Another interesting aspect of some 'Anglo-Saxon' metalwork in Britain, is the appearance on some of it of enamelling, a process that is a major feature of Celtic metalwork, but not of continental Anglo-Saxon metalwork.[263]

There's a rather similar situation with early Anglo-Saxon housing. It has long been noted that the longhouse, very common in the continental homelands of the Anglo-Saxons, has no parallels in Britain. Instead the main Anglo-Saxon house in Britain is a simple rectangular hut built from wooden posts. The method of building these huts is paralleled on the continent, though continental examples tend to have internal posts (and divisions). However, it has been suggested that the significant differences between housing on the continent and in Britain must represent a significant British presence among the builders, with Britons choosing from the menu of Anglo-Saxon housing the type of building that suited them and that was similar to buildings they already knew, while ignoring the larger and more complex longhouse that didn't suit their needs and was not similar to buildings they knew. Certainly, if Britons were looking for a simple form of building to replace some of the more complex constructions of the Roman period, these would have been a good choice and they are very similar to simple huts of the Roman period at Dunston's Clump.[264] Very often, as noted previously, early Anglo-Saxon settlement seems to take place close to Roman-period settlements and while some of this may represent new Anglo-Saxon owners of a farm or village, there is a suspicion that some of it may also represent existing British occupants building themselves new Anglo-Saxon-style accommodation on greenfield sites close to, but not in the middle of, the 'ruins' of their old lives.

Most of what is known about early Anglo-Saxons in Britain comes from their cemeteries and here too some archaeologists increasingly suspect the influence, and indeed the presence, of significant numbers of Britons.

A common way of dealing with the dead in the continental homelands of the Angles and Saxons was cremation, though inhumation is also known. In Britain, where inhumation was normal by the end of the Roman period, there are cremations particularly in the culturally Angle area, but there are numerous inhumations as well, particularly in the Saxon areas, and inhumation seems to become more common with time.

This spread of inhumation could perhaps show Anglo-Saxons adopting local customs, and/or it could show the presence of significant numbers of Britons within cemeteries in the Anglo-Saxon area. Christians of this period were traditionally buried without grave goods and there are significant numbers of inhumations without grave goods both in supposedly Anglo-Saxon cemeteries and occasionally separately. These burials could just be those of the extremely poor but they could also easily be those of Christian Britons. Equally though, many of those burials with grave goods could be of pagan Britons, or of Christian Britons whose families were unconcerned about a theological ban on all grave goods that may not have been anything like as watertight as is often assumed, with Christian burials of high status figures on the continent in the fifth and sixth centuries often incorporating grave goods.[265] While some burials are richly furnished with a range of items, many graves contain perhaps a brooch or two or a belt buckle or knife, and there is, in any case, no necessary reason why all burials with Anglo-Saxon grave goods need to belong to ethnic Anglo-Saxons, any more than all earlier British graves with Roman goods always belonged to ethnic Romans. This is particularly true since a significant number of 'Anglo-Saxon' inhumations also show

189 Newly identified fragment of fifth-century Quoit Brooch Style metalwork. It is, as with much Quoit Brooch Style metalwork, highly decorated

what may be British traits. Sometimes this is a British penannular brooch, or brooches worn in a British way, or grave goods from the Roman period in Britain, or burial forms that may be specifically British, including burying the body crouched or with its head decapitated.[266] Not even all the cremation burials have to be those of ethnic Anglo-Saxons. Cremation was the norm in early Roman Britain before, for reasons unknown, inhumation became the fashion. If cremation had been acceptable to Britons in that period of Roman Britain, then it could have become so again in post-Roman Britain.

Finally we come to the question of language. It has often been said that the English people must be mainly ethnic Anglo-Saxons because they speak English, the language of the Anglo-Saxons, with very few Celtic words and very few Celtic place names;

whereas in France, for instance, the Franks eventually adopted the language of the locals.

At first glance this argument has an attractive simplicity (even though there are more Germanic words in modern French than is sometimes thought) but increasingly it's being found that the situation in England is a bit more complicated than that.

The two main problems are that we simply don't know enough about what was being spoken in the Romanised part of Britain during the Roman period, and that we don't know enough about what was being spoken in the Anglo-Saxon kingdoms for the first few hundred years of Anglo-Saxon rule.

As discussed in Chapter 3, it is generally assumed that when the Romans arrived in Britain all of Britain was speaking various Celtic languages. However, since there

190 The Roman walls of London. Britons defeated by Anglo-Saxons in a battle in the post-Roman period are said to have taken refuge here

are almost no inscriptions in any Celtic language from the pre-Roman or Roman period in Britain, this is an assumption largely based on survival of Celtic languages in the West, a comment in Tacitus that the Britons spoke a similar language to that of the Gauls, and a few British names. Some people have, however, raised the question of whether a form of Germanic language may have been spoken by some Britons in the far east of the country.

From the Roman period in Britain, we have only two inscriptions in any Celtic languages. We have official and com-memorative inscriptions in Latin, we have brief messages in other contexts, such as, for instance, in mosaics, and occasional brief examples of graffiti in Latin. On the evidence of Gaul, it can probably be assumed that, by the end of the Roman period in Britain, Latin was being fairly widely spoken in the Romanised parts but with a Celtic language or languages still spoken elsewhere and pockets of people speaking a Celtic language even in more remote parts of the Romanised region. It is probably fair to see the Romanised part of Britain being in a transitional language phase heading towards Latin being gener-ally spoken.

We don't really know anything for the next few hundred years, until a few docu-ments begin to appear written in Old English. However, it's hard to know to what extent the Anglo-Saxon documents we do have represent what was being spoken by ordinary people in the different parts of the different Anglo-Saxon kingdoms for the first few hundred years. Some people argue that we don't get a proper view of what ordinary people in England were actually speaking until the Norman period.[267]

191 Example of Roman chip-carving from Britain

192 Example of Anglo-Saxon chip-carving

It's worth reminding ourselves at the start of this investigation of language change, of the probable linguistic vulnerability of the Britons at the time of the Anglo-Saxon arrival. If the Romanised part of Britain was in a period of linguistic transition from a Celtic language to Latin, then this would have made its attachment to either language weak, and its attachment to Latin such as it was, as with its attachment to the rest of Roman culture, would have dropped dramatically in the period immediately after 410. By the time the Anglo-Saxons turned up, Britons who had been speaking Latin either as their main or second language might have been keen to speak something else – in a development perhaps in some ways similar to the decline in importance of Russian language tuition in some areas of former Soviet influence immediately after the end of the Soviet Union. It's also worth pointing out that, while Cornwall has, as you would expect, plenty of place names with a Celtic origin, next door Devon (also conquered late by the Anglo-Saxons, and where nobody is suggesting mass extinction of the local Britons) has far fewer Celtic place names, and not that many more than are found much further east in places like Kent and Essex.[268]

We have already noted that Old English contained a significant number of Latin loan words by the time the Anglo-Saxons arrived in England, something which would have helped ease the transition to Old English for any Latin speakers. Only a few Celtic and additional Latin words seem to have been adopted into Old English after the arrival of the Anglo-Saxons in England but, as research shows, in some cases of large-scale language shift, the transfer of vocabulary from old language to new language can indeed be minimal.[269]

We certainly know that the early Anglo-Saxons did live alongside and talk to Britons, because the Anglo-Saxons adopted a lot of place names from them. Even in the parts of eastern England where Anglo-Saxon settlement was most heavy, most major cities and many major rivers have Celtic names and the number of Celtic names increases as you move further west. Some of the Anglo-Saxon kingdoms acquired new Anglo-Saxon names, as one might expect, but a number of them retained British names, based either on the tribe, as in the case of Kent, or on the main town of the kingdom, as in the case of Deira and Lindsey, or some other attribute, as in the case of Bernicia.

193 Anglo-Saxon annular brooch

There has been a tendency to play down the number of Celtic place names that have survived in England but there are a number of key points to make about this. Firstly, as mentioned, there are plenty of Anglo-Saxon place names, even in the far west of England (excluding Cornwall), where their presence has to be explained by some other reason apart from population replacement. Equally, the years after the end of Roman rule saw much settlement discontinuity which would probably mean name discontinuity as well, and the absence of a literate administrative system in the early Anglo-Saxon period can't have helped. Thirdly, since we only know a very few names from the Roman period it's hard to be sure how many of them actually have gone. There are a number of cases where we know that names, which at first sight seem Anglo-Saxon, are actually British names that have been Anglo-Saxonised. York, for instance, is ultimately derived from *Eboracum*, the Roman-period name, but without knowing the Roman-period name, we wouldn't know this and might try to deduce some kind of Anglo-Saxon derivation. The same applies to Rochester, ultimately derived from a cut-down version of the Roman-period name *Durobrivae*, and Speen, which comes from the Roman-

194 'Anglo-Saxon' disc brooch. This type of brooch may be one sign of British tastes influencing the culture of the Anglo-Saxon period

195 Excavated early Anglo-Saxon urns at Cleatham, Lincolnshire. *Courtesy of Kevin Leahy*

196 Roman material in the fabric of St Martin's, Canterbury. Kent is a continuation of the Roman-period name of the area (the *civitas* of the Cantii) and Canterbury, remaining the capital of the area, also contains the same name-element

197 The late Roman Multiangular Tower in
Eboracum/York. The name York ultimately
derives from the Roman-period name, but if
we did not already know the Roman name,
we might be tempted to think it was an
Anglo-Saxon or Viking name

period name *Spinae*. If we knew more names from the Roman period then we might well find a lot more cases of this. If we look at the problem from the other side, and say not 'what percentage of modern names have Roman-period roots?' but instead say 'what percentage of Roman-period names that we know, continue in some form into the Anglo-Saxon period?' then we get figures that suggest a much higher percentage of names surviving. Admittedly, these names are mostly of major sites, where names are more likely to survive, so place name continuity wouldn't be perhaps as high as that suggests, but it may be significantly more than currently recognised.

Increasingly, though, people are looking beyond vocabulary and place names, to the very structure of English itself, to identify the influence of the Britons. In significant ways the very structure of English seems to have been influenced by people originally speaking a Celtic language. The arguments are often highly technical but broadly speaking they take the view that when willingly learning a new language, you do not intentionally introduce vocabulary from your own language into it because you know that is not 'correct', but you may unintentionally introduce patterns of grammar, syntax and sound that seem less obviously to you 'incorrect'.[270] The evidence from these new lines of investigation does seem to suggest a significant Celtic influence on the Old English language, liable to have come from Britons changing from speaking a Celtic language to an Anglo-Saxon one, perhaps, in some cases, with a period of Latin in between. As a result of this and the work mentioned earlier on language shifts without large vocabulary transfer, a number of linguistic experts now think the case for widespread Anglo-Saxonisation of Britons is linguistically strong.

When all the evidence surrounding the Anglo-Saxon arrival in Britain is examined in detail it seems very unlikely that all the Britons in the area of early Anglo-Saxon settlement were simply wiped out or driven out, and it seems much more likely that many of them swapped what was left of their Roman and British culture for a new Anglo-Saxon import. Assuming therefore that Britons did adopt Anglo-Saxon culture and language, it is perhaps worth concluding this chapter with brief reflections on why they might have adopted an Anglo-Saxon identity more thoroughly than they adopted a Roman identity.

We have already touched upon perhaps the main reason. This is simply that when the Romans came to Britain, the Britons had a vibrant, thriving culture of their own. By the time the Anglo-Saxons came, the Britons had a culture which has left few archaeological traces, and Britons in the previously Romanised area must have been particularly culturally demoralised and probably ready to adopt pretty much any useful culture, particularly one so close to certain core British traditions. The rise of Anglo-Saxon political power is only likely to have made the attractions of Anglo-Saxon culture stronger. We know of a number of members of Gallo-Roman families with Germanic names under new Frankish rulers. Thus, for example, we know of Gallo-Roman senators who had Germanic names like Gundulfus or Beregesilus, while a couple with the Gallo-Roman names Gaudentius and Austadiola gave their son the Germanic name Gaugeric. No doubt plenty of this happened in Britain as well.[271]

In addition, though, the nature of the Anglo-Saxon presence was very different to that of Rome. Rome's presence was one imposed from the top by comparatively small numbers of people. The majority of outsiders in Roman Britain, certainly in the early period, were probably also soldiers who, after the initial invasion period, spent much of their time in a few specific locations, many of them far from British population centres. By contrast, if the final figure of about 100,000 Anglo-Saxon settlers over a period of 100 years is about right, then the Anglo-Saxons must by the end of that time have formed a significant percentage of the local population, particularly in East Anglia and the area just to the north of that, where immigration was perhaps most intense.

We can only guess about the speed of Britons and Anglo-Saxons becoming one society. In mainland Europe some incoming Germanic regimes made some attempts for a few generations to control intermarriage. Some did not. In both cases, though, the situation probably became rather similar to that in England after the Norman Conquest, where the senior Norman aristocrats tended to marry within their own families, but there were plenty of English mistresses and some marrying of English noblewomen, while further down the social scale, mixing was rather more free.[272] Just over 100 years after the invasion, it was said to be impossible to tell the difference between Normans and English. In a society where paperwork was minimal, the only real way to tell whether somebody was British or Anglo-Saxon would be through his culture. If a Briton changed his clothes, his name and his language, Anglo-Saxon society would almost certainly accept him, or certainly his children as Anglo-Saxon. The Anglo-Saxon law code of Ine does draw a distinction between Britons and Anglo-Saxons, but it is not the apartheid document it has sometimes been portrayed as. Anglo-Saxons are valued more highly than Britons (perhaps in a similar sense to the way that, for instance, Roman citizens were valued more highly than non-citizens in the early Empire), but a British noble is, for example, still valued more highly than an ordinary Anglo-Saxon. It is very similar to the law codes instituted by Germanic regimes in mainland Europe after they took over new territories and prior to integration of the Germanic newcomers with the indigenous population. In the context of Wessex, therefore, it is most likely to be referring to new, culturally British, Britons incorporated into Wessex after its expansion into western Britain. It is hard to think that a kingdom that seems to have had several kings with distinctly British names was massively prejudiced against Britons.

Ultimately, though, perhaps the final reason for the different outcomes of Romanisation and Anglo-Saxonisation is that while the Romans left, the Anglo-Saxons stayed and, in time, the Britons of the Anglo-Saxon kingdoms and ethnic Anglo-Saxons created a unified English identity, defining themselves as different to Welsh, Cornish and Scottish societies. If the Romans had managed to remain in England a few centuries longer, perhaps we'd all be speaking a Latin-based language today instead.

10

UNROMAN BRITAIN
THROUGH HISTORY

EVER since the end of Roman Britain, Britons have been looking back on it, wondering what it all meant.

The earliest whose thoughts on the subject have survived is, of course, Gildas, a man born at a time when the grandparents, and even parents, of some of those living would actually have experienced it. His verdict, as we have seen, is fascinating and reflects a lot of what has been said in this book. For Gildas Britain was a land a long way from Rome, a land on its own:

> The island of Britain lies at almost the very ends of the earth … it is surrounded by the ocean, with curving bays, and the sea forms a strong defence, an impassable barrier, I would say, except on the south side.[273]

It was a divided land:

> For it has always been the way with our people, as now, to be powerless in repelling foreign enemies, but powerful and bold in making civil war.[274]

It was a land of rebels:

> This island, stubborn to the core, from the time people first lived here, rebels ungratefully sometimes against God, sometimes against its own citizens, and often against foreign kings and their subjects.[275]

Fundamentally, it was for Gildas a land that had acquired a veneer of Roman culture under the weight of Roman might, but one where Britons never actually became Romans, and where, when Roman power had gone, the Britons were still there as they always had been.

Inevitably Gildas' views were affected by the climate of his day, in the sense that there may by his time have seemed an inevitability about the end of Roman Britain that would not have been apparent to someone living in the early fourth century. And yet, it would be unwise to dismiss his views entirely. Gildas after all is our earliest witness whose evidence has survived and he must also have been one of the Britons of his day most appreciative of Roman culture. He was a member of a Church that inherited significant elements of Roman culture, he wrote in Latin, had presumably read Latin authors, and spent more time castigating the sins of the Britons then he ever did the sins of Rome. If Gildas viewed Roman Britain as still, in many ways, a fairly UnRoman phenomenon then it is worth listening to him. As we have seen in this book, there is plenty of archaeological and historical evidence to support his view.

However, as the years eroded memories of the reality of the Romans in Britain, perhaps inevitably inhabitants of the island began to take a more enthusiastic view of Rome and its presence here. We all love the big characters in history, and they don't come much bigger

198 The sun setting over Hadrian's Wall just as the sun finally set on both Rome's and Britain's empires

199 Milecastle on Hadrian's Wall

200 A Roman design (Venus bathing) created in a rather UnRoman way – the Roman Britain that Britain later wanted to forget. *Courtesy of Great North Museum*

than Rome, the small village that grew to create one of the mightiest empires ever seen, a name that even today conjures up instant mental pictures of power, wealth, luxury and conquest. Both British and Anglo-Saxon dynasties seem to have been happy, from early on, to adopt some of the trappings of Rome, to imply that, in some ways, their kings of small tribal kingdoms were the successors to, and equals of, the mighty emperors of Rome. This, of course, was not just something that was happening in Britain. The phenomenon of later rulers adopting the trappings of Roman power to bolster their own importance was a firmly established tradition across much of the former territory of the Empire and in some areas beyond it as well.

Culturally, too, the legacy of Rome was a vibrant one, even in areas such as Britain where the realities of Roman culture under Roman rule had not always been universally appreciated. In the Middle Ages, Latin was not just the language of religion, it was also the language of learning, and classical authors remained a key element of the most advanced education available. And this respect for Roman culture was, of course, given a huge boost by the Renaissance. Now it was not just Roman learning and symbols of power that were valued but classical Roman art and architecture as well. And this love affair with Roman culture gradually grew and expanded during the seventeenth, eighteenth and nineteenth centuries in Britain. Take a look at Bath. The original temple complex was dedicated to a British goddess, Sulis Minerva, and over her temple was a pediment featuring a head with curving Celtic patterns in his hair, and staring Celtic eyes. But when the Georgians came to rebuild the

201 Detail of the Rudston mosaic. *Courtesy of Hull and East Riding Museum*

baths, they did so in as classical a style as they could think of, complete with Ionic, Doric and Corinthian capitol-capped columns and with Roman figures on the roof.

Above all, though, it was the expansion in the nineteenth century of the British Empire, and the rise in Britain of an ideology of empire that came to shape British attitudes to Roman Britain and which to some extent still does.

Many Britons came to see close parallels between the Roman Empire and Victoria's empire. Nineteenth-century Britons didn't just want to feel good about their empire being the most powerful in the world, they also wanted to feel that it was a force for good in the world, that it had moral as well as military and commercial power. In this scenario, the Romans were seen as spreading 'civilisation', with laws, roads, education,

sewers, water pipes etc., across the world, in the same way that Britons in the nineteenth century thought the British Empire was doing. This phenomenon can only have been boosted by the fact that studying Latin and Greek authors was the main component of the education of many of the British Empire's administrators.[276]

With this interpretation of history, many Britons of the nineteenth and early twentieth centuries found it much easier to sympathise with the Roman authorities controlling Britain, than they did with Britons unenthusiastic about Rome and Roman culture. To them, it was the imperial administrators who seemed worthy, not the rebellious locals, much in the same way that they looked across the British Empire and imagined they saw noble British administrators struggling to civilise

202 Late third- or early fourth-century tombstone of Vellibia Ertola, aged four. *Courtesy of Corbridge Museum*

and 'Roman Britain'. They are both phrases in regular use in the nineteenth and early twentieth centuries. Yet now we look back at so-called 'British India' and see clearly how India, in fact, still remained in so many ways *not* British during its time as part of the British Empire, while too often today we still use the phrase 'Roman Britain' without seeing the UnRoman aspects hidden by this useful shorthand for 'Britain under Roman control'.

In a Britain that no longer mainly defines the British Empire as a civilising force and is much more accepting of other cultures than nineteenth- and early twentieth-century Britain, views such as those of Fletcher and Kipling seem, in many ways, strange. And yet, some of the concepts that formed the basis of their perspective do still affect thinking about Roman Britain among today's Britons.

Many people would still see Roman culture as more 'civilised' and more modern than local British culture of the time and would, therefore, still find it easier to understand, sympathise with, and be interested in, the Romans and those Britons who enthusiastically adopted Roman culture than those Britons who did not. Inevitably when people look at History, they have a slight tendency to see what they want to see. If people want to see a Britain full of Britons keenly learning to be Roman, then that, to some extent, is what they are likely to see. The reverse is, of course, also true, but in this book we have tried to be objective, and in any event, after so much concentration in the past on the Roman side of Roman Britain, it seems important to take a fresh look at the undoubtedly also present UnRoman side.

Analogies between past and present history can obviously be dangerous. However,

often rebellious and ungrateful locals. As Fletcher and Kipling put it in 1911, 'It was ... a misfortune for Britain that Rome never conquered the whole island. The great warrior, Agricola, did ... penetrate far into Scotland; but he could leave no trace of civilization behind him, and Ireland he never touched at all'.[277]

It's also interesting at this point briefly to compare the two phrases 'British India'

203 Classical mosaic from a classical villa: the Roman Britain that Britain later wanted to remember

they can equally be vital in coming to a real sense of what happened in the past, and how the past really looked beyond the bare outline details available to us from archaeology and texts from the time.

Some people today would see analogies between the Roman army's presence in Britain and the recent history of US and British armies in Iraq and Afghanistan. Clearly there are huge and obvious differences which hardly need to be pointed out here. However, it is at least worth considering one aspect of the analogy.

Both Iraq and Afghanistan, Iraq particularly, have adopted significant portions of western culture (used here in its broadest sense to include items that ultimately derive from a western tradition even if created, and added to, by other cultures) in terms of artefacts and architecture. Major Iraqi and Afghan cities have many buildings built using western construction techniques and to basically western designs. People drive around in western cars, use western technology like mobile phones, TVs, fridges, air conditioning, some will wear western suits, some serve in

204 The Georgian recreation of
Bath. The combination of British
and Roman ideas and themes
in the original has become a
Georgian fantasy of Rome

armies trained by westerners and equipped with western uniforms and western guns, more now have learnt the English language than did before. Yet, much of the countryside in Iraq and Afghanistan has much lower levels of westernisation than the cities and, as the de-westernisation of Kabul at the end of the Soviet period shows, westernisation, like Romanisation, is not an irreversible process. Ultimately neither in Iraq nor Afghanistan do the people see themselves as westerners. They see themselves as Iraqis and Afghans as well as having other more local identities which have often recently taken priority over their national identities. The ambivalent attitude of Iraqis and Afghans to western cul-

ture is something very important to think about for anyone who assumes that just because a Briton of the Roman period had some of the trappings of Roman culture, they, therefore, saw themselves as Roman. Yes, Rome had a large impact on the culture of Britain during the years of Roman control. However, much of that was restricted to towns, military areas and the homes of the better off. Almost all of Roman culture disappeared rapidly after Roman control ended and ultimately, local identities probably always meant more to most Britons than their identities as forming a minor, remote, rebellious and perhaps largely (by Rome) unloved part of the Roman Empire.

NOTES

1 Anonymous *Story of Mac Dathó's Pig* i.
2 Anonymous *Story of Mac Dathó's Pig* x-xi.
3 Petronius *Satyricon* 5 xxxi-xxxiv.
4 James Whittington, BBC World Service business reporter, 13 June 2005: http://news.bbc. co.uk/1/hi/business/4077294.stm. The report also notes that a complicating factor in the supply of adequate amounts of electricity was the sudden extra demand for fridges, electric fans, air conditioners and other goods previously unavailable.
5 Reece 1988, 5. The relative 'isolation' of rural communities is something which is rarely assessed in the context of 'Roman' society.
6 Whitney 1867. In this work Whitney describes 'Italy after its first Romanization'. We are grateful to Guy de la Bédoyère for this particular reference.
7 Tacitus *Agricola* 21.
8 Cunliffe 1988 Greeks, Romans and Barbarians: spheres of interaction, 124. Calculating the size of ancient populations is a notoriously precarious thing to do, although some have at times suggested that the pre-Roman population of Gaul numbered around a million, of whom only a third remained after 50 BC. Although Caesar's war in Gaul was a particularly brutal one, this does appear, perhaps, to be an over-exaggeration.
9 Hawkes & Crummy 1995; Crummy 1997, 9-28. Contrary to most discussions on the nature of the Lexden burial, we do not know, and probably never will, the identity of the man buried there.
10 Strabo *Geography* IV, 5, 3.
11 Suetonius *Augustus* 48.
12 Suetonius *Caligula* 44.
13 An early fort, possibly demolished before AD 30, and associated granary buildings have been found at Fishbourne, beneath the later palace structure (Cunliffe 1971; Manley & Rudkin 2003; Russell 2006, 23-30) whilst another military installation at Gosbecks seems to pre-date a section of the Iron Age *oppidum* (Creighton 2001, 9; Russell 2006, 30). Neither fort has been securely dated.
14 Caesar *The Alexandrian Wars* 33.
15 Suetonius *Caligula* 44.
16 Suetonius *Claudius* 17.
17 Dio Cassius *History of Rome* LX, 19, 1.
18 There remains significant debate over precisely where, or indeed in what order, Roman troops landed in Britain. The traditional view is that they first established a base in Kent (e.g. Peddie 1987), although the natural harbours in the Chichester – Southampton area of Sussex/Hampshire remain a plausible alternative (e.g. Hind 1989; Black 2000; Russell 2010, 91-115). The debate is a lively one and seems, at the present time, to be no closer to resolution.
19 Fulford, Clarke & Eckhardt 2006.
20 Russell 2006, 55-148.
21 Cunliffe 1971; Russell 2006, 97-106.

22 Gregory 1991.
23 Davies 2009; we are also very grateful to Amanda Chadburn for discussing this aspect of her PhD thesis.
24 Tacitus *Annals* XIV, 31.
25 Tacitus *Annals* XIV, 31.
26 Dio Cassius *Roman History* LXII, 2.
27 Dio Cassius *Roman History* LXII, 4.
28 Tacitus *Annals* XIV, 31.
29 Crummy Benfield, Crummy, Rigby & Shimmin (2007).
30 Tacitus *Annals* XIV, 31.
31 Niblett 1999; Niblett & Thompson 2005. As with the rich burials recorded from Colchester, there is unfortunately no way that a positive identification between the man buried at Folly Lane and a British aristocrat recorded from coins or from the Roman histories can be made. Without clear evidence of a tombstone, recording the name of the individual concerned, archaeology alone can never be that precise.
32 Wheeler 1954; C. Haslegrove, P. Turnbull and R. Fitts 1990, Stanwick, North Yorkshire, Recent Research and Previous Archaeological Investigations: *Archaeological Journal* 147. Wheeler interpreted the site as the centre of a prominent anti-Roman faction in the north, something that has perhaps seemed less likely in the light of further Roman imports.
33 Harding 2004, 162-3.
34 Tacitus *Histories* III, 45.
35 Tacitus *Agricola* XIV, 17.
36 Crummy 1992; Crummy 1997, 73-84.
37 Tacitus *Annals* XIV, 33.
38 Laycock 2008, 7-14.
39 Tacitus *Annals* XIV, 33.
40 Cunliffe 1964. Despite Cunliffe's observations at the time, the possibility that Winchester may have been hit during the revolt has tended to be overlooked by more recent writers as it was not one of the cities noted by the account by Roman historians Tacitus and Dio Cassius.
41 Michael Fulford personal communication 2009.
42 Caesar *Gallic Wars* V, 13.
43 Henig 2002, 48-54.
44 Russell 2006, 225-8.
45 Woodward & Leach 1993.
46 Woodward 1992, 22-3, 35-7.
47 Millett 1990, 195-6.
48 Strabo *Geography* IV, 5.
49 Caesar *Gallic War* V, 12.
50 Strabo *Geography* IV, 5.
51 Pliny the Elder *Natural History* XXXIV, 164.
52 Brodribb & Cleere 1988.
53 Burnham & Burnham 2004.
54 Creighton 2000 features extensive analysis of the ways in which pre-Roman dynasties in Britain used classical designs on their coins to project messages about the power of the dynasties and their links to Rome.
55 Laing 2000, 109-110.
56 See Millet 1990, 175-6 for discussion of the phenomenon.
57 Henig 1995, 80. See also comment that British art under Rome remains more distinctive than in Gaul.
58 See Laycock 2008, figs 50a, 50d. See also Hawkes & Dunning 1961, fig. 15, n, o, q.

59 See Laing 1993.
60 See Bruce-Mitford & Raven 2005.
61 Tacitus *Agricola* XXI.
62 Mattingly 2006, 319.
63 Wild 2006, 299-306. Allason-Jones 2008, 95-96.
64 Wild 2006, 299-306.
65 Kilbride-Jones 1980, 159-169. Wild 1970.
66 Bayley & Butcher 2004, 194.
67 Bayley & Butcher 2004, 196.
68 Kilbride-Jones 1980, 170-183.
69 Bayley & Butcher 2004, 175-176.
70 Swift 2003, 19-20. Bayley & Butcher 2004, 185-186.
71 Laing 2000, 90.
72 Vindolanda Tablet 164.
73 Claudianus *De Consulatu Stilichonis* 2, 247-250.
74 Ausonius *Epigrams* 110, 111.
75 Creighton 2006, 123-156.
76 Millet 1990, fig. 68 and 172-174.
77 Millet 1990, 174-176.
78 L'Hour 1987, 113-131.
79 Woolf 1998, 3.
80 Knight 2007, 182-184.
81 The Gallic phenomenon of tribal capitals being called after the tribes only seems to happen in Britain in the case of Canterbury, but this is probably to be attributed to a break in occupation at most, maybe all, Roman-period tribal capitals in Britain.
82 Woolf 1998, 91-93.
83 Creighton 2000, 89-94.
84 Tacitus *Agricola* XI.
85 See the work of Daphne Nash-Briggs, plus Oppenheimer 2006, 267-307.
86 Mattingly 2006, 201-202.
87 Tacitus *Agricola* XXI.
88 Woolf 1998, 90.
89 Woolf 1998, 81-82.
90 Mattingly 2006, 460.
91 Mattingly 2006, 461.
92 de la Bédoyère 2006, 221.
93 Mullen 2007.
94 Schrijver 2007, 166-167.
95 Tacitus *Annals* XII, 39.
96 Tacitus *Annals* XII, 39.
97 Tacitus *Agricola* XXXIX, 26.
98 Herodian *History of the Empire* III, 14.
99 Cunliffe 1968.
100 Pitts & St Joseph 1985. In fact, the demolition seems to have occurred before the fortress had been completed, the foundations for the commanding officer's house not having been set out.
101 Fronto *Parthian War* 2, 220.
102 *Scriptores Historiae Augustae Hadrian*, 5, 1.
103 *Scriptores Historiae Augustae Hadrian*, 11, 2.
104 Harding 2004.
105 Vindolanda Tablet 291.
106 Vindolanda Tablet 233.
107 Vindolanda Tablet 346.

108 Vindolanda Tablet 164.

109 Russell 2006, 181-93; McWhirr 1981.

110 Palladius *Lausiac History* LXI.

111 Tacitus *Annals* III.

112 Tacitus *Histories* 4.69.

113 See Dark 2000, 43.

114 Thanks to Christopher Wrigley for this.

115 Laycock 2008, 85-108.

116 Zosimus *New History* 4, 114.

117 de la Bédoyère 2006, 103.

118 Mattingly 2006, 168.

119 de la Bédoyère 2001, 209-210. Erdkamp 2007, 183, 193, 196, 257, 421 etc. Goldsworthy, 80.

120 Mattingly 2006, 168-169, 222, 251.

121 Herodian *Roman History* 3, 6.

122 Dobson & Mann 1973, 205.

123 Yann Le Bohec 2000, 81.

124 Ammianus Marcellinus 20, 4, 1-5 and 20, 4, 16.

125 See the interesting maps of inscriptions of the different emperors in Bourne 2001, 23-24.

126 See, de la Bédoyère 2003, 127-138. For coin types, see Bourne 2001, Appendix 4-Appendix 6.

127 Drinkwater 1987, 43.

128 *Historia Augusta, The Thirty Pretenders*, 3, 3.

129 *Historia Augusta, Aurelian*, 34, 2.

130 de la Bédoyère 2003, 131.

131 Bourne 2001, 23-24.

132 Pearson 2002, 56-66.

133 Drinkwater 1987, 229.

134 Faulkner 2000, 116 and fig. 8. Mattingly 2006, 338, note the striking extent of the change in British towns and its earliness.

135 Faulkner 2000, figs 18, 19. See also fig.7 for levels of occupancy in towns being sustained.

136 Faulkner 2000, fig. 29.

137 Drinkwater 1987, 131.

138 Casey 1995, 71-76.

139 de la Bédoyère 2003, 146.

140 Casey 1995, 124-125. Pearson, 59-60.

141 Thomas 1994, 202, 205.

142 Salway 1993, 225.

143 de la Bédoyère 1999, 73.

144 King 1990, 189-201.

145 Salway 1993, 245.

146 Hunter 2010, 96-110.

147 Faulkner 2000, fig. 19.

148 Brooks 1986, 77-102.

149 Faulkner 2000, fig. 29.

150 Also, for example, Aurrecoechea Fernandez says that such buckles and other belt fittings are rare in southern Spain and southern France – personal comment. Professor Maurizio Buora says that as far as he knows there are extremely few such buckles and other belt fittings (at least published) in south Italy – personal comment.

151 Mark Corney, who has been working on horsehead buckles and connected belt fittings in western Britain, finds evidence in his work that may suggest military or official regulation of production and distribution of that category – Swift 1999, 15. Griffiths, who has been working with Corney, states that broadly, most buckles and associated fittings of the late Roman period in Britain are clearly official issue in some sense, Griffiths 2001, 53.

152 Aurrecoechea Fernandez 2001. Laycock 2008, 116-117.

153 Esmond Cleary 1989, 134.

154 At Wasperton, for instance, see buckles in Inhumation 10, Inhumation 22, Inhumation 23, Inhumation 115, Inhumation 135, Inhumation 142 etc. Carver, Hills, Scheschkewitz 2009.

155 Laycock 2008, 113-118.

156 MacMullen 1967, 135-139.

157 Burns 1995, 36.

158 Sidonius Apollinaris *Letters*, 3, 3.

159 Jordanes *The Origins and Deeds of the Goths*, 36, 191.

160 Rob Collins personal comment on scarcity in Hadrian's Wall area and see Coulston 2010, 62-63. See Bishop & Coulston 2006, 216 on scarcity of shield fittings.

161 For such knives in military-style burials in mainland Europe see e.g. Sommer 1984, Tafel 27, 28, 29, 31, 38, 56, 69. Böhme 1974, Tafel 63.

162 Often spearheads found on late Roman civilian sites in Britain seem to be relatively small types for javelins. This type is also common on late Roman military sites and in burials with weapons on the continent. See Bishop & Coulston 2006, fig. 93 and fig. 127; also note the figure of the soldier at fig. 94, 3. For burials on the continent see Sommer 1984, Tafel 71, 76, 80.

163 Fowler *Fyfod Working Paper FWP 64*.

164 For the Barnsley Park site, see Webster and Smith 1982. For Shakenoak Farm villa see Brodribb, Hands, Walker 2005. For the villa at Castle Copse, Great Bedwyn see Hostetter & Howe 1997. See Laycock 2009, 57 for more about finds of weighted military darts at civilian sites, where buckles and belt fittings have been found on the same site or very nearby – Caerwent, Wroxeter, Cirencester, Nettleton, Kenchester.

165 Hingley 2006, 213-257.

166 Frere 1989, 319.

167 Southern & Dixon 2000, 68-69.

168 Halsall 1982, 205-207.

169 See Pearson 2002, 163, fig. 77.

170 Laycock 2008, 118-125.

171 It is interesting to note a few similarities but rather more significant differences in the distribution of other metal items of dress, suggesting there are specific *civitas* factors at work in the distribution of late buckles and belt fittings. Compare, for instance, distribution of late buckles and other fittings with early and late pins, Cool 1983, 111-113, or for late bracelets see Swift 1999, figs. 145-227. Generally, in the late Roman west, there is not much evidence of buckles and other belt fittings being made in the same workshops as bracelets, Swift 1999, 116-117.

172 Wickham 2005, 334-336.

173 Wickham 2005, 334-339.

174 Zosimus *New History* 4, 114.

175 Saint Jerome *Letter 133*.

176 Gildas *On the Ruin of Britain*, 4.

177 Sozomen *Ecclesiastical History*, 7, 13.

178 Laycock 2009, 27-28.

179 Laycock 2009, 31-33.

180 Zosimus *New History*, 6.5.2-3.

181 Procopius *The Vandal War*, 3.2.38.

182 On Canterbury see Dark 2000, 82, 101-2. For *Verulamium*, see Niblett 2001, 131, 132, 145.

183 White 2007, 180-185.

184 White 2007, 169.

185 Esmonde-Cleary 1989, 158-159.

186 Dark 2000, 108.

187 Halsall 2007, 376-568.

188 See Knight 2007, Chapters 4 and 5, for instance.
189 Esmonde-Cleary 1989, 125.
190 Watts 1998, 18-19.
191 Gildas *On the Ruin of Britain*, 12.
192 Perring 2003, 97-127.
193 Watts 1998, 58-59.
194 Gerrard 2005, 371-373.
195 Pryor *Britain AD*, 113-116.
196 Delmaire & Delmaire 1990, 697-735.
197 L'Hour 1987, 113-131.
198 Salvian *De Gubernatione Dei*, 5.7.
199 Salvian *De Gubernatione Dei*, 5.8.
200 Mattingly 2006, 532-533.
201 See Jones 1996, 73-98.
202 Gildas *On the Ruin of Britain*, 24.
203 Dark 2000, 48-49.
204 Jones 1996, 169-171.
205 *Panegyrici Latini*, 10, 4, 3.
206 Zosimus, 5, 41, 4.
207 Mattingly 2006, 532.
208 Jones 1996, 204.
209 Dark & Dark 1998, 144.
210 Dark & Dark 1998, 143-144. Jones 1996, 228.
211 See, for instance, Wickham 2005, 306.
212 See Laycock 2008, Chapter 8. See also Henson 2006, 80-82.
213 White 2007, 196-199.
214 Bowen & Eagles 1990, 40-41. Cunliffe 1993, 280.
215 See Erskine 2007, 105-106.
216 See Laycock 2008, 140-152 for general discussion. Also see Chester-Kadwell 2009.
217 Malim, Penn, Robinson, Wait, Walsh 1996.
218 Laycock 2008, 140-144. Also see Erskine 2007, 100.
219 See Laycock 2008, Chapter 6 for an examination of this issue. See also Henson 2006.
220 Wickham 2005, 334-339.
221 Swift 2000, 69-77.
222 For more on all this, see Laycock 2008, Chapter 6.
223 Gildas *On the Ruin of Britain*, 22.
224 Wickham 2005, 330-332 also sees political fragmentation in post-Roman Britain as the key element in destroying the economy and culture of Roman Britain, though he hypothesises fragmentation to an even smaller scale.
225 See, for instance, fourth-century shipments of grain from Britain to the army on the Rhine frontier.
226 Puttnam 2000, 67-8.
227 See Dark 2000, Chapters 3, 4 on this.
228 Dark 2000, 188-190. Thomas 1994, Chapters 4-7.
229 Giot, Guigon & Merdrignac 2003, Chapter 5.
230 Dark 2000, 125-127.
231 Schrijver 2007, 166-167.
232 Jordanes *The Origins and Deeds of the Goths*, 45, 237-8.
233 Gildas *On the Ruin of Britain*, 24.
234 See the careers of Hengest, Ælle and Cerdic in terms of slaughtering Britons. But also see Laycock 2009 for reasons to think that the *Anglo-Saxon Chronicle* may be interpreting in simplistic terms, originally much more complex stories.

235 Bede *Ecclesiastical History of the English People*, 1, 15.
236 See, for instance, Dark 2000, 131 on brooches.
237 See Laycock 2008, 174-193, 224, 229 etc.
238 Hingley & Miles 2002, 153.
239 Wickham 2005, 508.
240 See Jones 1996, Chapter 6.
241 Eagles 2004, 234-240. And see Laycock 2008, 174-179.
242 Gregory of Tours *History of the Franks*, 2, 19.
243 Gregory of Tours *History of the Franks*, 5, 19 and 10, 9.
244 See Suzuki 2000.
245 Laycock 2008, Chapter 8. See also Henson 2006, 80-82.
246 Eugippius *The Life of St Severinus*, 5.
247 Eugippius *The Life of St Severinus*, 5.
248 Eugippius *The Life of St Severinus*, 19.
249 Procopius *Gothic Wars*, 4.20.8.
250 Jones 1996, 26-28. See also Wickham 2005, 312.
251 See Sykes 2006, 286 and Oppenheimer 2006, 356-376 for the debate on this.
252 Hills 2003, 63.
253 Hills 2003, 63.
254 Tacitus *Agricola*, 11.
255 Niblett 2001, 131, 132, 145.
256 Halsall 1995, 228-231.
257 Dark 2000, 75-76.
258 Freeborn 2006, 71-72.
259 Laycock 2008, 193-196.
260 See Hines 1993 for differences between those types of clasps found in both Scandinavia and Britain and those types just found in Britain.
261 Laing 200, 47-53.
262 Swanton 1973, 40-50.
263 Laing 2007, 44-46.
264 James, Marshall and Millett 1999, 50-51.
265 Dark 2000, 78.
266 See O'Brien 1999.
267 For instance, see Tristram 2007, 192-214.
268 Padel 2007, 217.
269 Tristram 2007, 192-214. Filppula, Klemola, Paulasto 2008, 131-132.
270 Tristram 2007, 192-214. Filppula, Klemola, Paulasto 2008.
271 Halsall 1995, 29-30. Hen 1995, 15.
272 Thomas 2003, Chapter 10, 138-160, 175-176, 190-196.
273 Gildas *On the Ruin of Britain*, 3.
274 Gildas *On the Ruin of Britain*, 21.
275 Gildas *On the Ruin of Britain*, 4.
276 Hingley 2000, 9-10.
277 Hingley 2000, 128-129.

BIBLIOGRAPHY

Abdy, R.A. (2002) *Roman-British Coin Hoards*, Oxford: Shire

Alcock, J. (1996) *Life in Roman Britain*, London: Batsford

Aldsworth, F. & Rudling, D. (1995) 'Excavations at Bignor Roman Villa, 1985-1990', *Sussex Archaeological Collections* 133, 103-188

Allason-Jones, L. (2008) *Daily Life in Roman Britain*, Oxford and Westport, CT: Greenwood World Publishing

Allason-Jones, L. & Miket, R. (1984) The catalogue of Small Finds from South Shields Roman Fort, Society of Antiquaries, Newcastle upon Tyne

Allen, D. (1989) *Rockbourne Roman Villa*, Hampshire County Council

Appels, A. & Laycock, S. (2007) *Roman Buckles & Military Fittings*, Witham: Greenlight

Applebaum, S. (1966) 'Peasant economy and types of agriculture' in C. Thomas (ed.), *Rural Settlement in Roman Britain*, 99-107, York: Council for British Archaeology

Arnold, C.J. (1984) *Roman Britain to Saxon England*, London: Routledge

Arnold, C.J. & Davies, J.L. (2000) *Roman & Early Medieval Wales*, Stroud: Sutton Publishing

Aurrecoechea Fernandez, J. (1999) 'Late Roman Belts in Hispania', *Journal of Roman Military Equipment Studies* 10, 55-62

Aurrecoechea Fernandez, J. (2001) *Los Cinturones Romanos en la Hispania del Bajo Imperio*, Monographies instrumentum 19

Barrett, A. (1979) 'The career of Tiberius Claudius Cogidubnus', *Britannia* 10, 227-242

Bassett, S. (1989) *The Origins of Anglo-Saxon Kingdoms*, Leicester: Leicester University Press

Bayley, J. & Butcher, S. (2004) *Roman Brooches in Britain*, London: Society of Antiquaries

Bean, S.C. (2000) *The Coinage of the Atrebates and Regni*, Oxford: Oxford University School of Archaeology

Bedwin, O. (1980) 'Excavations at Chanctonbury Ring, Wiston, West Sussex 1977', *Britannia* 11, 173-222

Bedwin, O. (1981) 'Excavations at Lancing Down, West Sussex 1980', *Sussex Archaeological Collections* 119, 37-56

Bennett, P., Riddler, I. & Sparey-Green, C. (2010) *The Roman Watermills and Settlement at Ickham Kent*, Canterbury: Canterbury Archaeological Trust

Birley, R. (1979) *The People of Roman Britain*, London: Batsford

Bishop, M.C. (1991) 'Soldiers and military equipment in the towns of Roman Britain' in *Roman Frontier Studies*, V. Maxfield and M. Dobson, Exeter, 21-7

Bishop, M.C. & Coulston, J.C.N. (2006) *Roman Military Equipment*, Oxford: Oxbow

Black, E. (1986) 'Romano-British Burial Customs and Religious Beliefs in South East England', *The Archaeological Journal* 14, 201-239

Black, E. (1987) *The Roman Villas of South-East England*, British Archaeological Reports, British Series 171

Black, E. (1994) 'Villa-owners: Romano-British Gentlemen and Officers', *Britannia* 25, 99-110

Black, E. (1995) 'Cursus Publicus: the infrastructure of government in Roman Britain', British Archaeological Research Report 241

Black, E.W. (2000) 'Sentius Saturninus and the Roman invasion of Britain', *Britannia* 31, 1-10

Black, E. (1997) 'Afterthoughts' in R.M. & D.E. Friendship Taylor (eds), *From Round 'house' to Villa*, Fascicle 3 of the Upper Nene Archaeological Society, 59-61

Blair, J. (1994) *Anglo-Saxon Oxfordshire*, Stroud: Sutton Publishing

Böhme, H.W. (1974) *Germanische Grabfunde des 4. bis 5. Jahrhunderts Zwischen unterer Elbe und Loire*, München: Beck

Böhme, H.W. (1986) 'Das Ende der Römerherrschaft in Britannien und die Angelsachsische Besiedlung Englands im 5. Jahrhundert', *Jahrbuch des Römisch-Germanischen Zentralmuseum Mainz 33* 469-574

Böhme, H.W. (1987) 'Gallien in der Spatantike', *Jahrbuch des Römisch-Germanischen Zentralmuseum Mainz 34* 770-3

Bourne, R.J. (2001) *Aspects of the Relationship between the Central and Gallic Empires in the Mid to Late Third Century AD with Special Reference to Coinage Studies*, British Archaeological Reports, International Series 963

Bowen, H.C. & Eagles, B.N. (1990) *The Archaeology of Bokerley Dyke*, London: HMSO

Bowles, C.R. (2006) *Rebuilding the Britons: The Postcolonial Archaeology of Culture and Identity in the Late Antique Bristol Channel Region*, Thesis

Branigan, K. (1977) *The Roman Villa in South-West England*, Bradford-on-Avon: Moonraker Press

Branigan, K. (1985) *The Catuvellauni*, Stroud: Sutton Publishing

Breeze, D.J. & Dobson, B. (1985) 'Roman Military Deployment in North England', *Britannia* 16, 1-19

Breeze, D.J. & Dobson, B. (2000) *Hadrian's Wall*, London: Penguin

Brodribb, A.C.C., Hands, A.R. & Walker D.R. (2005) *The Roman Villa at Shakenoak Farm, Oxfordshire, Excavations 1960-1976*, British Archaeological Reports, British Series 395

Brodribb, G. & Cleere, H. (1988) 'The Classis Britannica Bath-house at Beauport Park, East Sussex' in *Britannia* 11, 217-274

Brooks, D.A. (1986) 'A Review of the Evidence for Continuity in British Towns in Fifth and Sixth Centuries' in *Oxford Journal of Archaeology* 5, 1, 77-102

Brooks, N. (1989) 'The creation and early structure of the kingdom of Kent' in S. Bassett (ed.) *The Origins of Anglo-Saxon Kingdoms*, Leicester: Leicester University Press, 55-74

Brown, A. (1995) *Roman Small Towns in Eastern England and Beyond*, Oxford: Oxbow

Bruce-Mitford, R. & Raven, S. (2005) *The Corpus of Late Celtic Hanging Bowls. With an Account of the Bowls found in Scandinavia*, Oxford: Oxford University Press

Buora, M. (2002) *Miles Romanus dal Po al Danubio nel Tardoantico*, Pordenone: Lucaprint

Buora, M. (2002) 'Militari e militaria ad Aquileia e nell'attuale Friuli', in *Miles Romanus dal Po al Danubio nel Tardoantico*, Pordenone: Lucaprint

Burnham, B.C. (1987) 'The Morphology of Romano-British "Small Towns"', *Archaeological Journal* 144, 156-90

Burnham, B.C. (1986) 'The Origins of Romano-British Small Towns', Oxford Journal of Archaeology 5, 185-203

Burnham, B.C. & H. (2004) *Dolaucothi-Pumsaint: Survey and Excavation at a Roman Gold-Mining Complex (1987-1999)*, Oxford: Oxbow

Burnham, B.C. & Wacher, J. (1990) *The Small Towns of Roman Britain*, London: Batsford

Burns, T.S. (1995) *Barbarians within the Gates of Rome*, Indiana: Indiana University Press

Campbell, J. (1991) *The Anglo-Saxons*, London: Penguin

Carver, M., Hills, C. & Scheschkewitz, J. (2009) *Wasperton, A Roman, British and Anglo-Saxon Community in Central England*, Woodbridge: The Boydell Press

Casey, P.J. (1979) 'Magnus Maximus: a reappraisal' in P.J. Casey (ed.) *The End of Roman Britain*, British Archaeological Reports, British Series 71

Casey, P.J. (1983) 'Imperial campaigns and 4th century defences in Britain', CBA Research Report 51, 121-4

Casey, P.J. (1995) *Carausius & Allectus*, Yale University Press

Casey, P.J., Davies, J.L. & Evans., J. (1993) *Excavations at Segontium (Caernarfon) Roman Fort, 1975-1997*, CBA Research Report 90

Castle, S.A. (1975) 'Excavations in Pear Wood, Brockley Hill, Middlesex 1948-73' in *Transactions of London Middlesex Archaeological Society 26*, 267-77

Chadburn, A. & Corney, M. (2001) 'Iron Age Resource Assessment' in *Archaeological Research Agenda for the Avebury World Heritage Site*, Trust for Wessex Archaeology 19-23

Chester-Kadwell, M. (2009) *Early Anglo-Saxon Communities in the Landscape of Norfolk*, British Archaeological Reports, British Series 481

Clarke, G. (1979) *The Roman Cemetery at Lankhills*, Winchester Studies 3, Oxford

Clarke, R. (1955) 'The Fossditch – a Linear Earthwork in South West Norfolk' in *Norfolk Archaeology 31*, 178-196

Cleere, H. & Crossley, D. (1985) *The Iron Industry of the Weald*, Leicester University Press

Coates, R. (2007) 'Invisible Britons: Linguistics' in N.J. Higham (ed.) *Britons in Anglo-Saxon England*, Woodbridge: The Boydell Press

Coates, R., Breeze, A. & Horovitz, D. (2000) *Celtic Voices. English Places*, Stamford: Shaun Tyas

Collingwood, R. (1929) *Town and country in Roman Britain*, Antiquity 3, 261-76

Collingwood, R. & Wright, R. (1965) *The Roman Inscriptions of Britain. 1: Inscriptions on Stone*, Oxford: Clarendon

Collingwood, R. & Wright, R. (1995) *The Roman Inscriptions of Britain. 1: Inscriptions on Stone* (revised second edition), Oxford: Clarendon

Collins, R. (2005) *Decline, Collapse, or Transformation? Hadrian's Wall in the 4th-5th Centuries AD*, Thesis

Collins, R. & Allason-Jones, L. (2010) *Finds from the Frontier, Material Culture in the 4th-5th Centuries*, CBA Research Report 162

Collins, R. & Gerrard, J. (eds) (2004) *Debating Late Antiquity in Britain AD 300-700*, British Archaeological Reports, British Series 365, 123-132

Collis, J. (2007) 'The Polities of Gaul, Britain and Ireland in the Late Iron Age' in Haselgrove & Moore (eds) *The Later Iron Age in Britain and beyond*, Oxford: Oxbow

Cooke, N. (1998) *The definition and interpretation of Late Roman burial rites in the Western Empire*, Thesis

Cool, H.E.M. (1983) *A Study of the Roman Personal Ornaments made of metal, excluding Brooches, from Southern Britain*, Thesis

Cool, H.E.M. (2006) *Eating and Drinking in Roman Britain*, Cambridge: Cambridge University Press

Corney, M. (2001) 'The Romano-British nucleated settlements of Wiltshire' in P. Ellis (ed) *Roman Wiltshire and After, Papers in Honour of Ken Annable*, Wiltshire Archaeological and Natural History Society, 5-38

Coulston, J.C.N. (2010) 'Military Equipment of the "long" 4th century on Hadrian's Wall' in R. Collins & L. Allason-Jones (eds) *Finds from the Frontier*, York: Council for British Archaeology

Creighton, J. (1994) 'A time of change: the Iron Age to Roman Monetary Transition in East Anglia' in *Oxford Journal of Archaeology 13*, 325-34

Creighton, J. (2000) *Coins and Power in Late Iron Age Britain*, Cambridge: Cambridge University Press

Creighton, J. (2001) 'The Iron Age-Roman Transition' in S. James and M. Millett (eds), *Britons and Romans: advancing an archaeological agenda*, Council for British Archaeology Research Report 125, 4-11

Creighton, J. (2006) *Britannia, The creation of a Roman province*, London: Routledge

Crickmore, J. (1984) *Romano-British urban defences*, British Archaeological Reports, British Series 126

Crummy, P. (1992) *Excavations at Culver Street, the Gilberd School and Miscellaneous sites in Colchester 1971-85*, Colchester Archaeological Reports

Crummy, P. (1997) *City of Victory*, Colchester Archaeological Trust

Crummy, P., Benfield, S., Crummy, N., Rigby, V. & Shimmin, D. (2007) *Stanway: An Elite Burial Site at Camulodunum*, Britannia Monographs 24

Cunliffe, B. (1964) *Winchester Excavations*, Winchester: Winchester Museum

Cunliffe, B. (1968) *Fifth Report on the Excavations of the Roman Fort of Richborough, Kent*, Society of Antiquaries of London Research Reports 26

Cunliffe, B. (1971) *Excavations at Fishbourne 1961-1969, Vol. 1: The Site*, Society of Antiquaries of London Research Reports 26

Cunliffe, B. (1971b) *Excavations at Fishbourne 1961-1969, Vol. 11: The Finds*, Society of Antiquaries of London Research Reports 27

Cunliffe, B. (1973) *The Regni*, London: Duckworth

Cunliffe, B. (1975) *Excavations at Portchester Castle. Volume I: Roman*, Society of Antiquaries of London Research Reports 32

Cunliffe, B. (1980) 'Excavation at the Roman Fort at Lympne, Kent 1976-78' in *Britannia* 11, 227-288

Cunliffe, B. & Davenport, P. (1985) *The temple of Sulis Minerva at Bath. Vol 1: The Site*, Oxford: Oxford University Committee for Archaeology

Cunliffe, B. (1988) *Greeks, Romans and barbarians: spheres of interaction*, London: Guild

Cunliffe, B. (1991) *Iron Age communities in Britain* (3rd edn), London: Routledge

Cunliffe, B. (1993) *Wessex to A.D. 1000*, Longman

Cunliffe, B. (1998) *Fishbourne Roman palace*, Stroud: Tempus

Cunliffe, B., Down, A. & Rudkin, D. (1996) *Chichester Excavations 9, Excavations at Fishbourne 1969-1988*, Chichester: District Council

Cunliffe, B. (2003) *Danebury Hillfort*, Stroud: Tempus

Cunliffe, B. (2004) *Iron Age Britain*, English Heritage

Cunliffe, B. (2005) *Iron Age Communities in Britain*, London: Routledge

Curchin, L.A. (1991) *Roman Spain, Conquest and Assimilation*, London: Routledge

Curchin, L.A. (2003) *The Romanization of Central Spain*, London: Routledge

Curteis, M. (1996) 'An Analysis of the circulation patterns of Iron Age Currency from Northamptonshire' in *Britannia* 27, 17-42

Curwen, C. (1933) 'Excavations on Thundersbarrow Hill, Sussex' in *Antiquaries Journal* 13

Dark, K. (1994) *Civitas to Kingdom, British Political Continuity 300-800*, Studies in the Early History of Britain, Leicester

Dark, K. (2000) *Britain and the End of the Roman Empire*, Stroud: Tempus

Dark, K. & Dark, P. (1998) *The Landscape of Roman Britain*, Stroud: Sutton Publishing

Davey, J. (2004) 'The Environs of South Cadbury in the Late Antique and Early Medieval Periods' in R. Collins & J. Gerrard (eds) *Debating Late Antiquity in Britain AD 300-700*, British Archaeological Reports, British Series 365, 43-54

Davies, J. (2009) *The Land of Boudica: prehistoric and Roman Norfolk*, Cirencester: Heritage

Davies, J. & Williamson, T. (1999) *Land of the Iceni*, Norwich: University of East Anglia

de la Bédoyère, G. (1989) *The finds of Roman Britain*, London: Batsford

de la Bédoyère, G. (1991) *The buildings of Roman Britain*, London: Batsford

de la Bédoyère, G. (1999) *The Golden Age of Roman Britain*, Stroud: Tempus

de la Bédoyère, G. (2001) *Eagles over Britannia*, Stroud: Tempus

de la Bédoyère, G. (2002) *Gods with thunderbolts: religion in Roman Britain*, Stroud: Tempus

de la Bédoyère, G. (2003a) *Defying Rome, The Rebels of Roman Britain*, Stroud: Tempus

de la Bédoyère, G. (2003b) *Roman towns in Britain*, Stroud: Tempus

de la Bédoyère, G. (2006) *Roman Britain*, London: Thames & Hudson

Delmaire, B. & Delmaire, R. (1990) 'Les limites de la cité des Atrébates (nouvelle approche d'un vieux problème)', *Revue du Nord* 72, 697-735

Dickinson, T.M. (1982) 'Fowler's Type G penannular brooches reconsidered', *Medieval Archaeology* 26, 41-68

Dixon, P.H. (1993) 'The Anglo-Saxon Settlement at Mucking', *Anglo-Saxon Studies in Archaeology and History* 6, Oxford University Committee for Archaeology, 125-147

Dobson, B. & Mann, J.C. (1973) 'The Roman Army in Britain and Britons in the Roman Army', *Britannia* 205

Draper, S. (2006) *Landscape, Settlement and Society in Roman and Early Medieval Wiltshire*, British Archaeological Reports, British Series 419

Drinkwater, J.F. (1983) *Roman Gaul: the three provinces, 58 BC – AD 260*, London: Croom Helm

Drinkwater, J.F. (1987) *The Gallic Empire. Separatism and Continuity in the North-Western Provinces of the Roman Empire A.D. 260-274*, Stuttgart: Steiner

Drury, P.J. (1984) 'The Temple of Claudius at Colchester Reconsidered', *Britannia* 15, 7-50

Dumville, D.N. (1985) 'The West Saxon Genealogical Regnal List and the Chronology of Wessex', *Peritia* 4, 21-66

Dumville, D.N. (1986) 'The West Saxon Genealogical Regnal List: manuscripts and texts', *Anglia* 104, 1-32

Eagles, B. (2001) 'Anglo-Saxon Presence and Culture in Wiltshire c.AD 450 – c.675' in P. Ellis (ed) *Roman Wiltshire and After, Papers in Honour of Ken Annable*, Oxford: Oxbow, 199-233

Eagles, B. (2004) 'Britons and Saxons on the Eastern Boundary of the Civitas Durotrigum', *Britannia* 34, 234-40

Eckhardt, H. & Crummy, N. (2006) ' "Roman" or "native" bodies in Britain: the evidence of late Roman nail-cleaner strap-ends', *Oxford Journal of Archaeology* 25, 1, 83-103

Effros, B. (2003) *Merovingian Mortuary Archaeology*, Berkeley: University of California Press

Ellis, P. (1999) 'North Leigh Villa, Oxfordshire: A Report on Excavation and Recording in the 1970s', *Britannia* 30

Erdkamp, P. (ed.) (2007) *A Companion to the Roman Army*, Oxford: Wiley-Blackwell

Erskine, J. (2007) 'The West Wansdyke: an appraisal of the dating, dimensions and construction techniques in the light of excavated evidence', *Archaeological Journal* 164, 1, 80-108

Esmonde-Cleary, A.S. (1987) *Extra-Mural Areas of Romano-British Towns*, British Archaeology Reports British Series 169

Esmonde-Cleary, A.S. (1989) *The Ending of Roman Britain*, London: Routledge

Esmonde-Cleary, A.S. (1992) 'Small towns, past and future', *Britannia* 13, 341-4

Faulkner, N. (2000) *The Decline & Fall of Roman Britain*, Stroud: Tempus

Feugère, M. (2002) *Weapons of the Romans*, Stroud: Tempus

Filppula, M., Klemola, J. & Paulasto, H. (2008) *English and Celtic in Contact*, London: Routledge

Finch Smith, R. (1987) *Roadside settlements in lowland Britain*, British Archaeological Reports, British Series 157

Fincham, G. (2002) *Landscapes of Imperialism: Roman and native interaction in the East Anglian Fenland*, British Archaeological Reports, British Series 338

Fleuriot, L. (1999) *Les origines de la Bretagne*, Lausanne: Libraire Payot

Foard, G., *An Archaeological Resource Assessment of Anglo-Saxon Northamptonshire (400-1066)*, Northamptonshire Heritage

Fowler, P.J. *Fyfod Working Paper FWP 64, The Excavation of a settlement of the fourth and fifth centuries AD on Overton Down, West Overton, Wiltshire*

Freeborn, D. (2006) *From Old English to Standard English*, Basingstoke: Palgrave Macmillan

Frere, S. (1967) *Britannia – A History of Roman Britain*, London: Routledge

Frere, S. (1989) 'Roman Britain in 1988' in *Britannia* 20, 1989

Fulford, M.G. (1989) 'Byzantium and Britain: a Mediterranean perspective on Post-Roman Mediterranean imports in western Britain and Ireland', *MedArch* 33, 1-6

Fulford, M. (2000) 'Human Remains from the North Gate, Silchester', *Britannia* 31, 356-8

Fulford, M. (2001) 'Links with the Past: Pervasive "Ritual" Behaviour in Roman Britain', *Britannia* 32, 199-218

Fulford, M., Clarke, A. & Eckardt, H. (2006) *Life and Labour in Late Roman Silchester: Excavations in Insula IX from 1997*, Britannia Monograph 22

Gardner, A. (2007) *An Archaeology of Identity, Soldiers & Society in Late Roman Britain*, Walnut Creek, USA: Left Coast Press

Gerrard, J. (2004) 'How late is late? Pottery and the fifth century in southwest Britain' in R. Collins & J. Gerrard (eds) *Debating Late Antiquity in Britain AD 300-700*, British Archaeological Reports, British Series 365, 65-75

Gerrard, (2005) 'A Possible Late Roman Silver "Hoard" from Bath', *Britannia* 2005, 371-373

Gidlow, C. (2005) *The Reign of Arthur, From History to Legend*, Stroud: The History Press

Gidlow, C. (2010) *Revealing King Arthur: Swords, Stones and Digging for Camelot*, Stroud: The History Press

Gil, E., Filloy, I. & Iriarte, A. (2000) 'Late Roman Military Equipment from the City of Iruña/ Veleia (Alava/Spain)', *Journal of Roman Military Equipment Studies* 11, 25-35

Giot, P., Guignon, P. & Merdrignac, B. (2003) *The British Settlement of Brittany*, Stroud: Tempus

Goldsworthy, A. (2003) *The Complete Roman Army*, London: Thames & Hudson

Goldsworthy, A. (2009) *The Fall of the West*, London: Weidenfeld & Nicolson

Gould, J. (1999) 'The Watling Street Burgi', *Britannia* 30, 185-198

Gracie, H.S. & Price, E.G. (1979) 'Frocester Court Roman Villa: Second Report' in *Transactions of the Bristol and Gloucestershire Archaeological Society* Vol. 97, 9-64

Green, M. (1983) *The gods of Roman Britain*, Oxford: Shire

Green, M. (1986) *The gods of the Celts*, Gloucester: Alan Sutton

Green, M. (ed.) (1995) *The Celtic World*, London: Routledge

Green, T. (2008) *Concepts of Arthur*, Stroud: Tempus

Greep, S. (ed.) (1993) *Roman Towns: The Wheeler Inheritance: A Review of 50 Years' Research*, Council for British Archaeology Research Report 93

Gregory, T. (1991) *Excavations in Thetford, 1980-1982*, East Anglian Archaeology Report 53

Griffiths, N. (2001) 'The Roman Army in Wiltshire' in P. Ellis (ed) *Roman Wiltshire and After, Papers in Honour of Ken Annable*, Wiltshire Archaeological and Natural History Society, 39-72

Hadley, D.M. (2006) *The Vikings in England – Settlement, Society and Culture*, Manchester: Manchester University Press

Halsall, G. (1982) 'The origins of the *Reihengraberzivilisarion*: forty years on' in J. Drinkwater & H. Elton (eds) *Fifth-century Gaul: a crisis of identity?*, Cambridge: Cambridge University Press

Halsall, G. (1995) *Settlement and Social Organization, The Merovingian Region of Metz*, Cambridge: Cambridge University Press

Halsall, G. (2007) *Barbarian Migrations and the Roman West 376-568*, Cambridge: Cambridge University Press

Hamerow, H. (2002) *Early Medieval Settlements, The Archaeology of Rural Communities in North-West Europe 400-900*, Oxford: Oxford University Press

Harding, D.W. (2004) *The Iron Age in Northern Britain – Celts and Romans, Natives and Invaders*, London: Routledge

Härke, H. (2007) 'Invisible Britons: Culture Change' in N.J. Higham (ed) *Britons in Anglo-Saxon England*, Woodbridge: The Boydell Press

Harris, A. (2003) *Byzantium, Britain and the West*, Stroud: Tempus

Hartley, B. & Fitts, L. (1988) *The Brigantes*, Stroud: Sutton Publishing

Hawkes, S.C. (1974) 'Some recent finds of Late Roman Buckles', *Britannia* 5, 386-93

Hawkes, S.C. & Crummy, P. (1995) *Camulodunum 2*. Colchester Archaeological Report 11

Hawkes, S.C. & Dunning, G.C. (1961) 'Soldiers and settlers in Britain, fourth to fifth century', *Medieval Archaeology* 5, 1-70

Hawkes, S.C. & Grainger, G. (2003) *The Anglo-Saxon Cemetery at Worthy Park, Kingsworthy near Winchster, Hampshire*, Oxford: Oxford University School of Archaeology

Hawkes, S.C. & Hull, M. (1947) *Camulodunum*, Society of Antiquaries of London Research Reports 14

Hen, Y. (1995) *Culture and Religion in Merovingian Gaul AD 481-751*, Leiden: Brill

Hendy, M.F. (1985) *Studies in the Byzantine Monetary Economy c.300-1450*, Cambridge: Cambridge University Press

Henig, M. (1984) *Religion in Roman Britain*, London: Batsford

Henig, M. (1995) *The Art of Roman Britain*, London: Routledge

Henig, M. (2002) *The Heirs of King Verica, Culture & Politics in Roman Britain*, Stroud: Tempus

Henig, M. (2004) *Roman Sculpture from the North West Midlands*, London: The British Academy

Henig, M. (2004) 'Remaining Roman in Britain AD 300-700' in N.J. Higham (ed.) *Debating Late Antiquity in Britain AD 300-700*, British Archaeological Reports, British Series 365, 13-23

Henig, M. & Nash, D. (1982) 'Amminus and the kingdom of Verica', *Oxford Journal of Archaeology* 1, 243-246

Henson, D. (2006) *The Origins of the Anglo-Saxons*, Ely: Anglo-Saxon Books

Higham, N.J. (1992) *Rome, Britain and the Anglo-Saxons*, London: Routledge

Higham, N.J. (2002) *King Arthur, Myth-Making and History*, London: Routledge

Higham, N.J. (ed.) (2007) *Britons in Anglo-Saxon England*, Woodbridge: The Boydell Press

Hill, J. (1995) *Ritual and rubbish in the Iron Age of Wessex*, British Archaeological Reports, British Series 242

Hills, C. (2003) *Origins of the English*, London: Duckworth

Hind, J.G.F. (1977) 'The "Genounian" Part of Britain', *Britannia* 8, 229-234

Hind, J.G.F. (1989) 'The invasion of Britain in AD 43: an alternative strategy for Aulus Plautius', *Britannia* 20, 1-21

Hines, J. (1984) *The Scandinavian Character of Anglian England in the pre-Viking Period*, British Archaeological Reports, British Series 124

Hines, J. (1993) *Clasps Hektespenner Agraffen*, Upsala: Almquist and Wiksell

Hingley, R. (2000) *Roman Officers and English Gentlemen*, London: Routledge

Hingley, R., (2005) *Globalizing Roman Culture*, London: Routledge

Hingley, R. (2006) 'The Deposition of Iron Objects during the Later Prehistoric and Roman Periods', *Britannia* 37, 213-257

Hingley, R. & Miles, D. (2002) 'The Human Impact on the Landscape in the Roman Era' in P. Salway (ed) *The Roman Era, Short Oxford History of the British Isles*, Oxford: Oxford University Press

Hingley, R. & Unwin, C. (2005) *Boudica, Iron Age Warrior Queen*, London: Hambledon Continuum

Hostetter, E., Howe, T.N. & Allison, E.P. (1997) *The Romano-British Villa at Castle Copse, Great Bedwyn*, Indiana: Indiana University Press

Hunter, F. (2010) 'Beyond the frontier: interpreting late Roman Iron Age indigenous and imported material culture', in R. Collins & L. Allason-Jones (eds) *Finds from the Frontier*, CBA Research Report 162

Huskinson, J. (1994) *Roman Sculpture from Eastern England*, London: The British Academy

Inker, P. (2000) 'Technology as Active Material Culture: The Quoit-brooch Style', *Medieval Archaeology* 2000, 25-52

Ireland, S. (1986) *Roman Britain: a sourcebook*, London: Routledge

Jackson, K. (1970) 'Romano-British names in the Antonine itinerary', *Britannia* 1, 68-82

James, S., Marshall, A. & Millett, M. (1999) 'An Early Medieval Building Tradition' in C.E. Karkov (ed.) *The Archaeology of Anglo-Saxon England: Basic Readings*, London: Routledge

James, S. & Millett. M. (eds) (2000) *Britons and Romans: advancing an archaeological agenda*, Council for British Archaeology Research Report 125

Johnson, P. (1987) *Romano-British Mosaics*, Oxford: Shire

Johnson, S. (1976) *The Roman Forts of the Saxon Shore*, London: Paul Elek

Johnson, S. (1989) *Hadrian's Wall*, Swindon: English Heritage

Johnston, D.E. (ed.) (1977) *The Saxon Shore*, CBA Research Report 18

Johnston, D.E. (2004) *Roman Villas*, Oxford: Shire

Jones, B. & Mattingly, D. (1990) *An Atlas of Roman Britain*, Oxford: Blackwell

Jones, M. (1996) *The End of Roman Britain*, New York: Cornell University Press

Jones, S. (1997) *The Archaeology of Ethnicity*, London: Routledge

Karkov, C.E. (ed.) (1999) *The Archaeology of Anglo-Saxon England: Basic Readings*, London: Routledge

Kemble, J. (2001) *Prehistoric & Roman Essex*, Stroud: Tempus

Kilbride-Jones, H.E. (1980) *Celtic Craftsmanship in Bronze*, New York: St Martin's Press

King, A. (1990) *Roman Gaul and Germany*, Berkeley: University of California Press

King, A. & Soffe, G. (1994) 'The Iron Age and Roman temple on Hayling Island' in A. Fitzpatrick & E. Morris (eds) *The Iron Age in Wessex: recent work*, Salisbury: Trust for Wessex Archaeology, 114-16

Knight, J. (1996) 'Late Roman and Post-Roman Caerwent, Some Evidence from metalwork', *Archaeologia Cambrensis* 145, 35–65

Knight, J. (2001) *Roman France: an archaeological field guide*, Stroud: Tempus

Knight, J. (2007) *The End of Antiquity*, Stroud: Tempus

Kulikowski, M. (2004) *Late Roman Spain and its Cities*, London: The John Hopkins University Press

Laing, J. (2000) *Art & Society in Roman Britain*, Barton under Needwood: Wrens Park Publishing

Laing, L. (1993) *A Catalogue of Celtic Ornamental Metalwork in the British Isles c.A.D. 400-1200*, British Archaeological Reports, British Series 229

Laing, L. (2007) 'Romano-British Metalworking and the Anglo-Saxons' in N.J. Higham (ed.) *Britons in Anglo-Saxon England*, Woodbridge: The Boydell Press

Laing, L. (2010) *European Influence on Celtic Art*, Dublin: Four Courts Press

Laing, L. & Laing, J. (1986) 'Scottish and Irish metalwork and the '*conspiratio barbarica*', *Proc Soc Antiq Scot* 116, 211-221

Lambert, P. (1997) *La Langue Gauloise*, Paris: Errance

Laycock, S. (2006) 'The Threat Within', *British Archaeology*, March/April 2006, 11-15

Laycock, S. (2008) *Britannia the Failed State, Tribal Conflicts and the End of Roman Britain*, Stroud: The History Press

Laycock, S. (2009) *Warlords, The Struggle for Power in Post-Roman Britain*, Stroud: The History Press

Leahy, K.A. (1985) 'Late Roman and Early Germanic Metalwork from Lincolnshire' in N. Field, & A. White (eds) *A Prospect of Lincolnshire*, Lincoln: F.N. Field & A.J. White

Leahy, K.A. (1996) in *Dragonby*, Ed. May, J., Oxbow Monographs 61, 267-268

Leahy, K. (2007) *The Anglo-Saxon Kingdom of Lindsey*, Stroud: Tempus

Leahy, K. (2007) *Interrupting the Pots, The Excavation of Cleatham Anglo-Saxon Cemetery*, York: Council for British Archaeology

Le Bohec, Y. (2000) *The Imperial Roman Army*, London: Routledge

Leeds, E.T. (1945) 'Distribution of the Angles and Saxons Archaeologically Considered', *Archaeologia* 91, 1-106

L'Hour, M. (1987) 'Un site sous-marin sue la côte de l'Armorique. L'épave antique de Ploumanac'h', *Revue Archéologique de l'Ouest*, 113-131

Liddle, P. (2000) *An Archaeological Resource Assessment of Anglo-Saxon Leicestershire and Rutland*, Leicester: Leicestershire Museums

Lucy, S. (2000) *The Anglo-Saxon Way of Death*, Stroud: Sutton Publishing

Lyne, M. (1999) 'Fourth Century Roman Belt Fittings from Richborough', *Journal of Roman Military Equipment Studies* 10, 103-113

Lynn, M.A.B. & Jefferies, R.S. (1979) *The Alice Holt/Farnham Roman pottery industry*, Council for British Archaeology Research Report 30

Lysons, S. (1817) 'An Account of the Remains of a Roman Villa, discovered in Bignor, in Sussex', *Archaeologia* 18, 203-221

Lysons, S. (1819) *Reliquiae Britannico-Romanae Vol. 111, Remains of a Roman Villa Discovered in Bignor in Sussex*, London

Lysons, S. (1821) 'An Account of Further Discoveries of the Remains of a Roman Villa at Bignor in Sussex', *Archaeologia* 19, 176-177

MacDowall, S. (1995) *Late Roman Cavalryman*, London: Osprey

MacGregor, A. & Bolick, E. (1993) *A Summary Catalogue of the Anglo-Saxon Collections: Non-ferrous Metals*, British Archaeological Reports, British Series 230

MacMullen, R. (1965) 'The Celtic Renaissance', *Historia: Zeitschrift für Alte Geschichte 14*, 1, 93-104

MacMullen, R. (1967) *Soldier and civilian in the later Roman Empire*, Cambridge/Massachusetts: Harvard University Press

McWhirr, A. (1981) *Roman Gloucestershire*, Stroud: Sutton Publishing

Malim, T. with Penn, Robinson, Wait & Walsh (1996) 'New Evidence on the Cambridgeshire Dykes and Worsted Street Roman Road', *Proceedings of the Cambridge Antiquarian Society 85*, 27-122

Manley, J. (2002) *AD 43, The Roman Invasion of Britain – a Reassessment*, Stroud: Tempus

Manley, J. (2003) 'Inside/outside: architecture and the individual at Fishbourne Roman palace' in D. Rudling (ed.) *The Archaeology of Sussex to AD 2000*, King's Lynn: University of Sussex

Manley, J. & Rudkin, D. (2003) *Facing the Palace*, Lewes: Sussex Archaeological Society

Manning, W.H. (ed.) (1986) *Catalogue of the Roman-British Iron Tools, Fittings and Weapons in the British Museum*, London: British Museum Press

Marzinzik, S. (2003) *Early Anglo-Saxon Belt Buckles*, British Archaeological Reports, British Series 357

Mason, D. (2003) *Roman Britain and the Roman Navy*, Stroud: Tempus

Mattingly, D. (2006) *An Imperial Possession, Britain in the Roman Empire*, London: Penguin

Maxfield, V. (ed.) (1989) *The Saxon Shore: A Handbook*, Exeter: Exeter University Press

Middleton, A. (1997) 'Tiles in Roman Britain' in L. Freestone and D. Gaimster (eds), *Pottery in the making*, London: British Museum Press

Millett, M. (1987) 'Boudicca: the First Colchester Pottery Shop and the Dating of Neronian Samian', *Britannia* 18, 93-124

Millett, M. (1990) *The Romanization of Britain*, Cambridge: Cambridge University Press

Millett. M. (2005) *Roman Britain*, Swindon: English Heritage

Millett, M. & Graham, D. (1986) *Excavations on the Romano-British small town at Neathan, Hampshire, 1969-1979*, Hampshire Field Club Monograph 3

Moore, T. & Reece, R. (2001) 'The Dobunni', *Glevensis* 37, 17-26

Moorhead, J. (2001) *The Roman Empire divided*, London: Longman

Moorhead, T.S.N. (2001) 'Roman Coin Finds from Wiltshire' in P. Ellis (ed) *Roman Wiltshire and After, Papers in Honour of Ken Annable*, Devises: Wiltshire Archaeological and Natural History Society

Morris, C. with Batey, Brady, Harry, Johnson & Thomas (1990) 'Recent Work at Tintagel', *Medieval Archaeology* 43, 206-215

Mullen, A. (2007) 'Linguistic Evidence for "Romanization"', *Britannia* 38, 35-61

Myres, J.N.L. (1986) *The English Settlements*, Oxford: Oxford University Press

Niblett, R. (1999) *The Excavation of a Ceremonial Site at Folly Lane, Verulamium*, Britannia Monographs 14

Niblett, R. (2001) *Verulamium, the Roman City of St. Albans*, Stroud: Tempus

Niblett, R., Manning, W. & Saunders, D. (2006) 'Verulamium: excavations within the Roman town 1986-88', *Britannia* 37, 53-188

Niblett, R. & Thompson, I. (2005) *Alban's Buried Towns: An Assessment of St Albans' Archaeology up to AD 1600*, Oxford: Oxbow

Noble, T.F.X. (2006) *From Roman Provinces to Medieval Kindgoms*, London: Routledge

O'Brien, E. (1999) *Post-Roman Britain to Anglo-Saxon England: Burial Practices Reviewed*, British Archaeological Reports, British Series 289

Oppenheimer, S. (2006) *The Origins of the British, a Genetic Detective Story*, London: Constable

Ordnance Survey (1966) *Map of Britain in the Dark Ages*

Padel, O.J. (2007) 'Place-Names and the Saxon Conquest of Devon and Cornwall' in N.J. Higham (ed) *Britons in Anglo-Saxon England*, Woodbridge: The Boydell Press

Pearson, A. (2002) *The Roman Shore Forts*, Stroud: Tempus

Peddie, J. (1987) *Invasion: the Roman Conquest of Britain*, Stroud: Sutton Publishing

Perring, D. (2003) 'Gnosticism in Fourth Century Britain: The Frampton Mosaics Reconsidered', *Britannia* 2003, 97-127

Petts, D. (2000) *Burial, Religion and Identity in sub-Roman and early medieval Britain: AD 400-800*, Thesis

Philp, B. (1981) *The excavation of the Roman forts of the Classsis Britannica at Dover 1970-77*, Kent Archaeological Monograph 3

Pitts, L. & St. Joseph, J.K. (1985) *Inchtuthil, the Roman Legionary Fortress*, Britannia Monograph Series 6

Poulter, A.G. (2007) *The Transition to Late Antiquity on the Danube and Beyond*, Oxford: Oxford University Press for the British Academy

Potter, T.W. (2002) 'The Transformation of Britain from 55 BC to AD 60' in P. Salway (ed) *The Roman Era, Short Oxford History of the British Isles*, Oxford: Oxford University Press

Potter, T.W. & Johns, C. (2005) *Roman Britain*, London: British Museum Press

Pryor, F. (2004) *Britain AD*, London: Harper Collins

Puttnam, B. (2000) *Discover Dorset: The Romans*, Wimborne Minster: Dovecote Press

Puttnam, B. (2007) *Roman Dorset*, Stroud: Tempus

Rance, P. (2001) 'Attacotti, Déisi and Magnus Maximus: The Case for Irish Federates in Late Roman Britain' in *Britannia* 32, 243-70

Reece, R. (1988) *My Roman Britain*, Cotswold Studies

Reece, R. (1997) *The Future of Roman Military Archaeology*, National Museums and Galleries of Wales

Reece, R. (2002) *The Coinage of Roman Britain*, Stroud: Tempus

Reece, R. (2007) *The Later Roman Empire, An Archaeology AD 150-600*, Stroud: Tempus

Rivet, A.L.F. (1964) *Town and Country in Roman Britain*, 2nd edition, London: Hutchinson

Rivet, A.L.F. & Smith, R. (1979) *The Place-Names of Roman Britain*, London: Batsford

Robertson, A.S. (2000) *An Inventory of British Coin Hoards*, London: Royal Numismatic Society Special Publication 20

Robinson, P. (1994) 'The Late Roman Hoard from Blagan Hill, Wiltshire', *Minerva* 5, 4, 14-15

Rodwell, W.J. (1975) 'Trinovantian towns and their setting' in W.J. Rodwell & R.T. Rowley (eds) '*Small towns' of Roman Britain*, British Archaeological Reports 15, 85-102

Rodwell, W.J. (1976) 'Coinage, oppida and the rise of Belgic power in south-eastern Britain' in B.W. Cunliffe & R.T. Rowley (eds) *Oppida: the beginnings of urbanisation in barbarian Europe*, British Archaeological Reports S11, 184-367

Room, A. (2003) *The Penguin Dictionary of British Place Names*, London: Penguin

Rudling, D. (1979) 'Invasion and Response: Downland Settlement in East Sussex' in B.C. Barnham and R.B. Johnson (eds), *Invasion and Response: The Case of Roman Britain*, British Archaeological Reports, British Series 73, 339-356

Rudling, D. (1997) 'Round "house" to Villa: The Beddingham and Watergate Villas' in R.M. & D.E. Friendship-Taylor (series eds), *From Round 'house' to Villa*, Fascicle 3 of the Upper Nene Archaeological Society

Rudling, D. (2001) 'Chanctonbury Ring revisited, The excavations of 1988-1991', *Sussex Archaeological Collections* 139, 75-121

Russell, M. (2006) *Roman Sussex*, Stroud: Tempus

Russell, M. (2010) *Bloodline: The Celtic Kings of Roman Britain*, Amberley Publishing

Salway, P. (1993) *The Oxford Illustrated History of Roman Britain*, Oxford: Oxford University Press

Salway, P. (2002) *The Roman Era, Short Oxford History of the British Isles*, Oxford: Oxford University Press

Scott, E. (1993) *A Gazetteer of Roman Villas in Britain*, Leicester Archaeology Monographs No.1

Sealey, P. (1997) *The Boudican Revolt Against Rome*, Oxford: Shire

Sear, F. (2000) *Roman architecture*, London: Routledge

Schrijver, P. (2007) 'What Britons Spoke around 400 AD' in N. J. Higham (ed.) *Britons in Anglo-Saxon England*, Woodbridge: The Boydell Press

Schulze-Dörrlamm, M. (2002) *Byzantinische Gürtelschnallen und Gürtelbeschläge im Römisch-Germanischen Zentralmuseum*, Mainz: Verlag des Römisch-Germanischen Zentralmuseums

Shotter, D. (1996) *The Roman Frontier in Britain*, Preston: Carnegie

Simpson, C.J. (1976) 'Belt-Buckles and Strap-Ends of the Later Roman Empire: A Preliminary Survey of Several New Groups', *Britannia* 7, 192-223

Sims-Williams, P. (1983) 'The settlement of England in Bede and the Chronicle', *Anglo-Saxon England* 12, 1-41

Smith, J. (1997) *Roman villas: a study in social structure*, London: Routledge

Snyder, C. (1998) *An Age of Tyrants: Britain and the Britons*, AD 400-600, Stroud: Sutton Publishing

Snyder, C. (2003) *The Britons*, Oxford: Blackwell

Sommer, M. (1984) *Die Gürtel und Gürtelbeschläge des 4. und 5. Jahrhunderts im Römischen Reich*, Bonner Hefte zur Vorgeschichte 22, Bonn

Southern, P., & Dixon, K.R. (2000) *The Late Roman Army*, London: Routledge

Stead, I.M. (1979) *The Arras Culture*, York: Yorkshire Philosophical Society

Stenton, F.M. (1971) *Anglo-Saxon England*, Oxford: Clarendon Press

Stevens, C.E. (1937) 'Gildas and the Civitates of Britain' in *English Historical Review* 52, 193-203

Sumner, G. (2009) *Roman Military Dress*, Stroud: The History Press

Suzuki, S. (2000) *The Quoit Brooch Style and Anglo-Saxon Settlement*, Woodbridge: The Boydell Press

Swanton, M.J. (1973) *The Spearheads of the Anglo-Saxon Settlements*, London: The Royal Archaeological Institute

Swift, E. (1999) *Regionality in the Late Roman West: through the study of crossbow brooches, bracelets, beads & belt sets*, Thesis

Swift, E. (2000) *The End of the Western Roman Empire, An Archaeological Investigation*, Stroud: Tempus

Swift, E. (2003) *Roman Dress Accessories*, Oxford: Shire

Swift, E. (2009) *Style and Function in Roman Decoration, Living with Objects and Interiors*, Farnham: Ashgate

Sykes, B. (2006) *Blood of the Isles*, London: Bantam

Tainter, J. (1988) *The Collapse of Complex Societies*, Cambridge: Cambridge University Press

Taylor, A. (1998) *Archaeology of Cambridgeshire, South-East Cambridgeshire and the Fen Edge*, Cambridge: Cambridgeshire County Council

Taylor, A. (2001) *Burial Practice in Early England*, Stroud: Tempus

Taylor, J. (2007) *An atlas of Roman rural settlement in England*, York: Council for British Archaeology

Thomas, C. (1994) *And Shall These Mute Stones Speak?* Cardiff: University of Wales Press

Thomas, H.M. (2003) *The English & The Normans, Ethnic Hostility, Assimilation and Identity 1066-c. 1220*, Oxford: Oxford University Press

Todd, M. (1970) 'The small towns of Roman Britain', *Britannia* 1, 114-30

Todd, M. (1991) *The Coritani*, Stroud: Sutton Publishing

Todd, M. (2004) *The Early Germans*, Oxford: Blackwell

Todd, M. (2006) *A Companion to Roman Britain*, Oxford: Wiley Blackwell

Toynbee, J. (1962) *Art in Roman Britain*, London: Phaidon

Tristram, H. (2007) 'Why Don't the English Speak Welsh' in N.J. Higham (ed) *Britons in Anglo-Saxon England*, Woodbridge: The Boydell Press

Tyers, P., *Potsherd Atlas of Roman Pottery*, www.potsherd.uklinux.net/index.php

Tyers, P. (2003) *Roman Pottery in Britain*, London: Routledge

Van Arsdell, R.D. (1989) *Celtic Coinage of Britain*, London: Spink

Van Arsdell, R.D. (1994) *The Coinage of the Dobunni: Money Supply and Coin Circulation in Dobunnic Territory*, Oxford: Oxford University School of Archaeology

Wacher, J.S. (1962) 'A survey of Romano-British Town Defences of the early and middle second century', *Archaeological Journal* 119, 103-13

Wacher, J.S. (1966) *The civitas capitals of Roman Britain*, Leicester: Leicester University Press

Wacher, J.S. (1995) *The Towns of Roman Britain*, London: Batsford

Wade-Martins, P. (1974) 'The Linear Earthworks of West Norfolk', *Norfolk Archaeology* 36, 23-38

Walton Rogers, P. (2007) *Cloth and Clothing in Early Anglo-Saxon England* AD 450-700, CBA Research Report 145

Ward-Perkins, B. (2005) *The Fall of Rome and the End of Civilization*, Oxford: Oxford University Press

Warner, P. (1996) *The Origins of Suffolk*, Manchester: Manchester University Press

Watts, D. (1998) *Religion in late Roman Britain*, London: Routledge

Webster, G. & Smith, L. (1982) 'The Excavation of a Romano-British Rural Settlement at Barnsley Park: Part II' in *Transactions of the Bristol and Gloucestershire Archaeological Society* Vol. 100, 65-189

Webster, J. & Cooper, N. (eds) (1996) *Roman Imperialism: Post-Colonial Perspectives*, Leicester: Leicester University Press

West, S. (1998) *A Corpus of Anglo-Saxon Material from Suffolk*, East Anglian Archaeology 84, Ipswich: Suffolk County Council

Wheeler, M. (1954) *The Stanwick Fortifications*, Oxford: Oxford University Press for the Society of Antiquaries, London

Wheeler, R. & Wheeler, T. (1932) *Report on the excavation of the prehistoric, Roman and post Roman site in Lydney Park, Gloucestershire*, Oxford: Oxford University Press for The Society of Antiquaries, London

White, R. (1987) *Roman and Celtic objects in Anglo-Saxon cemeteries of the Pagan period: a Catalogue and an interpretation of their use*, Thesis

White, R. (2007) *Britannia Prima*, Stroud: Tempus

Whitney, W.D. (1867) *Language and the Study of Language: Twelve Lectures on the Principles of Linguistic Science*

Whyman, M. (2001) *Late Roman Britain in Transition, AD 300 – 500: A Ceramic Perspective from East Yorkshire*, Thesis

Wickham, C. (2005) *Framing the Early Middle Ages*, Oxford: Oxford University Press

Wickham, C. (2010) *The Inheritance of Rome*, London: Penguin

Wild, J.P. (1970) 'Button-and-Loop fasteners in the Roman Provinces', *Britannia* 1, 137-155

Wild, J.P. (2006) 'Textiles and Dress' in M. Todd (ed.) *A Companion to Roman Britain*, Oxford: Wiley-Blackwell

Williams, D. & Vince, A. (1997) 'The characterization and interpretation of early to middle Saxon granitic tempered pottery in England' in *Medieval Archaeology* 41, 214-220

Wilmott, T. (2002) 'Roman Commanders, Dark Age Kings', *British Archaeology* 63

Wilmott, T. & Wilson, P. (eds) (2000) *The Late Roman Transition in the North*, British Archaeological Reports, British Series 299

Witts, P. (2005) *Mosaics in Roman Britain, Stories in Stone*, Stroud: Tempus

Wolseley, G., Smith, R. & Hawley, W. (1927) 'Prehistoric and Roman Settlement on Park Brow', *Archaeologia* 76, 140

Wood, M. & Queiroga, F. (1992) *Current Research on the Romanization of the Western Provinces*, British Archaeological Reports, International Series S575

Woodfield, C. (1995) 'New thoughts on town defences in the western territory of Catuvellauni' in A.E. Brown (ed.) *Roman Small Towns in Eastern England and Beyond*, Oxford: Oxbow

Woodward, A. (1992) *Shrines and Sacrifice*, London: Routledge

Woodward, A. & Leach, P. (1993) *The Uley Shrines*, Swindon: English Heritage

Woolf, G. (1998) *Becoming Roman, The Origins of Provincial Civilization in Gaul*, Cambridge: Cambridge University Press

Yorke, B. (1983) 'Joint kingship in Kent, c.560-785', *Archaeologia Cantiana* 99, 1-20

Yorke, B. (1989) 'The Jutes of Hampshire and Wight and the origins of Wessex' in S. Bassett (ed.) *The Origins of Anglo-Saxon Kingdoms*, Leicester: Leicester University Press

Yorke, B. (1990) *Kings and Kingdoms of Early Anglo-Saxon England*, London: Routledge

Yorke, B. (1993) 'Fact or Fiction? The written evidence for the fifth and sixth centuries AD' in *Anglo-Saxon Studies in Archaeology and History 6*, Oxford: Oxford University Committee for Archaeology

INDEX

Italics refer to illustration numbers.